BLOOM'S

HOW TO WRITE ABOUT

George Orwell

KIM E. BECNEL

Introduction by Harold Bloom

BLOOM'S
LITERARY CRITICISM
An imprint of Infobase Publishing

Bloom's How to Write about George Orwell

Bloom's Literary Criticism
An imprint of Infobase Publishing
132 West 31st Street
New York NY 10001

Library of Congress Cataloging-in-Publication Data
Becnel, Kim.
  Bloom's how to write about George Orwell / Kim E. Becnel ; introduction by Harold Bloom.
    p. cm. — (Bloom's how to write about literature)
  Includes bibliographical references and index.
  ISBN 978-1-60413-703-3 (hardcover)
  1. Orwell, George, 1903–1950—Criticism and interpretation. 2. Criticism—Authorship. I. Bloom, Harold. II. Title.
  PR6029.R8Z5875 2010
  828'.91209—dc22
                        2010015752

Bloom's Literary Criticism books are available at special discounts when purchased in bulk quantities for businesses, associations, institutions, or sales promotions. Please call our Special Sales Department in New York at (212)967-8800 or (800)322-8755.

You can find Bloom's Literary Criticism on the World Wide Web at http://www.chelseahouse.com

Text design by Annie O'Donnell
Cover design by Ben Peterson
Composition by Mary Susan Ryan-Flynn
Cover printed by Art Print, Taylor, PA
Book printed and bound by Maple Press, York, PA
Date printed: October 2010
Printed in the United States of America

10 9 8 7 6 5 4 3 2 1

All links and Web addresses were checked and verified to be correct at the time of publication. Because of the dynamic nature of the Web, some addresses and links may have changed since publication and may no longer be valid.

CONTENTS

SERIES
INTRODUCTION

Bloom's How to Write about Literature series is designed to inspire students to write fine essays on great writers and their works. Each volume in the series begins with an introduction by Harold Bloom, meditating on the challenges and rewards of writing about the volume's subject author. The first chapter then provides detailed instructions on how to write a good essay, including how to find a thesis; how to develop an outline; how to write a good introduction, body text, and conclusion; how to cite sources; and more. The second chapter provides a brief overview of the issues involved in writing about the subject author and then a number of suggestions for paper topics, with accompanying strategies for addressing each topic. Succeeding chapters cover the author's major works.

The paper topics suggested within this book are open-ended, and the brief strategies provided are designed to give students a push forward in the writing process rather than a road map to success. The aim of the book is to pose questions, not answer them. Many different kinds of papers could result from each topic. As always, the success of each paper will depend completely on the writer's skill and imagination.

HOW TO WRITE ABOUT GEORGE ORWELL: INTRODUCTION

by Harold Bloom

I N 2010, 60 years after Orwell's death, he is known to general readers only for his two political allegories, *1984* and *Animal Farm*. They both are period pieces and, in time, will fade away. Orwell had no gifts as a writer of prose fiction: He was an inadequate storyteller and could not create personalities. I reread him now as an essayist and as the memoirist of *Homage to Catalonia*, where he fought against the Fascists in 1936–37. I have trouble rereading Hemingway's *For Whom the Bell Tolls* but return to Orwell's Catalan odyssey every decade. It remains extraordinarily poignant.

I am also still moved by Orwell's dark early novel, *Keep the Aspidistra Flying*, which is winning despite its formal ineptitude. Orwell, however, survives best as a moral essayist, where his temperament and his capabilities fuse into an available form wholly adequate to them.

How to write about George Orwell? His world is gone as my own soon will be. The judgment that he mastered the English "plain style" of writing seems fair enough. The inventor of that style was the great translator William Tyndale, whose work survives in the King James Bible of 1611, where it appears as about 70 percent of the Hebrew Bible (the Christian Old Testament) and 85 percent of the Greek New Testament. Tyndale's narrative mode became that of John Bunyan's *The Pilgrim's Progress* and

Daniel Defoe's novels and tracts. Orwell can be regarded as one of the final legatees of Tyndale's tradition.

I suggest that one highly useful way of writing about Orwell is to investigate his narrative style and his argumentative vigor, which depends on his fine plainness of style.

Orwell will go on finding readers because of his passionate sincerity, which would count for little if his means of expression could not persuade us that his plain speaker was a truth teller. At his best, he reminds me of William Hazlitt, a great literary critic and a personal essayist worthy of Montaigne and of Emerson. Orwell is not of Hazlitt's eminence, but he did carry Hazlitt's concerns forward into a very bad time.

HOW TO WRITE
A GOOD ESSAY

By Laurie A. Sterling and Kim E. Becnel

WHILE THERE are many ways to write about literature, most assignments for high school and college English classes call for analytical papers. In these assignments, you are presenting your interpretation of a text to your reader. Your objective is to interpret the text's meaning in order to enhance your reader's understanding and enjoyment of the work. Without exception, strong papers about the meaning of a literary work are built upon a careful, close reading of the text or texts. Careful, analytical reading should always be the first step in your writing process. This volume provides models of such close, analytical reading, and these should help you develop your own skills as a reader and as a writer.

As the examples throughout this book demonstrate, attentive reading entails thinking about and evaluating the formal (textual) aspects of the author's works: theme, character, form, and language. In addition, when writing about a work, many readers choose to move beyond the text itself to consider the work's cultural context. In these instances, writers might explore the historical circumstances of the time period in which the work was written. Alternatively, they might examine the philosophies and ideas that a work addresses. Even in cases where writers explore a work's cultural context, though, papers must still address the more formal aspects of the work itself. A good interpretative essay that evaluates Charles Dickens's use of the philosophy of utilitarianism in his novel *Hard Times,* for example, cannot adequately address the author's treatment of the philosophy without firmly grounding this discussion in the book itself. In other words, any analytical paper about a text, even one that seeks to evaluate the work's cultural context, must also have a firm handle on the work's themes, characters, and language. You must look for and evaluate these aspects of a work, then, as you read a text and as you prepare to write about it.

WRITING ABOUT THEMES

Literary themes are more than just topics or subjects treated in a work; they are attitudes or points about these topics that often structure other elements in a work. Writing about theme therefore requires that you not just identify a topic that a literary work addresses but also discuss what the work says about that topic. For example, if you were writing about the culture of the American South in William Faulkner's famous story "A Rose for Emily," you would need to discuss what Faulkner says, argues, or implies about that culture and its passing.

When you prepare to write about thematic concerns in a work of literature, you will probably discover that, like most works of literature, your text touches upon other themes in addition to its central theme. These secondary themes also provide rich ground for paper topics. A thematic paper on "A Rose for Emily" might consider gender or race in the story. While neither of these could be said to be the central theme of the story, they are clearly related to the passing of the "old South" and could provide plenty of good material for papers.

As you prepare to write about themes in literature, you might find a number of strategies helpful. After you identify a theme or themes in the story, you should begin by evaluating how other elements of the story—such as character, point of view, imagery, and symbolism—help develop the theme. You might ask yourself what your own responses are to the author's treatment of the subject matter. Do not neglect the obvious, either: What expectations does the title set up? How does the title help develop thematic concerns? Clearly, the title "A Rose for Emily" says something about the narrator's attitude toward the title character, Emily Grierson, and all she represents.

WRITING ABOUT CHARACTER

Generally, characters are essential components of fiction and drama. (This is not always the case, though; Ray Bradbury's "August 2026: There Will Come Soft Rains" is technically a story without characters, at least any human characters.) Often, you can discuss character in poetry, as in T. S. Eliot's "The Love Song of J. Alfred Prufrock" or Robert Browning's "My Last Duchess." Many writers find that analyzing character is one of the most interesting and engaging ways to work with a piece of literature and to shape a paper. After all, characters generally are human, and we all know something about being human and living in the world. While it is always important to remember that these figures are not real people but creations of the writer's imagination, it can be fruitful to begin evaluating them as you might evaluate a real person. Often you can start with your own response to a character. Did you like or dislike the character? Did you sympathize with the character? Why or why not?

Keep in mind, though, that emotional responses like these are just starting places. To truly explore and evaluate literary characters, you need to return to the formal aspects of the text and evaluate how the author has drawn these characters. The 20th-century writer E. M. Forster coined the terms *flat* characters and *round* characters. Flat characters are static, one-dimensional characters that frequently represent a particular concept or idea. In contrast, round characters are fully drawn and much more realistic characters that frequently change and develop over the course of a work. Are the characters you are studying flat or round? What elements of the characters lead you to this conclusion? Why might the author have drawn characters like this? How does their development affect the meaning of the work? Similarly, you should explore the techniques the author uses to develop characters. Do we hear a character's own words, or do we hear only other characters' assessments of him or her? Or, does the author use an omniscient or limited omniscient narrator to allow us access to the workings of the characters' minds? If so, how does that help develop the characterization? Often you can even evaluate the narrator as a character. How trustworthy are the opinions and assessments of the narrator? You should also think about characters' names. Do they mean anything? If you encounter a hero named Sophia or Sophie, you should probably think about her wisdom (or lack thereof), since *sophia* means "wisdom" in Greek. Similarly, since the name Sylvia is derived from the word *sylvan*, meaning "of the wood," you might want to evaluate that character's relationship with nature. Once again, you might look to the title of the work. Does Herman Melville's "Bartleby, the Scrivener" signal anything about Bartleby himself? Is Bartleby adequately defined by his job as scrivener? Is this part of Melville's point? Pursuing questions such as these can help you develop thorough papers about characters from psychological, sociological, or more formalistic perspectives.

WRITING ABOUT FORM AND GENRE

Genre, a word derived from French, means "type" or "class." Literary genres are distinctive classes or categories of literary composition. On the most general level, literary works can be divided into the genres of drama, poetry, fiction, and essays, yet within those genres there are classifications that are also referred to as genres. Tragedy and comedy, for example, are genres of drama. Epic, lyric, and pastoral are genres of poetry. *Form,* on the other hand, generally refers to the shape or structure of a work. There are many clearly defined forms of poetry that follow specific patterns of meter, rhyme, and stanza. Sonnets, for example, are poems that follow a fixed form of 14 lines. Sonnets generally follow one of two basic sonnet forms, each with its own distinct rhyme scheme. Haiku is another example of poetic form, traditionally consisting of three unrhymed lines of five, seven, and five syllables.

While you might think that writing about form or genre might leave little room for argument, many of these forms and genres are very fluid. Remember that literature is evolving and ever changing, and so are its forms. As you study poetry, you may find that poets, especially more modern poets, play with traditional poetic forms, bringing about new effects. Similarly, dramatic tragedy was once quite narrowly defined, but over the centuries playwrights have broadened and challenged traditional definitions, changing the shape of tragedy. When Arthur Miller wrote *Death of a Salesman,* many critics challenged the idea that tragic drama could encompass a common man like Willy Loman.

Evaluating how a work of literature fits into or challenges the boundaries of its form or genre can provide you with fruitful avenues of investigation. You might find it helpful to ask why the work does or does not fit into traditional categories. Why might Miller have thought it fitting to write a tragedy of the common man? Similarly, you might compare the content or theme of a work with its form. How well do they work together? Many of Emily Dickinson's poems, for instance, follow the meter of traditional hymns. While some of her poems seem to express traditional religious doctrines, many seem to challenge or strain against traditional conceptions of God and theology. What is the effect, then, of her use of traditional hymn meter?

WRITING ABOUT LANGUAGE, SYMBOLS, AND IMAGERY

No matter what the genre, writers use words as their most basic tool. Language is the most fundamental building block of literature. It is essential that you pay careful attention to the author's language and word choice as you read, reread, and analyze a text. Imagery is language that appeals to the senses. Most commonly, imagery appeals to our sense of vision, creating a mental picture, but authors also use language that appeals to our other senses. Images can be literal or figurative. Literal images use sensory language to describe an actual thing. In the broadest terms, figurative language uses one thing to speak about something else. For example, if I call my boss a snake, I am not saying that he is literally a reptile. Instead, I am using figurative language to communicate my opinions about him. Since we think of snakes as sneaky, slimy, and sinister, I am using the concrete image of a snake to communicate these abstract opinions and impressions.

The two most common figures of speech are similes and metaphors. Both are comparisons between two apparently dissimilar things. Similes are explicit comparisons using the words *like* or *as*; metaphors are implicit comparisons. To return to the previous example, if I say, "My boss, Bob, was waiting for me when I showed up to work five minutes late today—the snake!" I have constructed a metaphor. Writing about his experiences fighting in World War I, Wilfred Owen begins his poem "Dulce et decorum est," with a string of similes: "Bent double, like old beggars under sacks, / Knock-kneed, coughing like hags, we cursed through sludge." Owen's goal was to undercut clichéd notions that war and dying in battle were glorious. Certainly, comparing soldiers to coughing hags and to beggars underscores his point.

"Fog," a short poem by Carl Sandburg, provides a clear example of a metaphor. Sandburg's poem reads:

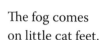

The fog comes
on little cat feet.

It sits looking
over harbor and city
on silent haunches
and then moves on.

Notice how effectively Sandburg conveys surprising impressions of the fog by comparing two seemingly disparate things—the fog and a cat.

Symbols, by contrast, are things that stand for, or represent, other things. Often they represent something intangible, such as concepts or ideas. In everyday life we use and understand symbols easily. Babies at christenings and brides at weddings wear white to represent purity. Think, too, of a dollar bill. The paper itself has no value in and of itself. Instead, that paper bill is a symbol of something else, the precious metal in a nation's coffers. Symbols in literature work similarly. Authors use symbols to evoke more than a simple, straightforward, literal meaning. Characters, objects, and places can all function as symbols. Famous literary examples of symbols include Moby Dick, the white whale of Herman Melville's novel, and the scarlet *A* of Nathaniel Hawthorne's *The Scarlet Letter.* As both of these symbols suggest, a literary symbol cannot be adequately defined or explained by any one meaning. Hester Prynne's Puritan community clearly intends her scarlet *A* as a symbol of her adultery, but as the novel progresses, even her own community reads the letter as representing not just *adultery,* but *able, angel,* and a host of other meanings.

Writing about imagery and symbols requires close attention to the author's language. To prepare a paper on symbolism or imagery in a work, identify and trace the images and symbols and then try to draw some conclusions about how they function. Ask yourself how any symbols or images help contribute to the themes or meanings of the work. What connotations do they carry? How do they affect your reception of the work? Do they shed light on characters or settings? A strong paper on imagery or symbolism will thoroughly consider the use of figures in the text and will try to reach some conclusions about how or why the author uses them.

WRITING ABOUT HISTORY AND CONTEXT

As noted above, it is possible to write an analytical paper that also considers the work's context. After all, the text was not created in a vacuum. The author lived and wrote in a specific time period and in a specific cultural context and, like all of us, was shaped by that environment. Learning more about the historical and cultural circumstances that surround the author and the work can help illuminate a text and provide you with productive material for a paper. Remember, though, that when you write analytical papers, you should use the context to illuminate the text. Do not lose sight of your goal—to interpret the meaning of the literary work. Use historical or philosophical research as a tool to develop your textual evaluation.

Thoughtful readers often consider how history and culture affected the author's choice and treatment of his or her subject matter. Investigations into the history and context of a work could examine the work's relation to specific historical events, such as the Salem witch trials in 17th-century Massachusetts or the restoration of Charles II to the English throne in 1660. Bear in mind that historical context is not limited to politics and world events. While knowing about the Vietnam War is certainly helpful in interpreting much of Tim O'Brien's fiction, and some knowledge of the French Revolution clearly illuminates the dynamics of Charles Dickens's *A Tale of Two Cities*, historical context also entails the fabric of daily life. Examining a text in light of gender roles, race relations, class boundaries, or working conditions can give rise to thoughtful and compelling papers. Exploring the conditions of the working class in 19th-century England, for example, can provide a particularly effective avenue for writing about Dickens's *Hard Times*.

You can begin thinking about these issues by asking broad questions at first. What do you know about the time period and about the author? What does the editorial apparatus in your text tell you? Similarly, when specific historical events or dynamics are particularly important to understanding a work but might be somewhat obscure to modern readers, textbooks usually provide notes to explain historical background. With this information, ask yourself how these historical facts and circumstances might have affected the author, the presentation of theme, and the presentation of character. How does knowing more about the work's specific historical context illuminate the work? To take a well-known example, understanding the complex attitudes toward slavery during the time Mark Twain wrote

Adventures of Huckleberry Finn should help you begin to examine issues of race in the text. Additionally, you might compare these attitudes to those of the time in which the novel was set. How might this comparison affect your interpretation of a work written after the abolition of slavery but set before the Civil War?

WRITING ABOUT PHILOSOPHY AND IDEAS

Philosophical concerns are closely related to both historical context and thematic issues. Like historical investigation, philosophical research can provide a useful tool as you analyze a text. For example, an investigation into the working class in Dickens's England might lead you to a topic on the philosophical doctrine of utilitarianism in *Hard Times.* Many other works explore philosophies and ideas quite explicitly. Mary Shelley's famous novel *Frankenstein,* for example, explores John Locke's tabula rasa theory of human knowledge as she portrays the intellectual and emotional development of Victor Frankenstein's creature. As this example indicates, philosophical issues are more abstract than investigations of theme or historical context. Some other examples of philosophical issues include human free will, the formation of human identity, the nature of sin, or questions of ethics.

Writing about philosophy and ideas might require some outside research, but usually the notes or other material in your text will provide you with basic information, and often footnotes and bibliographies suggest places you can go to read further about the subject. If you have identified a philosophical theme that runs through a text, you might ask yourself how the author develops this theme. Look at character development and the interactions of characters, for example. Similarly, you might examine whether the narrative voice in a work of fiction addresses the philosophical concerns of the text.

WRITING COMPARISON AND CONTRAST ESSAYS

Finally, you might find that comparing and contrasting the works or techniques of an author provides a useful tool for literary analysis. A comparison and contrast essay might compare two characters or themes in a single work, or it might compare the author's treatment of a theme in two works. It might also contrast methods of character development or analyze an author's differing treatment of a philosophical concern in two works. Writing comparison and contrast essays, though, requires some special consideration. While they generally provide you with plenty of material to use, they also come with a built-in trap: the laundry list. These papers often become mere lists of connections between the works. As this chapter will discuss, a strong thesis must make an assertion that you want to prove or validate. A strong comparison/contrast thesis, then, needs to comment on the significance of the similarities and differences you observe. It is not enough merely to assert that the works contain similarities and differences. You might, for example, assert why the similarities and differences are important and explain how they illuminate the works' treatment of theme. Remember, too, that a thesis should not be a statement of the obvious. A comparison/contrast paper that focuses only on very obvious similarities or differences does little to illuminate the connections between the works. Often, an effective method of shaping a strong thesis and argument is to begin your paper by noting the similarities between the works but then to develop a thesis that asserts how these apparently similar elements are different. If, for example, you observe that Emily Dickinson wrote a number of poems about spiders, you might analyze how she uses spider imagery differently in two poems. Similarly, many scholars have noted that Hawthorne created many "mad scientist" characters, men who are so devoted to their science or their art that they lose perspective on all else. A good thesis comparing two of these characters—Aylmer of "The Birthmark" and Dr. Rappaccini of "Rappaccini's Daughter," for example—might initially identify both characters as examples of Hawthorne's mad scientist type but then argue that their motivations for scientific experimentation differ. If you strive to analyze the similarities or differences, discuss significances, and move beyond the obvious, your paper should move beyond the laundry-list trap.

PREPARING TO WRITE

Armed with a clear sense of your task—illuminating the text—and with an understanding of theme, character, language, history, and philosophy, you are ready to approach the writing process. Remember that good writing is grounded in good reading and that close reading takes time, attention, and more than one reading of your text. Read for comprehension first. As you go back and review the work, mark the text to chart the details of the work as well as your reactions. Highlight important passages, repeated words, and image patterns. "Converse" with the text through marginal notes. Mark turns in the plot, ask questions, and make observations about characters, themes, and language. If you are reading from a book that does not belong to you, keep a record of your reactions in a journal or notebook. If you have read a work of literature carefully, paying attention to both the text and the context of the work, you have a leg up on the writing process. Admittedly, at this point, your ideas are probably very broad and undefined, but you have taken an important first step toward writing a strong paper.

Your next step is to focus, to take a broad, perhaps fuzzy, topic and define it more clearly. Even a topic provided by your instructor will need to be focused appropriately. Remember that good writers make the topic their own. There are a number of strategies—often called "invention"—that you can use to develop your own focus. In one such strategy, called *freewriting*, you spend 10 minutes or so just writing about your topic without referring back to the text or your notes. Write whatever comes to mind; the important thing is that you just keep writing. Often this process allows you to develop fresh ideas or approaches to your subject matter. You could also try *brainstorming*: Write down your topic and then list all the related points or ideas you can think of. Include questions, comments, words, important passages or events, and anything else that comes to mind. Let one idea lead to another. In the related technique of *clustering*, or *mapping*, write your topic on a sheet of paper and write related ideas around it. Then list related subpoints under each of these main ideas. Many people then draw arrows to show connections between points. This technique helps you narrow your topic and can also help you organize your ideas. Similarly, asking journalistic questions—Who? What? Where? When? Why? and How?—can lead to ideas for topic development.

Thesis Statements

Once you have developed a focused topic, you can begin to think about your thesis statement, the main point or purpose of your paper. It is imperative that you craft a strong thesis; otherwise, your paper will likely be little more than random, disorganized observations about the text. Think of your thesis statement as a kind of road map for your paper. It tells your reader where you are going and how you are going to get there.

To craft a good thesis, you must keep a number of things in mind. First, as the title of this subsection indicates, your paper's thesis should be a statement, an assertion about the text that you want to prove or validate. Beginning writers often formulate a question that they attempt to use as a thesis. For example, a writer exploring the theme of love in Orwell's *1984* might ask, Why does Winston jump so quickly into a relationship with a woman he has previously despised? What is he trying to accomplish, and is he successful? While a question like this is a good strategy to use in the invention process to help narrow your topic and find your thesis, it cannot serve as the thesis statement because it does not tell your reader what you want to assert about love. You might shape this question into a thesis by instead proposing an answer to that question: In *1984*, Winston subconsciously associates rebellion and love and so begins an intense romantic relationship. This relationship, in turn, helps him to understand that love is a powerful tool of a rebellion because of its capacity to preserve the humanity that Big Brother seeks to strip people of. Unfortunately, in part because of the society he has grown up in, Winston has trouble experiencing and understanding real love. In particular, he does not understand that the most powerful potential of love comes from one's willingness to sacrifice oneself for the beloved, and as a result, love cannot protect him after all. Notice that this thesis provides an initial plan or structure for the rest of the paper, and notice, too, that the thesis statement does not necessarily have to fit into one sentence.

Second, remember that a good thesis makes an assertion that you need to support. In other words, a good thesis does not state the obvious. If you tried to formulate a thesis about love by simply saying, Love plays a central role in Orwell's *1984*, you have done nothing but rephrase the obvious. Every reader of *1984* will come away already aware that love is an important theme in the novel. Your job as a writer is to help your reader see something new or appreciate the text in a deeper way. To do that, instead of making a generic or obvious statement as your thesis, you would want to work on answering the questions you initially posed about love, including why Winston enters into a relationship with Julia, what he hopes to get out of that relationship, and whether or not he is successful. It is helpful to remember that your thesis should take considerable time and effort to construct. As the foundation of your essay, it needs to be thoughtful and strong.

As the comparison with the road map suggests, your thesis should appear near the beginning of the paper. In relatively short papers (three to six pages) the thesis almost always appears in the first paragraph. Some writers fall into the trap of saving their thesis for the end, trying to provide a surprise or a big moment of revelation, as if to say, "TA-DA! I've just proved that in *1984*, Orwell indicates that self-sacrifice born of love is the key to preserving humanity." Placing a thesis at the end of an essay can seriously mar the essay's effectiveness. If you fail to define your essay's point and purpose clearly at the beginning, your reader will find it difficult to assess the clarity of your argument and understand the points you are making. When your argument comes as a surprise at the end, you force your reader to reread your essay in order to assess its logic and effectiveness.

Finally, you should avoid using the first person ("I") as you present your thesis. Though it is not strictly wrong to write in the first person, it is difficult to do so gracefully. While writing in the first person, beginning writers often fall into the trap of writing self-reflexive prose (writing *about* their paper *in* their paper). Often this leads to the most dreaded of opening lines: "In this paper I am going to discuss . . ." Not only does this self-reflexive voice make for very awkward prose, but it frequently allows writers to boldly announce a topic while completely avoiding a thesis statement. An example might be a paper that begins as follows: Animal Farm and 1984 both depict societies in which the citizens are oppressed and stripped of many basic rights. In this essay, I am going to discuss one of the techniques that the leaders of these societies use to control their citizens: the manipulation and revision of history. The author of this paper has done little more than announce a general topic for the paper. To improve this "thesis," the writer would need to back up a couple of steps and ask some questions. What is similar and different about the way the leaders of these two societies manipulate and revise history? Are they equally successful? Why or why not? Examining the texts for the answers to these questions might lead to a thesis such as the following: "In Animal Farm, Napoleon creates a false version of history to persuade the animals to support his actions, and in 1984, Big Brother goes a step further, his constant revisions of the past creating not so much a skewed sense of history as a continuous present. In both instances, the citizens are deprived of an accurate sense of perspective and a faith in their own memories, and the result is that they have no fixed point from which to evaluate their rulers and the choices they are making. Though these techniques render most citizens powerless, when taken too far they can incite, rather than prevent, rebellion and thus become a potential liability to a totalitarian state.

Outlines

While developing a strong, thoughtful thesis early in your writing process should help focus your paper, outlining provides an essential tool for logically shaping that paper. A good outline helps you see—and develop—the relationships among the points in your argument and assures you that your paper flows logically and coherently. Outlining not only helps place your points in a logical order but also helps you subordinate supporting points, weed out any irrelevant points, and decide if there are any necessary points that are missing from your argument. Most of us are familiar with formal outlines that use numerical and letter designations for each point. However, there are different types of outlines; you may find that an informal outline is a more useful tool for you. What is important, though, is that you spend the time to develop some sort of outline—formal or informal.

Remember that an outline is a tool to help you shape and write a strong paper. If you do not spend sufficient time planning your supporting points and shaping the arrangement of those points, you will most likely construct a vague, unfocused outline that provides little, if any, help with the writing of the paper. Consider the following example.

Thesis: *In Animal Farm,* Napoleon creates a false version of history to persuade the animals to support his actions, and in *1984,* Big Brother goes a step further, his constant revisions of the past creating not so much a skewed sense of history as a continuous present. In both instances, the citizens are deprived of an accurate sense of perspective and a faith in their own memories, and the result is that they have no fixed point from which to evaluate their rulers and the choices they are making. Though these techniques render most citizens powerless, when taken too far they can incite, rather

than prevent, rebellion and thus become a potential
liability to a totalitarian state.

    I. Introduction and thesis

   II. In *Animal Farm,* Napoleon interferes with
       history and perspective
       A. Napoleon revises Snowball's history to
          make him a scapegoat.
          1. Revising the story of the Battle of
             the Cowshed
       B. The animals are persuaded that they are
          better off now than they were in the time
          of Farmer Jones.
       C. Napoleon plans to build the windmill.

  III. *1984* also illustrates that manipulation of
       memory and history, when taken too far, can
       incite rebellion.
       A. Psychological manipulation sparks Winston's
          rebellion.
          1. Winston's tendency to trust his own
             observations and memories
          2. Winston's work
       B. Big Brother regains control of Winston
          through torture.

   IV. In *1984*, Oceania creates a continuous present
       so that the citizens cannot criticize them.
       A. Rewriting of documents
       B. Manipulation of current reality
       C. Citizens rendered powerless to criticize
          government

    V. *Keep the Aspidistra Flying*

   VI. Conclusion

This outline has a number of flaws. First, the major topics labeled with the Roman numerals are not arranged in a logical order. It would make much more sense to present Roman numeral III after Roman number IV. This way, the paper would establish the manner in which Oceania manipulates history successfully before moving on to illustrate that those techniques can incite rebellion if pushed too far. Further, the thesis makes no reference to *Keep the Aspidistra Flying,* so Roman numeral V should be removed entirely. Third, in section II, the writer is going to discuss the ways that Napoleon revises history and distorts the animals' sense of perspective. The ideas under A and B, revising the story of Snowball and persuading the animals that their lives are better under Napoleon than they were under Jones, both support the main idea of the paragraph. Building the windmill, listed under C, does not and so should be removed. A fourth problem is the inclusion of a section 1 under Roman numeral II, letter A. An outline should not include an A without a B, a 1 without a 2, and so forth. The final problem with this outline is the overall lack of detail. None of the sections provide much information about the content of the argument, and it seems likely that the writer has not given sufficient thought to the content of the paper.

A better start to this outline might be the following:

Thesis: In *Animal Farm,* Napoleon creates a false version of history to persuade the animals to support his actions, and in *1984,* Big Brother goes a step further, his constant revisions of the past creating not so much a skewed sense of history as a continuous present. In both instances, the citizens are deprived of an accurate sense of perspective and a faith in their own memories, and the result is that they have no fixed point from which to evaluate their rulers and the choices they are making. Though these techniques render most citizens powerless, when taken too far they can incite, rather than prevent, rebellion and thus become a potential liability to a totalitarian state.

I. Introduction and thesis

In *Animal Farm*, Napoleon creates a false history and distorts the animals' perspective to prevent them from criticizing and challenging him.

   A. Napoleon gets rid of his main rival, Snowball, by creating a false history in which he is a traitor.

   B. The animals are convinced that they are better off now than they were in the time of Farmer Jones.

II. In *1984*, Oceania creates a continuous present so that the citizens cannot criticize them.

   A. Rewriting of documents to revise the past

   B. Manipulation of current reality as well as past keeps citizens completely off-balance.

   C. Citizens rendered powerless to criticize government

III. *1984* also illustrates that manipulation of memory and history, when taken too far, can incite rebellion.

   A. Extreme psychological manipulation sparks Winston's rebellion.

   B. Big Brother resorts to torture to get Winston to accept that his perceptions do not matter and that his very reality is constructed by the will of the party.

   C. Big Brother regains control of Winston, but perhaps there is hope for others.

IV. Conclusion

This new outline would prove much more helpful when it came time to write the paper.

An outline like this could be shaped into an even more useful tool if the writer fleshed out the argument by providing specific examples from the text to support each point. Once you have listed your main point and your supporting ideas, develop this raw material by listing related supporting ideas and material under each of those main headings. From there, arrange the material in subsections and order the material logically. For example, you might begin with one of the theses cited above: Because he subconsciously associates rebellion and love, Winston begins an intense romantic relationship. This relationship, in turn, helps him to understand that love is a powerful tool of a rebellion because of its capacity to preserve the humanity that Big Brother seeks to strip people of. Unfortunately, in part because of the society he has grown up in, Winston has trouble experiencing and understanding real love. In particular, he does not understand that the most powerful potential of love comes from one's willingness to sacrifice oneself for the beloved, and as a result, love cannot protect him after all.

As noted above, this thesis already gives you the beginning of an organization: Start by explaining the connection in Winston's mind between rebellion and love. Then, demonstrate the difficulty Winston has in feeling and understanding love. And finally, you will want to point out that it is this inability to fully love and understand love, particularly the sacrifice it can involve, that dooms Winston's rebellion. You might begin your outline, then, with three topic headings along these lines: (1) the connection between love and rebellion, (2) Winston's difficulty feeling and understanding love, and (3) the failure of Winston's rebellion stemming from his inability to sacrifice himself for love. Under each of those headings you could list ideas that support the particular point. Be sure to include references to parts of the text that help build your case.

An informal outline might look like this:

1. Introduction and thesis
2. Winston associates rebellion against Big Brother with love; this is why he is so eager to begin a relationship with Julia. As that relationship deepens, Winston discovers that the way love

helps one to rebel against Big Brother is by preserving one's humanity.

- From the start of the novel, Winston subconsciously connects rebellion against Big Brother and love.
  - The novel starts with Winston engaging in his most overt and dangerous act of rebellion against the party—writing in his diary.
  - The first thing he chooses to record is a movie scene in which a mother tries in vain to protect the child she loves from the violence of war.
- This connection between love and rebellion in Winston's mind explains why he jumps so quickly into a relationship with Julia.
- Eventually, Winston brings this connection between love and protection against Big Brother to the service of his thoughts; he comes to believe that love is key to rebellion because it preserves one's humanity.
  - As Winston's relationship with Julia progresses, he begins to think more and more about his mother.
- Finally, Winston connects the movie scene he writes about in his first diary entry to a memory of his mother holding his baby sister.
- Winston comes to understand that this love his mother felt for her children and the love displayed in the movie scene demonstrate "what mattered were individual relationships." He understands that his mother's "feelings were her own, and could not be altered from the outside. . . . If you loved someone, you loved him, and when you had nothing else to give, you still gave him love" (136).

- Winston thinks that this ability to privilege relationships and inner feelings makes people human and that it is this humanity that is the ultimate rebellion against Big Brother.

3. Winston's relationship with Julia demonstrates that simply deciding to love someone does not make it so; feeling love is not easy for someone who has grown up under Big Brother.
   - Initially, the relationship is in his head, not his heart.
   - Winston admits to himself while in custody that "he loved [Julia] and would not betray her; but that was only a fact, known as he knew the rules of arithmetic."
   - "He felt no love for her, and he hardly even wondered what has happened to her" (189).
   - Through torture and brainwashing, Big Brother gains control of Winston's brain; his intellectual devotion to Julia cannot prevent this.
   - Although Winston finally feels love for Julia, it is not an authentic, freely given love but one that is born out of his desperate attempt to stop Big Brother from taking control of his heart as well as his mind. It is much more about him than about her.
     - Having lost control of his mind, Winston determines that his heart will not become party property: "He obeyed the Party, but he still hated the Party. In the old days he had hidden a heretical mind beneath an appearance of conformity. Now he had retreated a step further: in the mind he had surrendered, but he had hoped to keep the inner heart inviolate" (230).

    ○ To protect his heart from being filled with the Party, he lets Julia in: "Julia! Julia! Julia, my love! Julia! For a moment he had an overwhelming hallucination of her presence. She had seemed to be not merely with him, but inside him. It was as though she had got into the texture of his skin. In that moment he had loved her far more than he had ever done when they were together and free" (230).

4. Winston fails to understand the biggest lesson he should have learned from his mother's example: that the real protection born of love is gained by someone's willingness to sacrifice himself for a loved one.
   - Winston's mother and the mother in the film did not simply love their children; each was willing to sacrifice herself—the movie mother to take bullets and Winston's own mother to starve—in attempts to save their children. It is this ability to put the welfare of a loved one ahead of one's own that is both supremely human and the ultimate weapon against Big Brother.
   - Unfortunately, Winston is unable to replicate that deep love with Julia.
   - When Winston's love is put to the test—he must choose whether to sacrifice himself or Julia—he chooses to preserve his own life and to sacrifice Julia, emphatically, yelling, "Do it to Julia! Do it to Julia! Not me! Julia! I don't care what you do to her. Tear her face off, strip her to the bones. Not me! Julia! Not me!" (236).
   - Faced with the same situation, Julia chooses to sacrifice Winston. When they meet on the

street after they have both been released from prison, they acknowledge that once you make the choice to sacrifice one you claim to love in your stead, "you don't feel the same toward that other person any longer" (240).

- They give up their love to save themselves, and they lose themselves as well. By refusing to sacrifice themselves for the other, Winston and Julia admit that their own well-being is primary to them. Since Big Brother controls that well-being, it controls them entirely and has little trouble reducing them to empty vessels filled with nothing but party ideology.

You would set about writing a formal outline with a similar process, though in the final stages you would label the headings differently. A formal outline for a paper that argues the thesis about *Animal Farm* and *1984* cited above might look like this:

Thesis: In *Animal Farm*, Napoleon creates a false version of history to persuade the animals to support his actions, and in *1984*, Big Brother goes a step further, his constant revisions of the past creating not so much a skewed sense of history as a continuous present. In both instances, the citizens are deprived of an accurate sense of perspective and a faith in their own memories, and the result is that they have no fixed point from which to evaluate their rulers and the choices they are making. Though these techniques render most citizens powerless, when taken too far they can incite, rather than prevent, rebellion and thus become a potential liability to a totalitarian state.

    I. Introduction and thesis
       In *Animal Farm*, Napoleon creates a false history and distorts the animals' perspective to prevent them from criticizing and challenging him.

A. Napoleon gets rid of his main rival, Snowball, by creating a false history in which he is a traitor.

    1. Napoleon, with help from Squeaker, even convinces the animals that their memories of the Battle of the Cowshed, in which they recall Snowball fighting bravely for their cause, are wrong. In the new version, "just at the moment when Jones and his men had got inside the yard, Snowball suddenly turned and fled" (80).

    2. After Squealer had "described the scene so graphically, it seemed to the animals that they did remember it that way" after all (80–81).

B. The animals are convinced that they are better off now than they were in the time of Farmer Jones.

    1. Squeaker presents reports replete with false data to prove that life for the animals is better under Napoleon than it was under Jones.

    2. The animals believe Squealer: "Jones and all he stood for had almost faded out of their memories. They knew that life nowadays was harsh and bare. . . . But doubtless it had been worse in the old days. They were glad to believe so" (106–07).

    3. Of course, conditions are actually worse than they had been under Jones, a fact that is made clear by the human farmers' comment that "the lower animals on Animal Farm did more work and received less food than any animals in the county" (125).

II. In *1984*, Oceania creates a continuous present so that the citizens cannot criticize them.

   A. Winston's job is rewriting of documents to revise the past.

   B. Manipulation of current reality as well as past keeps citizens completely off balance.

      1. To take one example, when Oceania shifts to being at war with Eastasia, no explanation is made. The official rhetoric simply changes mid-spiel and past documents are revised to match.

      2. The political speech "had been proceeding for perhaps twenty minutes when a messenger hurried onto the platform and a scrap of paper was slipped into the speaker's hand. He unrolled and read it without pausing in his speech. Nothing altered in his voice or manner, or in the content of what he was saying, but suddenly the names were different. Without words, a wave of understanding rippled through the crowd . . . Oceania was at war with Eastasia: Oceania had always been at war with Eastasia. A large part of the political literature of five years was now completely obsolete. Reports and records of all kinds, newspapers, books . . . all had to be rectified at lightning speed" (149).

   C. Citizens are rendered powerless to criticize government.

III. *1984* also illustrates that manipulation of memory and history, when taken too far, can incite rebellion.

   A. Extreme   psychological   manipulation
     sparks Winston's rebellion.
     1. Winston's tendency to trust his own
       observations and memories.
     2. Winston's work in the department
       that alters historical documents.
   B. Big Brother resorts to torture to get
     Winston to accept that his perceptions do
     not matter and that his very reality is
     constructed by the will of the party.
   C. Big Brother regains control of Winston,
     but perhaps there is hope for others.

IV. Conclusion

As in the previous example outline, the thesis provided the seeds of a structure, and the writer was careful to arrange the supporting points in a logical manner, showing the relationships among the ideas in the paper.

Body Paragraphs

Once your outline is complete, you can begin drafting your paper. Paragraphs, units of related sentences, are the building blocks of a good paper, and as you draft, you should keep in mind both the function and the qualities of good paragraphs. Paragraphs help you chart and control the shape and content of your essay, and they help the reader see your organization and your logic. You should begin a new paragraph whenever you move from one major point to another. In longer, more complex essays, you might use a group of related paragraphs to support major points. Remember that in addition to being adequately developed, a good paragraph is both unified and coherent.

Unified Paragraphs:

Each paragraph must be centered around one idea or point, and a unified paragraph carefully focuses on and develops this central idea without including extraneous ideas or tangents. For beginning writers, the best way to ensure that you are constructing unified paragraphs is to include a topic sentence in each paragraph. This topic sentence should convey the main point of the paragraph, and every sentence in the paragraph should relate to that topic sentence. Any sentence that strays from the central topic does not belong in the paragraph and needs to be revised or deleted. Consider the following paragraph about the difficulty Winston has feeling love for Julia in *1984*. Notice how the paragraph veers away from the main point:

> Even though Winston learns a great deal about love and its potential through his relationship with Julia and the memories and reflections that relationship encourages, he finds that growing up under Big Brother's thumb has conditioned him to think primarily of himself and the party. Even though he wants desperately to love Julia, Winston has great trouble truly experiencing love. Winston has difficulties in other areas of his life as well. He finds the intellectual challenge of his job pleasurable, but he is conflicted about the nature of the work he does. Winston is critical of the way the party simply revises history to accord with its present stance. Winston also has trouble with the party's demand that he participate regularly in group events, when he craves time alone to think and reflect.

Although the paragraph begins solidly, the author soon goes on a tangent. If the purpose of the paragraph is to demonstrate the difficulty that Winston experienced in his attempt to feel love, the sentences about Winston's job and his need for privacy do not belong here and should be deleted.

In addition to shaping unified paragraphs, you must also craft coherent paragraphs, paragraphs that develop their points logically with sentences that flow smoothly into one another. Coherence depends on the order of your sentences, but it is not strictly the order of the sentences that is important to paragraph coherence. You also need to craft your prose to help the reader see the relationship among the sentences. Consider the following paragraph about the difficulty that Winston encounters as he experiments with love in *1984*. Notice how the writer uses the same main idea as the paragraph above, and this time stays on topic, yet ultimately fails to help the reader see the relationships among the points.

Coherent Paragraphs:

Even though Winston learns a great deal about love and its potential through his relationship with Julia and the memories and reflections that relationship encourages, he finds that growing up under Big Brother's thumb has conditioned him to think primarily of himself and the party. Even though he wants desperately to love Julia, Winston has great trouble truly experiencing love. The relationship, it turns out, exists in Winston's head, rather than in his heart. Winston admits to himself that "he loved [Julia] and would not betray her; but that was only a fact, known as he knew the rules of arithmetic." "He felt no love for her, and he hardly even wondered what has happened to her" (189). Winston's intellectual love cannot stand up to the torture and brainwashing he suffers. Winston determines that his heart will not become party property: "in the mind he had surrendered, but he had hoped to keep the inner heart inviolate" (230). Orwell writes:

> "Julia! Julia! Julia, my love! Julia!" For a moment he had an overwhelming hallucination of her presence. She had seemed to be not merely with him, but inside him. It was as though she had got into the texture of his skin. In that moment he had loved her far more than he had ever done when they were together and free. (230)

Although Winston finally feels love for Julia, it is not an authentic, freely given love, but one that is born out of his desperate attempt to stop Big Brother from taking control of his heart as well as his mind. It is much more about him than about her.

This paragraph demonstrates that unity alone does not guarantee paragraph effectiveness. The argument is hard to follow because the author fails both to show connections between the sentences and to indicate how they work to support the overall point.

A number of techniques are available to aid paragraph coherence. Careful use of transitional words and phrases is essential. You can use transitional flags to introduce an example or an illustration *(for example, for instance)*, to amplify a point or add another phase of the same idea *(additionally, furthermore, next, similarly, finally, then)*, to indicate a conclusion or result *(therefore, as a result, thus, in other words)*, to signal a contrast or a qualification *(on the other hand, nevertheless, despite this, on the contrary, still, however, conversely)*, to signal a comparison *(likewise, in comparison, similarly)*, and to indicate a movement in time *(afterward, earlier, eventually, finally, later, subsequently, until)*.

In addition to transitional flags, careful use of pronouns aids coherence and flow. If you were writing about *The Wizard of Oz*, you would not want to keep repeating the phrase *the witch* or the name *Dorothy*. Careful substitution of the pronoun *she* in these instances can aid coherence. A word of warning, though: When you substitute pronouns for proper names, always be sure that your pronoun reference is clear. In a paragraph that discusses both Dorothy and the witch, substituting *she* could lead to confusion. Make sure that it is clear to whom the pronoun refers. Generally, the pronoun refers to the last proper noun you have used.

While repeating the same name over and over again can lead to awkward, boring prose, it is possible to use repetition to help your paragraph's coherence. Careful repetition of important words or phrases can lend coherence to your paragraph by reminding readers of your key points. Admittedly, it takes some practice to use this technique effectively. You may find that reading your prose aloud can help you develop an ear for effective use of repetition.

To see how helpful transitional aids are, compare the paragraph below to the preceding paragraph about Winston's relationship with Julia. Notice how the author works with the same ideas and quotations but shapes them into a much more coherent paragraph whose point is clearer and easier to follow.

```
Even though Winston learns a great deal about love and
its potential through his relationship with Julia and the
memories and reflections that relationship encourages,
he finds that growing up under Big Brother's thumb has
conditioned him to think primarily of himself and the
```

party. Despite the fact that he wants desperately to love Julia, Winston has great trouble truly experiencing love. For most of its existence, the feelings he has for her, it turns out, exist in Winston's head, rather than in his heart. After Winston has been taken into custody, he thinks to himself that "he loved [Julia] and would not betray her" but then immediately realizes that "that was only a fact, known as he knew the rules of arithmetic. He felt no love for her, and he hardly even wondered what has happened to her" (189). Contrary to his vow, Winston does betray Julia. His intellectual love cannot stand up to the torture and brainwashing he suffers. But having lost control of his mind, Winston determines that his heart will not become party property: "in the mind he had surrendered, but he had hoped to keep the inner heart inviolate" (230). To protect his heart from being filled with the party, he finally lets Julia in:

> "Julia! Julia! Julia, my love! Julia!" For a moment he had an overwhelming hallucination of her presence. She had seemed to be not merely with him, but inside him. It was as though she had got into the texture of his skin. In that moment he had loved her far more than he had ever done when they were together and free. (230)

Although Winston finally feels love for Julia, it is not an authentic, freely given love, but one that is born out of his desperate attempt to stop Big Brother from taking control of his heart as well as his mind. It is much more about him than about her.

Similarly, the following paragraph from a paper on the manipulation of history and distortion of perspective in *Animal Farm* demonstrates both unity and coherence. In it, the author argues that Napoleon successfully manipulates the other animals by creating a false history and distorting their sense of perspective.

Once Napoleon decides to take control of the farm and begins making decisions not based on the public good but to enhance his own power, he has to begin to deceive the other animals to get them to cooperate with him. He begins by getting rid of his main rival, Snowball, by labeling him a traitor and turning him into a scapegoat for all the problems suffered on the farm. To convince the animals of Snowball's guilt, Napoleon has to revise the group's communal history, eventually convincing the animals that Snowball was not the hero they remember but that he had always been a traitor to their cause. Napoleon, with help from Squeaker, even convinces the animals that their memories of the Battle of the Cowshed, in which they recall Snowball fighting bravely for Animal Farm, are mistaken. In the new version, "just at the moment when Jones and his men had got inside the yard, Snowball suddenly turned and fled" (80). Because Squealer had "described the scene so graphically, it seemed to the animals that they did remember it that way" after all (80–81). By creating a false history in which Snowball was a traitor all along, Napoleon gives the animals a misleading sense of the trajectory of their society, one in which Napoleon has consistently made the correct decisions for the safety and prosperity of the group. Napoleon also deliberately distorts the animals' sense of perspective. He has Squeaker convince the animals with false reports and misleading data that they are better off now than they were in the time of Farmer Jones. The animals "knew that life nowadays was harsh and bare. . . . But doubtless it had been worse in the old days. They were glad to believe so" (106–07). Of course, conditions were, in reality, worse than they had been under Jones, a fact that is made clear by the human farmers' comment that "the lower animas on Animal Farm did more work and received less food than any animals in the county" (125). Faced with a false narrative and robbed of their sense of perspective, the citizens of Animal Farm cannot identify grounds for criticizing

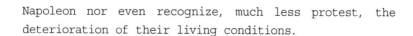

Napoleon nor even recognize, much less protest, the
deterioration of their living conditions.

Introductions

Introductions present particular challenges for writers. Generally, your
introduction should do two things: capture your reader's attention and
explain the main point of your essay. In other words, while your introduction should contain your thesis, it needs to do a bit more work than that.
You are likely to find that starting that first paragraph is one of the most
difficult parts of the paper. It is hard to face that blank page or screen,
and as a result, many beginning writers, in desperation to start somewhere, start with overly broad, general statements. While it is often a
good strategy to start with more general subject matter and narrow your
focus, do not begin with broad sweeping statements such as Everyone
likes to be creative and feel understood. Such sentences
are nothing but empty filler. They begin to fill the blank page, but they do
nothing to advance your argument. Instead, you should try to gain your
readers' interest. Some writers like to begin with a pertinent quotation
or with a relevant question. Or, you might begin with an introduction of
the topic you will discuss. Another common trap to avoid is depending
on your title to introduce the author and the text you are writing about.
Always include the work's author and title in your opening paragraph.

Compare the effectiveness of the following introductions.

1)   People need to have a sense of their history.
     Imagine what you would feel like if you did
     not know the history of your family, your
     community, or even your own history? While in
     Animal Farm the rulers create a new version of
     history to persuade the population to support
     their actions, in *1984,* Big Brother goes a step
     further, his constant revisions of the past
     creating not so much a skewed sense of history
     as a continuous present. In both instances, the
     citizens are deprived of an accurate sense of
     perspective and a faith in their own memories,
     and the result is that they have no fixed
     point from which to evaluate their rulers and

the choices they are making. They are rendered powerless.

2) Human beings have an innate need to make sense of the world around us and the events that happen in our lives. To gain a sense of control over our destinies, we fashion narratives or histories that explain the things that have happened to us in a way that we find satisfying or at least comprehensible. Framing our experiences this way enables us to evaluate and understand events in our lives and in our pasts. These kinds of stories also help us to plan for our futures by showing us what consequences lie ahead on various paths. In Orwell's *Animal Farm,* the rulers create a fake version of history to persuade the population to support their actions, and in *1984,* Big Brother goes a step further, his constant revisions of the past creating not so much a skewed sense of history as a continuous present. In both instances, the citizens are deprived of an accurate sense of perspective and a faith in their own memories, and the result is that they have no fixed point from which to evaluate their rulers and the choices they are making. They are rendered powerless.

The first introduction begins with a vague, overly broad sentence; cites unclear, undeveloped examples; and then moves abruptly to the thesis. The second introduction works with the same ideas and thesis but provides more detail and is consequently more interesting. It begins by discussing the importance of history and creating our own narratives and ends with the thesis, which focuses on what happens when the power of constructing meaningful narratives is removed.

The paragraph below provides another example of an opening strategy. It begins by introducing the author and the texts it will analyze, and then it moves on to catalog the different techniques used to control the citizens of *Animal Farm* and *1984* before narrowing the focus to the one technique that the essay will concentrate on: the destruction of a proper communal history and intentional distortion of perspective.

As Orwell's *Animal Farm* and *1984* are both critiques of totalitarian societies, the two works examine many ways in which people can be manipulated, including the use of rhetoric to persuade and influence, the creation of scapegoats to take on blame, and the threat and actual implementation of violence. All of these techniques work on people's psyches in different ways. Perhaps the most insidious, and most effective, are those used to prohibit people from maintaining a clear sense of their shared history and a stable perspective from which to evaluate their world. While in *Animal Farm* the rulers create a new version of history to persuade the population to support their actions, in *1984,* Big Brother goes a step further, his constant revisions of the past creating not so much a skewed sense of history as a continuous present. In both instances, the citizens are deprived of an accurate sense of perspective and a faith in their own memories, and the result is that they have no fixed point from which to evaluate their rulers and the choices they are making. They are rendered powerless.

Conclusions

Conclusions present another series of challenges for writers. No doubt you have heard the adage about writing papers: "Tell us what you are going to say, say it, and then tell us what you've said." While this formula does not necessarily result in bad papers, it does not often result in good ones, either. It will almost certainly result in boring papers (especially boring conclusions). If you have done a good job establishing your points in the body of the paper, the reader already knows and understands your argument. There is no need to merely reiterate. Do not just summarize your main points in your conclusion. Such a boring and mechanical conclusion does nothing to advance your argument or interest your reader. Consider the following conclusion to the paper about the manipulation of history in *Animal Farm* and *1984.*

In conclusion, *Animal Farm* and *1984* demonstrate that the manipulation of history and intentional distortion of memory and perspective can be a powerful tool

in controlling a group of citizens. *1984* also shows
that when pushed too far, those citizens are likely
to rebel. Unfortunately, however, Winston's rebellion
is unsuccessful, and Big Brother, though challenged,
remains in control.

Besides starting with a mechanical transitional device, this conclusion
does little more than summarize the main points of the outline (and it
does not even touch on all of them). It is incomplete and uninteresting
(and a little too depressing).

Instead, your conclusion should add something to your paper. A good
tactic is to build upon the points you have been arguing. Asking "why?" or
"what next?" often helps you draw further conclusions. For example, in the
paper on *Animal Farm* and *1984*, you might speculate on whether or not,
based on the text and what you've already argued, other citizens in Oceania would rebel in the same way that Winston did and how those rebel-
lions would play out. Another method for successfully concluding a paper
is to speculate on other directions in which to take your topic by tying it
into larger issues. You might do this by envisioning your paper as just one
section of a larger paper. Having established your points in this paper, how
would you build upon this argument? Where would you go next? Finally,
you could also use your conclusion to discuss the implications of your
argument outside of the text. In the following conclusion to the paper on
Animal Farm and *1984*, for example, the author ties the experiences of the
characters in the books to fundamental human characteristics and suggests that Orwell's novels provide lessons that can help us understand the
relationship between power and the human spirit in the real world.

Taken together, *Animal Farm* and *1984* demonstrate that
our perceptions of right and wrong, good and evil, and
fairness and injustice are not entirely personal or
internal notions; how we understand the world is greatly
determined by cultural and historical context that we
help to create through our experiences, memories, and
stories. Even more than that, our participation in the
creation of a communal narrative gives us the power to
shape that narrative, and in turn, our destinies and our
world. Leaders who corrupt or violate this process, who

try to strip human beings of their memories and their histories, can have great sway over the will of their people. But if Orwell's lessons in *1984* and *Animal Farm* are to be taken to heart, these strategies of manipulation and control must be used carefully, because the human tendency to trust our own perceptions and tell our own stories is strong and will always tend to struggle to the surface, seeking to break through any false histories or propaganda that threaten to smother it.

Similarly, in the following conclusion to a paper on love and rebellion in *1984*, the author summarizes the argument and speculates on its implications.

Ultimately, in Oceania, there are still those like Winston who believe in the power of love, but their suffocating society has made it a difficult emotion to experience. Unfortunately, it turns out that Winston was not only right when he surmised that it was his mother's pure love that made her fully human but also when he observed that this was an emotion that belonged to the past, that "you could not have pure love or pure lust nowadays. No emotion was pure, because everything was mixed up with fear and hatred" (105). As a result, even those like Winston who manage to feel real love are incapable of sacrificing themselves to protect a loved one or to preserve the integrity of their love. Without this capacity for sacrifice, love loses much of its power to make change in the world. Perhaps this means that Winston is right about one more thing: that the best hope for rebellion and revolution in Oceania is not skeptical party members but the Proles who have been allowed to conduct romances and relationships freely. Perhaps in their capacity to love lies Oceania's best chance for freedom.

Citations and Formatting

Using Primary Sources

As the examples included in this chapter indicate, strong papers on liter-ary texts incorporate quotations from the text in order to support their points. It is not enough for you to assert your interpretation without pro-viding support or evidence from the text. Without well-chosen quotations to support your argument you are, in effect, saying to the reader, "Take my word for it." It is important to use quotations thoughtfully and selectively. Remember that the paper presents *your* argument, so choose quotations that support *your* assertions. Do not let the author's voice overwhelm your own. With that caution in mind, there are some guidelines you should fol-low to ensure that you use quotations clearly and effectively.

Integrate Quotations

Quotations should always be integrated into your own prose. Do not just drop them into your paper without introduction or comment. Oth-erwise, it is unlikely that your reader will see their function. You can integrate textual support easily and clearly with identifying tags, short phrases that identify the speaker. For example:

> Winston remembers his sister as "a tiny, ailing, very silent child."

While this tag appears before the quotation, you can also use tags after or in the middle of the quoted text, as the following examples demonstrate:

> "I did not murder her," says Winston.

> "If you mean confessing," Julia said to Winston, "we shall do that, right enough. Everybody always confesses."

You can also use a colon to formally introduce a quotation:

> Winston's terror is clear: "Of all horrors in the world—a rat!"

When you quote brief sections of poems (three lines or fewer), use slash marks to indicate the line breaks in the poem:

As the poem ends, Dickinson speaks of the power of the imagination: "The revery alone will do, / If bees are few."

Longer quotations (more than four lines of prose or three lines of poetry) should be set off from the rest of your paper in a block quotation. Double-space before you begin the passage, indent it 10 spaces from your left-hand margin, and double-space the passage itself. Because the indentation signals the inclusion of a quotation, do not use quotation marks around the cited passage. Use a colon to introduce the passage:

O'Brien exploits Winston's deep fear of rats by threatening to allow them to attack Winston's face:

The wire door was a couple of hand-spans from his face. The rats knew what was coming now. One of them was leaping up and down; the other, an old scaly grandfather of the sewers, stood up, with his pink hands against he bars, and fiercely snuffed the air. Winston could see the whiskers and the yellow teeth. Again the black panic took hold of him. He was blind, helpless, mindless.

Facing his greatest fear, Winston is rendered entirely powerless and will do whatever O'Brien wishes.

The whole of Dickinson's poem speaks of the imagination:

To make a prairie it takes a clover and one bee,
One clover, and a bee,
And revery.
The revery alone will do,
If bees are few.

Clearly, she argues for the creative power of the mind.

It is also important to interpret quotations after you introduce them and explain how they help advance your point. You cannot assume that your reader will interpret the quotations the same way that you do.

Quote Accurately

Always quote accurately. Anything within quotations marks must be the author's exact words. There are, however, some rules to follow if you need to modify the quotation to fit into your prose.

1. Use brackets to indicate any material that might have been added to the author's exact wording. For example, if you need to add any words to the quotation or alter it grammatically to allow it to fit into your prose, indicate your changes in brackets:

   > According to O'Brien, the party is "not interested in the good of others; [they] are interested solely in power."

2. Conversely, if you choose to omit any words from the quotation, use ellipses (three spaced periods) to indicate missing words or phrases:

   > A guard collects one of the prisoners bound for Room 101: "The man was led out, walking unsteadily . . . [and] all the fight had gone out of him."

3. If you delete a sentence or more, use the ellipses after a period:

   > O'Brien explains to Winston that he has been sent to Room 101 for the failure of self-discipline that has resulted in his rebellion: "You are here because you have failed in humility, in self-discipline. . . . Only the disciplined mind can see reality, Winston."

4. If you omit a line or more of poetry, or more than one paragraph of prose, use a single line of spaced periods to indicate the omission:

```
To make a prairie it takes a clover and one bee,
. . . . . . . . . . . . . . . . . .
And revery.
The revery alone will do,
If bees are few.
```

Punctuate Properly

Punctuation of quotations often causes more trouble than it should. Once again, you just need to keep these simple rules in mind.

1. Periods and commas should be placed inside quotation marks, even if they are not part of the original quotation:

    ```
    O'Brien explains to Winston: "We are the priests
    of power."
    ```

    The only exception to this rule is when the quotation is followed by a parenthetical reference. In this case, the period or comma goes after the citation (more on these later in this chapter):

    ```
    O'Brien explains to Winston: "We are the priests
    of power" (217).
    ```

2. Other marks of punctuation—colons, semicolons, question marks, and exclamation points—go outside the quotation marks unless they are part of the original quotation:

    ```
    Why does the narrator say that Elisa's "work
    with the scissors was over-eager, over-
    powerful"?
    ```

    ```
    O'Brien tries to convince Winston that the Party,
    not the individual, is the entity that matters
    most, asking him, "Do you not understand . . .
    that the individual is only a cell?"
    ```

Documenting Primary Sources

Unless you are instructed otherwise, you should provide sufficient information for your reader to locate material you quote. Generally, literature papers follow the rules set forth by the Modern Language Association (MLA). These can be found in the *MLA Handbook for Writers of Research Papers* (sixth edition). You should be able to find this book in the reference section of your library. Additionally, its rules for citing both primary and secondary sources are widely available from reputable online sources. One of these is the Online Writing Lab (OWL) at Purdue University. OWL's guide to MLA style is available at http://owl.english.purdue.edu/owl/resource/557/01/. The Modern Language Association also offers answers to frequently asked questions about MLA style on this helpful Web page: http://www.mla.org/style_faq. Generally, when you are citing from literary works in papers, you should keep a few guidelines in mind.

Parenthetical Citations

MLA asks for parenthetical references in your text after quotations. When you are working with prose (short stories, novels, or essays), include page numbers in the parentheses:

> O'Brien explains to Winston: "We are the priests of power" (217).

When you are quoting poetry, include line numbers:

> Dickinson's speaker tells of the arrival of a fly: "There interposed a Fly— / With Blue—uncertain stumbling Buzz— / Between the light—and Me—" (12-14).

The Works Cited Page

These parenthetical citations are linked to a separate works cited page at the end of the paper. The works cited page lists works alphabetically by the authors' last name. An entry for the above reference to Orwell's *1984* would read:

> Orwell, George. *1984.* New York: Penguin, 1977.

The *MLA Handbook* includes a full listing of sample entries, as do many of the online explanations of MLA style.

Documenting Secondary Sources

To ensure that your paper is built entirely upon your own ideas and analysis, instructors often ask that you write interpretive papers without any outside research. If, on the other hand, your paper requires research, you must document any secondary sources you use. You need to document direct quotations, summaries or paraphrases of others' ideas, and factual information that is not common knowledge. Follow the guidelines above for quoting primary sources when you use direct quotations from secondary sources. Keep in mind that MLA style also includes specific guidelines for citing electronic sources. OWL's Web site provides a good summary: http://owl.english.purdue.edu/owl/resource/557/09/.

Parenthetical Citations

As with the documentation of primary sources, described above, MLA guidelines require in-text parenthetical references to your secondary sources. Unlike the research papers you might write for a history class, literary research papers following MLA style do not use footnotes as a means of documenting sources. Instead, after a quotation, you should cite the author's last name and the page number:

> When faced with his greatest fear, Winston "abandons his love for Julia which is his last link with ordinary humanity" (Symons 380).

If you include the name of the author in your prose, then you would include only the page number in your citation. For example:

> Daphne Patai, for instance, argues that Winston's relationship with Julia is likely nothing more than a "concession on Orwell's part to popular literature, as well as a vehicle for setting Winston's half-hearted rebellion in motion" (239).

If you are including more than one work by the same author, the parenthetical citation should include a shortened yet identifiable version of the title in order to indicate which of the author's works you cite. For example:

> "The animals were shocked beyond measure to learn
> that even Snowball could be guilty of such an action"
> (Orwell, Animal 72).

Similarly, and just as important, if you summarize or paraphrase the particular ideas of your source, you must provide documentation:

> Orwell included a romantic relationship in *1984* to make
> the novel more appealing to readers and to provide Winston
> with motivation to rebel against Big Brother (Patai 293).

The Works Cited Page

Like the primary sources discussed above, the parenthetical references to secondary sources are keyed to a separate works cited page at the end of your paper. Here is an example of a works cited page that uses the examples cited above. Note that when two or more works by the same author are listed, you should use three hyphens followed by a period in the subsequent entries. You can find a complete list of sample entries in the *MLA Handbook* or from a reputable online summary of MLA style.

WORKS CITED

Orwell, George. *1984.* New York: Penguin, 1977.

——. *Animal Farm.* New York: Penguin, 1972.

Patai, Daphne. *The Orwell Mystique: A Study in Male Ideology.* Amherst: U of Mass P, 1984.

Symons, Julian. "Power and Corruption." *Times Literary Supplement* (10 June 1949): 380.

Plagiarism

Failure to document carefully and thoroughly can leave you open to charges of stealing the ideas of others, which is known as plagiarism, and this is a very serious matter. Remember that it is important to include quotation marks when you use language from your source, even if you use just one or two words. For example, if you wrote, when Winston abandons his love for Julia, he also abandons his last link with ordinary humanity, you would be guilty of plagiarism, since you used Symons's distinct language without acknowledging him as the source. Instead, you should write: When Winston "abandons his love for Julia," he also "abandons his last link with ordinary humanity" (Symons 455). In this case, you have properly credited Symons.

Similarly, neither summarizing the ideas of an author nor changing or omitting just a few words means that you can omit a citation. Michael Shelden's biography of Orwell contains the following passages about *Animal Farm*:

> As a clever satire on Stalin's betrayal of the Russian Revolution, Animal Farm caught the popular imagination just when the Cold War was beginning to make itself felt. For many years "anticommunists" enjoyed using it as a propaganda weapon in that war, but this was a gross misrepresentation of the book and a violation of the spirit in which Orwell wrote it. He was not a fanatical opponent of the Soviet Union.

Below are two examples of plagiarized passages:

> The widespread use of Animal Farm as an argument against communism grossly oversimplifies Orwell's more nuanced stance regarding the Soviet Union.

> For many years "anticommunists" used Animal Farm as a propaganda weapon in the Cold War, but such a use was a gross misrepresentation of the book and a violation of the spirit in which Orwell wrote it (Shelden 369).

While the first passage does not use Shelden's exact language, it does include a main idea from Shelden's volume without crediting him, and this constitutes plagiarism. The second passage has shortened his passage, changed some wording, and included a citation, but some of the phrasing is Shelden's. The first passage could be fixed with a parenthetical citation. Because some of the wording in the second remains the same, though, it would require the use of quotation marks, in addition to a parenthetical citation. The passage below represents an honestly and adequately documented use of the original passage:

According to Michael Shelden, the use of Orwell's *Animal Farm* as "a propaganda weapon" in the Cold War "was a gross misrepresentation of the book and a violation of the spirit in which Orwell wrote it" (369).

This passage acknowledges that the interpretation is derived from Shelden while appropriately using quotations to indicate his precise language.

While it is not necessary to document well-known facts, often referred to as "common knowledge," any ideas or language that you take from someone else must be properly documented. Common knowledge generally includes the birth and death dates of authors or other well-documented facts of their lives. An often-cited guideline is that if you can find the information in three sources, it is common knowledge. Despite this guideline, it is, admittedly, often difficult to know if the facts you uncover are common knowledge or not. When in doubt, document your source.

Sample Essay

Harrison Wright
Ms. Formly
English III
November 25, 2009

THE FAILURE OF LOVE IN *1984*

George Orwell's *1984* features a protagonist, Winston Smith, who chafes against an oppressive regime that seeks to control every aspect of its citizens' lives. Winston rebels in secret ways while trying to put forth the appearance of a committed party member. He manages to find some enjoyment in the intellectual challenge of his work, even though it involves rewriting history to align with current party policy, a practice that Winston abhors. He buys a diary on the black market and arranges a space in his apartment where he can write down his true thoughts about the party in private. In essence, Winston is hanging on by a thread, barely surviving his suffocating life. He desperately wants to stand up to Big Brother, but he struggles to figure out how to do it in a meaningful way. Because he unconsciously associates rebellion and love, Winston begins an intense romantic relationship. This relationship, in turn, helps him to understand that love is a powerful tool of a rebellion because of its capacity to preserve the humanity that Big Brother seeks to strip people of. Unfortunately, in part because of the society he has grown up in, Winston has trouble experiencing and understanding real love. In particular, he does not understand that the most powerful potential of love comes from one's willingness to sacrifice oneself for the beloved, and as a result, love cannot protect him after all.

In Winston's unconscious mind, love and rebellion are closely connected; his relationship with Julia is sparked by this connection and eventually helps him to understand it. At the start of the novel, Winston's association of rebellion with love comes through clearly in one of the initial scenes of the novel, which present Winston engaging in his most overt and dangerous act of rebellion against the party thus far, writing in his diary. The first thing he chooses to record is a movie scene in which a mother tries in vain to protect the child she loves from the violence of war. He describes the scene as follows:

> a jewess sitting up in the bow with a little boy about three years old in her arms. little boy screaming with fright and hiding his head between her breasts as if he was trying to burrow right into her and the woman putting her arms round him and comforting him although she was blue with fright herself, all the time covering him up as much as possible as if she thought her arms could keep the bullets off him. (11)

That this scene depicting the love of a mother is the first thing Winston writes down when he decides to commit the act—journaling—which will likely get him killed reveals how closely love and rebellion are linked in Winston's mind. Even though Winston does not understand that connection, it is the one that motivates him to jump at the chance to experience love when Julia offers it. Some critics see Winston's relationship with Julia as a mere plot device; Daphne Patai, for instance, argues that Winston's relationship with Julia is likely nothing more than a "concession on Orwell's part to popular literature, as well as a vehicle for setting Winston's half-hearted rebellion in motion" (239). However, it would be more accurate to say that the relationship is the heart of Winston's rebellion and that it is the only act of rebellion he commits that has any real chance at saving him from annihilation by Big Brother. It is only after Winston and Julia have established a solid, if complicated, romantic relationship, after all, that Winston is able to connect the movie scene he writes about in his first diary entry to a memory of his mother holding his baby sister and come to a more fully realized appreciation of why love constitutes rebellion. Winston comes to understand that this love his mother felt for her children and the love displayed in the movie scene demonstrate that "what mattered were individual relationships." He understands that his mother's "feelings were her own, and could not be altered from the outside. . . . If you loved someone, you loved him, and when you had nothing else to give, you still gave him love" (136). Winston discovers that this ability to privilege relationships and inner feelings makes people human and that it is this humanity that is the ultimate rebellion against Big Brother.

Even though Winston learns a great deal about love and its potential through his relationship with Julia and the memories and reflections that relationship encourages, he finds that growing up under Big Brother's thumb has conditioned him to think primarily of himself and the party. Despite the fact that he wants desperately to love Julia, Winston has great trouble truly experiencing love. For most of its existence, the feelings he has for her, it turns out, exist in Winston's head, rather than in his heart. After Winston has been taken into custody, he thinks to himself that "he loved [Julia] and would not betray her" but then immediately realizes that "that was only a fact, known as he knew the rules of arithmetic. He felt no love for her, and he hardly even wondered what has happened to her" (189). Contrary to his vow, Winston does betray Julia. His intellectual love cannot stand up to the torture and brainwashing he suffers. But having lost control of his mind, Winston determines that his heart will not become party property: "in the mind he had surrendered, but he had hoped to keep the inner heart inviolate" (230). To protect his heart from being filled with the party, he finally lets Julia in:

> "Julia! Julia! Julia, my love! Julia!" For a moment he had an overwhelming hallucination of her presence. She had seemed to be not merely with him, but inside him. It was as though she had got into the texture of his skin. In that moment he had loved her far more than he had ever done when they were together and free." (230)

Although Winston finally feels love for Julia, it is not an authentic, freely given love, but one that is born out of his desperate attempt to stop Big Brother from taking control of his heart as well as his mind. It is much more about him than about her.

Once Winston succeeds in feeling love for Julia, he definitely thinks, and readers may even agree, that he has achieved some sort of protection against Big Brother, that at the least there will be dignity and humanity at his death. The problem, though, is that Winston fails to understand the biggest lesson he should have learned from his mother's example: that the only fail-safe protection born of love is gained by someone's willingness to sacrifice himself for a loved one.

When Winston refuses to make that sacrifice, he loses everything. Winston's examples of love, his own mother and the mother in the film he described in his journal, did not simply love their children; each was willing to sacrifice herself—the movie mother to take bullets and Winston's own mother to starve—in attempts to save them. It is this ability to put the welfare of a loved one ahead of one's own that is both supremely human and the ultimate weapon against Big Brother. Unfortunately, Winston is unable to replicate that deep love with Julia. When Winston's love is put to the test, when he faces the "threat of attack by [rats] Winston abandons his love for Julia which is his last link with ordinary humanity" (Symons 380). He yells: "Do it to Julia! Do it to Julia! Not me! Julia! I don't care what you do to her. Tear her face off, strip her to the bones. Not me! Julia! Not me!" (236). Faced with a similar situation, Julia also chooses to sacrifice Winston. When they meet on the street after they have both been released from prison, Julia speaks for the both of them: "You think there's no other way of saving yourself and you're quite ready to save yourself that way. You want it to happen to the other person. You don't give a damn what they suffer. All you care about is yourself" (240). She acknowledges that once you make the choice to sacrifice one you claim to love in your stead, "you don't feel the same toward that other person any longer" (240). Julia and Winston give up their love to save themselves, and in doing so, they lose themselves as well. By refusing to sacrifice themselves for the other, they admit that their own well-being and safety is primary to them. It is more important than other people and more important than the idea of love. Since Big Brother controls what is most important to them— their physical bodies—he controls them entirely and has little trouble reducing them to empty vessels filled with nothing but party ideology.

    In Oceania, there are still those like Winston who believe in the power of love, but their suffocating society has made it a difficult emotion to experience. Unfortunately, it turns out that Winston was not only right when he surmised that it was his mother's pure love that made her fully human but also when he observed that this was an emotion that belonged to the past, that "you could not have pure love or pure lust nowadays. No emotion was pure, because everything was mixed up with fear and hatred" (105). As a result, even those like Winston who manage to feel real love are incapable of sacrificing themselves to protect a loved one or to preserve the integrity of their love. Without this capacity for sacrifice, love loses much of its power to create change in the world. Perhaps this means that Winston is right about one more thing: that the best hope for rebellion and revolution in Oceania is not skeptical party members but the Proles who have been allowed to conduct romances and relationships freely. Perhaps in their capacity to love lies Oceania's best chance for freedom.

WORKS CITED

Orwell, George. *1984*. New York: Penguin, 1977.

Patai, Daphne. *The Orwell Mystique: A Study in Male Ideology*. Amherst: U of Mass P, 1984.

Symons, Julian. "Power and Corruption." *Times Literary Supplement* (10 June 1949): 380.

HOW TO WRITE ABOUT
GEORGE ORWELL

EVEN IF you know very little of the man himself, chances are you know at least a little something of George Orwell's works. Most adults in the United States have probably read either *1984, Animal Farm,* or both. Orwell's influence on Western culture has been so great, however, that even those few people who have never read a word of Orwell's writing may very well have used the not uncommon adjective *Orwellian* to describe an overly intrusive government or institution. References to Orwell's works permeate our popular culture, from takeoffs on the Animal Farm pigs' commandment, "All animals are equal, but some animals are more equal than others," to the popular reality television series *Big Brother.* Orwell created the concept of *doublethink,* a term commonly used in a pejorative sense in politics, and the frightening idea of the *thought police* comes straight out of *1984.* It is even suggested that Orwell coined the phrase *cold war* in a prescient essay published just after the conclusion of World War II. Clearly, when a writer has made such a wide-ranging impact on an entire culture, it can be very beneficial to join the cultural conversation by reading and thinking about his works. Of course, if you are a student, that decision may be made for you; *Animal Farm* and *1984,* along with a few of Orwell's other works, frequently are assigned reading in high school and college. Whether you are reading and writing about Orwell's works out of your own desire to become conversant with some of the great literature of the 20th century or you are required to read Orwell for a class, there are a few things you should keep in mind in order to maximize your experience with this major British author.

It can at times be easy to forget that Orwell wrote more than just two major works. While *1984* and *Animal Farm* are undeniably his most popular and widely read works, Orwell, in fact, produced six novels, three nonfiction books, and literally hundreds of essays and editorials in his relatively short writing career. While almost no one reads his few surviving poems or many of those editorials, most of his books are still read and studied today. If you are familiar only with one or both of Orwell's most famous books, you might be pleasantly surprised by the range he demonstrates in his other works. There is an air of the fantastical surrounding Orwell if you are only familiar with his two most popular books. After all, *1984* certainly contains major elements of science fiction and *Animal Farm* is a fable, complete with talking animals. Much of the rest of Orwell's canon, surprisingly, consists of works of gritty realism. *Down and Out in Paris and London,* for instance, recalls Orwell's days barely eking out an existence as a dishwasher in Paris and then living homelessly in London. *Homage to Catalonia* narrates in stunning detail Orwell's experiences fighting against the fascists in Spain's civil war. *The Road to Wigan Pier* constitutes a sort of anthropological experiment in which Orwell lived with the coal miners of northern England in order to describe to the world the abject poverty they had to endure because of deeply entrenched social inequities. Orwell's fiction is likewise varied. His first novel, *Burmese Days,* is a richly-textured, verbally and visually extravagant novel of love and intrigue set in Burma shortly after the end of World War I, while *Keep the Aspidistra Flying* is a spare and sometimes disturbing story of a young man who wants to escape the existing class structure but has no idea how. In other words, Orwell is anything but a one-trick pony. His works run the gamut from adventure to love, war to existentialism, the macabre to the mundane. If you are writing on Orwell as an assignment, your choice of texts may be limited by your instructor. If you are working on *1984* or *Animal Farm* and are allowed to include other texts, however—as in a compare and contrast essay, for instance—you should consider picking one of Orwell's less popular works as a complementary text. You will likely be surprised and delighted in the ways that Orwell's other works will deepen your understanding of his more famous novels.

Although Orwell's corpus covers a great deal of subject area, one thing remains the same throughout: He is a fiercely political writer. In fact, Orwell occupies a prominent place in a pantheon of socially conscious

authors writing about the same time as him. Pearl S. Buck, John Steinbeck, Upton Sinclair, Richard Wright, and Aldous Huxley are just a few
of Orwell's contemporaries whose works were primarily concerned with
exposing social and political inequities and promoting positive social
change. The previous generation of writers had largely identified with the
aesthetic movement, which believed in the credo "art for art's sake," or
with the naturalist movement, which was interested in the various forces
that drive people to behave in the ways that they do but with little attention paid to using that knowledge to make things better. Orwell's generation, on the other hand, felt that authors had an obligation to use their
words to try to better the world. These writers had seen the unimaginable
destruction wrought by World War I and were watching Hitler consolidate
power in Europe before triggering World War II and knew that politics
had very real, and often tragic, consequences. Believing that art could be
influential, they sought to enact fundamental changes to better society.
Thus, you find Orwell throwing off the privileges afforded to him by his
middle-class upbringing and living among the working class in order to
write more knowledgeably and authoritatively about their plight. Nor was
Orwell coy or apologetic for attempting to use his art to achieve political ends; quite the opposite, in fact. In a well-known essay titled "Why I
Write," Orwell admitted that his motivation to write arose from a "[d]esire
to push the world in a certain direction, to alter other people's idea of the
kind of society that they should strive after" (5). He then quite proudly pro-
claimed, "Every line of serious work that I have written since 1936 has been
written, directly or indirectly, *against* totalitarianism and *for* democratic
Socialism, as I understand it" (8). Knowing that this is the kind of writer
you are dealing with when approaching Orwell's work can help you understand some of the themes and undercurrents you will find there. Unfortunately, it can also prove a little intimidating at times. Once you realize
the heavy political baggage that comes with Orwell's books, you might feel
unprepared to try to interpret what is going on. This is a legitimate concern, but there are two successful strategies for dealing with this.

On the one hand, Orwell's literary works are just like every other
writer's literary works; they create a world unto themselves. The characters of these works—even the nonfiction works—inhabit a world that is
shaped and populated by Orwell himself, even if he is doing his best to
reflect the real world. Therefore, each work is complete in and of itself.

It is possible to engage with and make sense of any of Orwell's works on its own basis. You can read *Animal Farm* with no knowledge whatsoever of the Russian Revolution, and the novel will still carry several layers of meaning for you. It is true that understanding the ways that Orwell is using *Animal Farm* to comment on the rise of communism in Russia will open up new and useful interpretations of the novel for you, but they will only enhance the bountiful interpretive options already there for you. So the first option for dealing with a political writer like Orwell is simply to let the books stand on their own. Even in the explicitly propagandist nonfiction works, Orwell himself will provide you with enough details of the politics he is championing for the work to make sense.

The second option, of course, is to spend a little time and energy doing some outside research. This is a highly fruitful strategy that will not only open up entirely new avenues in your reading of Orwell but will also help you to comprehend and appreciate other authors' works as well. For instance, researching the causes and outcomes of the Spanish civil war will empower you to judge the veracity of Orwell's *Homage to Catalonia*. Without research, you are forced into a position of having to accept everything that Orwell himself tells you about the war. Because you know that he is trying to persuade you of a particular political point of view, there is little you can do to protect your objectivity as a reader if you must simply assume his version of events is true. Armed with the proper research, however, you are capable of determining how Orwell is manipulating the facts. You can identify which details he is omitting and which he is exaggerating. Furthermore, with your deeper understanding of the circumstances and political currents surrounding the Spanish civil war, you are now much better prepared to appreciate Ernest Hemingway's *For Whom the Bell Tolls*, Max Aub's *Field of Honor*, or even Pablo Picasso's famous painting *Guernica*. Obviously, this kind of research can pay large dividends and is not that difficult to conduct. At several points in this volume, specific suggestions are made to help you begin researching historical and cultural topics that will help you better understand and write about Orwell's works.

Whether you conduct extensive research or work only with Orwell's words, and whether you stick with *1984* or *Animal Farm* or dig deeper into Orwell's considerable canon of writing, you are sure to find him to be a challenging and rewarding writer whose works will provide you with a practically infinite number of essay topics.

TOPICS AND STRATEGIES

The sample topics provided below are designed to provide you some ideas for how you might approach writing an essay about a work of Orwell's. Many of the samples will give you the titles of some possible works to focus on. Keep in mind the length of your essay when you are deciding on which works, and how many of them, you want to consider. You will want to make sure that you have adequate space to give thorough treatment to each work you talk about in your essay. You are certainly free to select works not mentioned in the sample topics as well. Bear in mind, too, that if you choose multiple texts, it is good to have a rationale for grouping those texts in your essay. Ideally, you do not want the determining factor simply to be which texts you already happened to have read. Instead, you might choose works that were written at a certain period in history or works that explore similar themes, for example.

Themes

One of the most common methods of approaching a piece of literature is to consider its themes or major concerns. When we ask ourselves what a piece is really "about," or what it wants to say, we are trying to discern its themes. Of course, it is not enough to identify the topics with which a work is concerned. We must then investigate the text to discover what message the writer is conveying about a particular theme. Like many writers, Orwell revisits the same, or similar, themes in several of his works. For instance, as a writer deeply committed to socialism, Orwell writes frequently about poverty. He describes what life is like for the impoverished, how they came to be in that situation, and what can be done to help them break the cycle of poverty. Some of his nonfiction works take this theme up as their explicit subject matter and deal quite directly with it, while his fictional works may treat the subject a bit more subtly. In either case, poverty is a major theme of the work and will offer you plenty of material from which to craft an interesting and meaningful essay. Of course, the job of your essay is much more than merely identifying Orwell's theme. Presumably, any intelligent reader of Orwell's works will be able to discern that poverty is a primary concern in them. Rather, you are required to go further, to help your reader better understand what Orwell is up to when he writes about poverty. For instance, it is clear that one of the main themes of *The Road to Wigan Pier* is the poverty suffered by the coal miners. In your essay, you might analyze Orwell's reasoning for why the miners are so impoverished. Perhaps you might point out some flaws in his logic. Or you might trace out his proposed remedies to their logical conclusions and write an essay on about how they will or will not succeed and what implications that has on Orwell's understanding of poverty as a social ill.

Sample Topics:

1. **Poverty:** Quite nearly all of Orwell's works at least touch on the theme of poverty. Some, such as *The Road to Wigan Pier,* take poverty as their major focus, while others, like *Animal Farm,* only tangentially deal with it as an issue. How does Orwell conceive of poverty? Why does he think it exists? And what does he think we should do about it?

You have your pick of works to work on for this theme. If you choose one of the works concerned primarily with poverty, say *Wigan Pier* or *Down and Out in Paris and London,* you are going to want to delve a good bit beneath the surface. After all, in these works, Orwell has announced quite clearly what he thinks about poverty, its causes, and his proposed solutions. You will need to engage his ideas and intellectually test them out. Poverty, obviously, is an extraordinarily complex and persistent problem; are Orwell's explanations for it reasonable? Is his thinking on the subject comprehensive enough? Or does he have his favorite targets for criticism that blind him to other possibilities? Can you imagine a world in which his proposed solutions have been enacted? Are these solutions actually workable? What might be some unintended consequences that Orwell failed to consider? Orwell's other works deal with varying degrees of poverty, as well, even if in a less head-on fashion. The citizens of Oceania in *1984,* for instance, live with constant privations and are forced into creative solutions to deal with shortages in basic necessities. Certainly, this reflects some degree of poverty. For works like this, you will engage the same questions as above, but you will have to do a little more interpretive work to discover the ideas that Orwell is espousing. When working with an issue like this in the fictional pieces, remember also that you cannot necessarily equate what a character says with what Orwell believes.

If, for example, you are looking at a statement about poverty made by Gordon in *Keep the Aspidistra Flying*, do not automatically assume that Gordon is merely a mouthpiece for his author. Instead, examine the text for clues about whether you are supposed to see Gordon as a flawed character or if you should be reading what he says ironically.

2. **Revolution:** There are two fundamental strategies for changing the world: slow reformation or sudden revolution. This is a theme frequently visited in Orwell's works. Which strategy does Orwell appear to prefer? Does revolution, according to Orwell, lead to meaningful change?

   The list of works dealing with this theme is fairly long; *Animal Farm, 1984, Homage to Catalonia, The Road to Wigan Pier, Keep the Aspidistra Flying,* and "The Lion and the Unicorn" all take up this subject in one form or another. The starting point for your thinking about this theme is the question: Is revolution effective? Proponents of revolution claim that only violent ruptures in the texture of society are radical enough to introduce the entirely new paradigms needed to effect real change. According to them, any attempts at gradual reformation will simply be absorbed and neutralized by the existing power structure. Proponents of reformation, on the other hand, argue that revolution ultimately fails at meaningful reform. People desire stability and continuity, they reason, and so eventually all revolutions will suffer a backlash that will undo the progress that was made. How do you see this tension playing out in Orwell's works? The approach you take may depend on the particular work you pick. Orwell offers a number of scenarios involving revolution. There are the works in which revolution is apparently successful, such as *Animal Farm* or *Homage to Catalonia,* works in which revolution seems to fail, such as *1984* or *Keep the Aspidistra Flying,* and works through which Orwell proposes revolution, though it is not actually attempted, such as "The Lion and the Unicorn" and *The Road to Wigan Pier.* Evaluate how successful revolution is in the work you choose. Does revolution lead to permanent change? Why or why not? Where it fails, why does it? Does

Orwell propose true revolution in his political writings, or does he lean toward a slower process of reformation?

3. **The power of the written word:** As an author, Orwell obviously is quite concerned with the relative power of the written word. Many authors admit to vacillating between feeling that writing is one of the most persuasive forces available and the feeling that writing is ineffectual and completely incapable of effecting change. What do you see as Orwell's stance about the power of the written word?

In addition to being written works themselves, almost all of Orwell's works contain references to, discussions of, or scenes involving the written word. Two of his more famous essays, "Why I Write" and "Politics and the English Language," deal almost exclusively with writing. In *Animal Farm*, the pigs' ability to read and write, and their manipulation of written language, give them a great advantage over the other animals. Winston's decision to keep a diary represents his first step toward rebellion against Big Brother in *1984*. Orwell bemoans the role that the press played in the Spanish civil war in *Homage to Catalonia*. In *Keep the Aspidistra Flying*, Gordon is a published poet, working in a bookstore, who vacillates between rapture and disgust every time he tries to work on his new poetry. In each of these situations, some kind of value judgment is being made about the ability of the written word to accomplish something. Without writing, could the pigs have tyrannized the other animals? What about keeping a diary is so threatening to Big Brother that it deserves the death penalty? Examine all instances in which characters read and write or talk about the written word in the work you are reading. Does writing accomplish anything? If not, then why has Orwell himself written about it? What does it all say about the power of the written word?

Character

If you are having difficulty devising a topic or method of critical approach to a piece of literature, it can be helpful to begin with an examination of its characters. List all of the characters and their traits, noting whether or not they develop during the course of the story or novel. Record what you know about the characters' relationships with one another as well. Then, you might look for any patterns—is there something interesting to be said about Orwell's portrayals of certain groups of people? How does he depict the poor? The middle class? Or, perhaps you might choose to focus on a particular character who changes in an interesting way, analyzing his or her development and the reasons and results of this evolution. Or, there might be a particular relationship or group of relationships you can analyze and evaluate—dictators or women characters, for example.

Sample Topics:

1. **Female characters:** For a man who fought so tirelessly against the inequities of classism, Orwell had a much spottier record when it came to dealing with gender inequities. Ever since he became famous enough to draw attention from literary critics, Orwell has been roundly criticized for perpetuating patriarchal stereotypes and doing nothing to help women gain equality. Looking carefully at Orwell's work, what do you notice about his female characters? Are they mere stereotypes? Do they do anything to undercut the patriarchy?

   It is true that Orwell created very few memorable female characters. However, nearly all of this works do include some female characters, however minor. If you are working on *Animal Farm*, you might compare and contrast the two horses, Mollie and Clover. Certainly, Mollie seems to be a caricature of a particular female stereotype—weak, vain, and foolish. Clover may appear more levelheaded and likeable, but is she any more empowered than Mollie? Or is she just another stereotype herself? Does she really do anything more than support Boxer? Other female characters you may consider include Julia in *1984*, Mrs. Brooker in *The Road to Wigan Pier*, or Rosemary in *Keep the Aspidistra Flying*. Another interesting approach may be to address the lack of female characters in certain works. Although Orwell states that there are significantly fewer homeless women than men in England, what do you make of the almost total absence of women in *Down and Out in Paris and London?* Is it possible that a great number of women were suffering just as badly, or even worse, than the men Orwell was documenting, but he overlooked them? Is he making unverified and stereotypical assumptions when he suggests that women have resources for keeping themselves out of homelessness that men do not? All in all, do you find that Orwell is patronizing or dismissive toward women? Is he ultimately a sexist?

2. **The working class:** As a champion of the working class, Orwell, not surprisingly, populates his books with many working class characters. How does he choose to portray these people whose backgrounds are so different from his own? Does he romanticize them, or are his portrayals brutally honest and accurate?

Because Orwell was so committed to socialism and bettering the living conditions of the working class, working class characters show up in nearly everything he ever wrote. In some cases, such as *The Road to Wigan Pier* or *Down and Out in Paris and London,* the working classes are the primary focus. In other works, like *Keep the Aspidistra Flying* and *Animal Farm,* characters move between the middle and lower classes, illustrating the differences between the different strata. In *1984,* the working class, in the form of the Proles, make up the vast majority of the society but are nearly invisible. All of these portrayals tell us a great deal about Orwell's feelings about the working class. Of course, Orwell made no secret of his admiration for and concern for the people of the working class, so it does not require any interpretive work to get that far. What is worth studying, however, is how nuanced Orwell's treatment of the working class was. Did he have a sort of romantic obsession with the working class? If so, did that cause him to exaggerate their virtues and overlook their shortcomings? How much sense does it even make to speak of a large group of people like this? Do they, in fact, share enough common traits to allow such discussions, or are they all individuals who deserve to be depicted on an individual basis?

3. **Dictators:** Several of Orwell's works feature dictators as characters, either as direct participants in the plot or as looming forces

offstage. How does Orwell portray dictators and tyrants in his works? What motivates them? Where does the distinction lie between a strong, but benevolent, leader and a totalitarian ruler?

The "bad guys" in Orwell's works are often larger-than-life tyrants, leaders who use their power primarily to quash any perceived rebellion against their rule. What do these characters look and act like? How can you tell the difference between a good leader and a tyrant in Orwell's world? As a staunch pro-ponent of democratic socialism, Orwell presumably thought an ideal government would be relatively weak, leaving the people to govern themselves for the most part. Does this ideal color his ideas of what a dictator is? What does Orwell suggest motivates a despotic ruler? What is it that corrupts leaders? Works that would lend themselves to this topic include *Animal Farm, 1984, Homage to Catalonia,* and "The Lion and the Unicorn."

History and Context

Even when writing about times other than their own, authors write from within the context of their own culture and history. And some authors, like Orwell, write extensively about contemporary politics and culture. Much of the impetus of Orwell's writing lies in contemporary events, and, as a reader, if you do not understand what those events were, you will not fully appreciate what Orwell was trying to say. For instance, Orwell writes with a great sense of urgency in *The Road to Wigan Pier* about the need for England to adopt socialism. On the one hand, he has depicted in great detail the plight of the struggling coal workers, and it is a depiction that carries a great deal of persuasive power. On the other hand, he does not suggest that the entire coal industry is on the verge of collapse, and, while it is a sad truth, it is a fact that poverty has always plagued humankind. Thinking of it this way may leave you puzzled as to why Orwell's argument is infused with such a sense of urgency and may lead you to criticize him for being melodramatic. If, however, you consider that Orwell was writing with one eye cast toward the European continent, where Hitler was rapidly consolidating power and assembling a terrifying war machine, your con-clusions about the tone of the book will very likely change. If Orwell fore-saw the danger facing all of Europe and knew that England would need to be at its strongest to repel the Nazis, then you can understand his fear that the existing class stratification of England sapped the country's strength—consolidating privilege and power in the hands of a few while disenfranchising the majority of the citizens—and would ultimately lead to England being overrun by Germany in the impending war. Orwell's urgency makes a lot more sense in this context, and knowing this is likely to alter your interpretation of his argument. While doing historical research can seem like a lot of extra work sometimes, the benefits you reap from the research, as shown in the quality of your essay, will far outweigh the labor.

Sample Topics:

1. **English class structure:** It is virtually impossible to understand most of Orwell's writings without having at least a rudimentary understanding of the class system in Great Britain. Once you have a grasp of how the class structure works, you are in a better position to interpret and analyze Orwell's critiques of it.

   It can be extraordinarily difficult for a twenty-first century resident of the United States to understand the ways in which England's relatively rigid class structure permeated every single aspect of life in Orwell's time. Even today, the British class structure is far more robust than anything found in the U.S. Americans sometimes believe, somewhat naively, that someone can simply "opt out" of the class distinctions—if you do not care what people say if you call a lavatory a toilet, then the class system has no power over you—but that is very difficult to do when every single feature of life, from language, to clothing, to food, is a determining factor of class. Without understanding the class system, it can be nearly incomprehensible why Gordon, in *Keep the Aspidistra Flying,* refuses to spend the "Joey" for fear of being looked at askance by a shop girl, what Orwell means in the conclusion to *The Road to Wigan Pier* by "we have nothing to lose but our aitches" (204), or why the younger Orwell, in "Shooting an Elephant," feels compelled to kill the elephant even though he has no desire to. Learning about the intricacies of the class system in England will require a little research on your part. Two excellent sources to kick off your research are David Cannadine's *The Class in Britain* and Christopher Hibbert's *The English: A Social History, 1066–1945.* Once you have a good overview of the social class structure, you can approach Orwell's works with a fuller sense of what he is criticizing. Are the class distinctions as odious as he claims? What would be the consequences of scrapping the system? Would there be more to lose than he implies?

2. **The rise of fascism:** Much of Orwell's body of work was produced in the latter half of the 1930s and first half of the 1940s, as England increasingly faced the consequences of the bellicose ascendancy of fascism in Austria, Germany, Italy, and, to some extent, Spain. The anxiety this produced in Orwell forms a tangible subtext to all that he wrote in this period. Understanding the menacing political shifts occurring in Europe during the 1930s is fundamental to understanding Orwell's works from this period.

In order to appreciate fully what is going on in a great number of Orwell's work—"Politics and the English Language," *Homage to Catalonia, Animal Farm,* "The Lion and the Unicorn," *1984,* "Why I Write," and *The Road to Wigan Pier*—you must first appreciate what Hitler's rise to power meant to England. For the United States, World War II did not begin until the very end of 1941, and even then, the fighting was an ocean away. England, on the other hand, entered the war in 1939 and was heavily damaged by German bombings. Even before the war began, however, England watched nervously as Hitler and Mussolini consolidated power, stoked rabid nationalism, and brazenly ratcheted up their countries' militaries. The inevitability of war was apparent years before the actual outbreak, and the sort of tyrant Hitler was became all too clear well in advance of open hostilities. To understand the fears being faced by Orwell, do some research into the pre-war years in Europe. You might begin your research at the Internet Modern History Sourcebook (www.fordham.edu/halsall/mod/modsbook.html), which provides links to many primary historical sources dealing both with the lead up to WWII and with fascism. Two excellent print sources you will find helpful are *The Dark Valley: A Panorama of the 1930s* by Piers Brendon and *The Rise of Fascism* by F. L. Carsten. Once you have completed your research, return to the Orwell text on which you are working. While Hitler obviously was a very real and awful force in Europe, does Orwell in any way take advantage of Hitler's rise to try to make a point? In what ways does Orwell use the spread of fascism in his writing? Does history bear out Orwell's predictions, or was he a bit paranoid?

Philosophy and Ideas

Another way to approach a piece of literature is to think about what social ideas or philosophies it comments on or engages in some way. What ideological concerns does the work address? What "big ideas" are being debated in some way? To write an essay about philosophy and ideas, first think about the broad social concepts, ideologies, or complicated questions about human endeavors that are present in the work. Simply identifying those philosophical concerns is not enough, however. Next, determine what the work is saying about those ideas. This part may be trickier than it sounds at first. While you may recognize that Ravelston is merely a character in *Keep the Aspidistra Flying* and that, therefore, we must approach his statements about socialism with a certain amount of caution, you must also be aware that Orwell is likewise a character in his own nonfiction works, if for no other reason than Orwell the author is having to write about a younger incarnation of himself in his memoirs. Therefore, you have to be careful not to accept immediately and without criticism what Orwell the character may say about socialism in *The Road to Wigan Pier*. Consider the possibility that, by the time Orwell was writing his final revision of the book, his ideas may have evolved, and he may treat the ideas he had held the previous year with a touch of irony.

Sample Topics:

1. **Socialism:** Of all the ideologies that appear in Orwell's works, none is so prevalent or so dear to him as the social and economic philosophy of democratic socialism. What precisely does Orwell mean when he talks about socialism? Is his version of socialism an ideal, or could it be practically implemented in the ways he suggests? Does he truly believe in it, or is it more of a comforting thought for him?

   In "Why I Write," Orwell rather famously conceded, "Every line of serious work that I have written since 1936 has been written, directly or indirectly, *against* totalitarianism and *for* democratic

Socialism, as I understand it" (8). However, in *The Road to Wigan Pier*, he also asserted, "We all rail against class-distinctions, but very few people seriously want to abolish them. Here you come upon the important fact that every revolutionary opinion draws part of its strength from a secret conviction that nothing can be changed" (138). Is this a confession on Orwell's part? Is his socialism a sort of intellectual and moral security blanket rather than a real-world solution? Or is he counting himself among the very few who truly want to see a socialist revolution? And what does Orwell mean when he talks about socialism? In *Wigan Pier* he says that "the real Socialist is one who wishes—not merely conceives it as desirable, but actively wishes—to see tyranny overthrown" (194). That is his essential definition of socialism, though clearly that same desire could be shared by people of a number of political persuasions. Orwell may be coy about revealing the exact specifications of his brand of socialism, but he must know what they are. Why will he not be more specific? Looking at his works, what would you say are the fundamental tenets of socialism to Orwell? Why is he convinced that socialism is the best system? The more you understand about socialism, the better your essay is likely to turn out. You will find it worthwhile to do some research to understand just what is suggested by socialism. A great place to start is Thomas Fleming's *Socialism*. The Internet Modern History Sourcebook (www.fordham.edu/halsall/mod/modsbook.html) compiles a number of primary sources related to socialism that will also be quite helpful.

2. **The purpose of art:** The purpose of art has been hotly debated throughout human history. What does Orwell have to say about this topic? What is the purpose of literature according to Orwell? Is he an artist?

Questions about the form and function of art recur so often that an entire branch of philosophy, called aesthetics, is devoted to pondering them. There have been many different lines of thought on the subject, with some artists believing that art should inspire moral improvement in its viewers while other thinkers claim that art exists solely to be enjoyed. In the decades before Orwell produced and published his work, much of the Western literary world was controlled by the realists, naturalists, and the aesthetes. The realists and naturalists primarily believed that literature should be an accurate reflection of life. While it might reveal truths about human existence, it had no business in trying to effect change. The aesthetes took an even more radical view. They believed that art existed only to be enjoyed sensually. Art brought pleasure. Clearly, Orwell broke with both of these traditions. In "Why I Write," he explained that his motivation for writing came from a deep-seated "[d]esire to push the world in a certain direction, to alter other people's idea of the kind of society that they should strive after" (5). And he stated, without hesitation, "Every line of serious work that I have written since 1936 has been written, directly or indirectly, *against* totalitarianism and *for* democratic socialism, as I understand it" (8). Unlike the naturalists and the realists, Orwell describes the world not as it is but in ideal terms. In *1984*, for instance, he describes what the world might become if humans do not take steps to preserve their liberty. And, unlike the aesthetes, Orwell wants his writing to do much more than entertain or bring pleasure. In fact, the aesthetes would have claimed that Orwell's writing was not art at all. From their perspective, what he wrote was journalism at best, propaganda at worst. What is your opinion of Orwell's writing? Is it literature? Or is it reporting? Where do you draw the line? Is a pamphlet urging you to become a socialist literature? If not, then does *The Road to Wigan Pier* qualify as literature? If it is not, why then is it still so widely read and studied? What about Orwell's works of fiction? Does the fact that he has a political agenda in any way minimize the literary qualities of *1984* or *Animal Farm?*

Form and Genre

Paying careful attention to the craftsmanship behind a piece of literature can often yield valuable and surprising insights into its meaning and help you arrive at a deeper understanding and interpretation. To begin thinking about an essay of this kind, you might reread the piece while keeping in mind that it is a deliberate construction. The words are certainly of primary importance, but the ways in which the author put the piece together carry meaning, as well. Ask yourself why the author made the decisions he did when he was writing it, because an author has many decisions to make aside from developing the plot. When Orwell wanted to write about and comment on the Russian Revolution and Stalin's brutal dictatorship, he could have chosen any number of ways to approach it. Curiously enough, he chose to tell his story using talking animals that run the humans off their farm. When you consider all the various options he must have considered before coming to this one, you realize that making that choice must have carried a great deal of meaning for him. Writing the novel in the form of a fable, after all, put it at great risk of being dismissed as frivolous and silly. What does the fable offer that a more serious and straightforward treatment does not? These are the sorts of questions you find yourself asking when you write about form and genre. When you treat each aspect of a piece of literature as a well-considered decision, something the author carefully thought about, you find that meaning extends far beyond just the words on the page.

Sample Topics:

1. **Questions of genre:** Orwell has a knack for confounding easy classification. His works often seem to straddle categories of genre, drawing on multiple traditions while not quite fitting into any of them. What significance do questions of genre carry? Why are Orwell's works so difficult to classify? Does his work transcend traditional categories, or is it too sloppy to fit into an appropriate grouping?

   Orwell hardly produced a book-length work that does not defy easy classification. *Animal Farm* announces itself as a fable, yet it deals satirically with complex political situations—subject matter far outside the normal purview of the fable. *1984* is also a serious political commentary but shares a lot of features with science fiction, a genre not always taken as seriously as other forms of literature. *Homage to Catalonia* blends elements of memoir, history, and journalism, sometimes in very questionable ways. *The Road to Wigan Pier* has an unusual two-part structure, and many readers find that the two parts are so completely different that they question whether they constitute a single work. Is Orwell simply not a very careful writer? Or is he purposefully playing with genre? If he is, what's his game? Why might he want people to pay attention not only to the content of his works but to the forms as well? Why might he want people to stop and explicitly question the genres of his works?

2. **Structure and continuity in nonfiction works:** While Orwell was often applauded for the way he structured his works of fiction, he was just as often criticized for the curious structuring of his nonfiction. Why would there be a difference in his ability to form his thoughts depending on whether they are fictional or nonfictional? Could there be a reason that his nonfiction works have unusual structures?

Some of Orwell's decisions about the construction of his works earned him a great deal of criticism and caused his publishers much grief. In fact, his publishers have at times taken drastic measures to right what they saw as the mistakes in the forms of his books. In *Homage to Catalonia,* Orwell interrupts the flow of his mostly chronological narrative with two chapters of political analysis. Orwell himself recognized the rupture in the flow of the narrative and even suggested to his readers, "If you are not interested in the horrors of party politics, please skip" (46). Later editors of his works took the step of moving the two chapters into appendices. *Down and Out in Paris and London* was likewise dogged by charges of an inconsistent narration. According to the critics, the two large divisions of the plot—the Paris section and the London section—seemed to have little to do with one another. A similar criticism was leveled at *The Road to Wigan Pier.* The first half of the book is a relatively objective study of the coal miners of England, while the second half is a highly autobiographical and opinionated appeal for socialism. Orwell's publisher was so worried about the marketing implications of the incongruent parts that he published some copies of the book that contained only Part I. What does this string of questionable decisions about structure suggest to you? Was this a particular authorial weakness of Orwell's? Why does he not seem to have these kinds of troubles when it comes to fiction? Is he less adept at structuring nonfiction, or could it be that these decisions were quite intentional? What would justify forcing seemingly discordant elements together in a single work?

Symbols, Imagery, and Language

Works of literature are filled with symbols and images that can lead us to meaningful discoveries about the themes and meanings of these pieces. When reading, we should pay close attention to images that recur throughout a piece and to images that seem to be especially significant because of the attention the author devotes to them or their location near an important scene or character. Once you have identified potentially meaningful images and symbols, you will want to closely read the passages that include them. First, ask yourself what traditional associations these images or symbols carry, and then look closely at the particular way they are functioning in the literary work you are studying. Is the author enhancing an image's traditional associations or perhaps tweaking them in some way? Once you have some ideas about the meaning of a particular image, think about ways to connect your new knowledge to the central ideas of the work. How does what you have discovered about a symbol or image help you to interpret the story or novel? You can look at symbols and images within a single work or locate similar images in multiple works if you wish to consider Orwell's work as a body instead of focusing on a single text. In addition to symbols and imagery, you will want to pay close attention to the author's language as you read. It is helpful to keep in mind that the English language contains so many ways to say the same thing. Thinking about why the author chose exactly the words that he or she did and not the other options available will often lead to meaningful discoveries about a work's theme that can help you to construct or support a claim in your essay.

Sample Topics:

1. **The invisible enemy:** In many of Orwell's works, the greatest threats to freedom are enemies who never make a direct appearance in the work and who may not even actually exist. Why does Orwell rely on these invisible enemies? What is he suggesting about the nature of fear and propaganda?

   In Orwell's worlds, often the greatest source of fear and terror is someone you never actually see. In some cases, it is clear that the invisible enemy is merely a propaganda tool of the ruling class. Such is the case in *Animal Farm*, for instance. The reader is not expected to believe that Snowball is behind all of the sabotage that Napoleon accuses him of. However, the image of the conniving and evil Snowball works to consolidate the animals' loyalty to Napoleon. In other cases, the existence of the invisible enemy is questionable. Is there any evidence that Big Brother actually exists in *1984?* Does that uncertainty make him even more powerful? What about Emmanuel Goldstein? Does he exist? Is he responsible for all of the rebellious acts the party accuses him of? Or is he a creation of the party? What benefit does a created adversary bring to the party? Is a fictional opponent in some ways better than an actual one? Even in his nonfiction works, Orwell took advantage of the concept of the invisible enemy. In *Homage to Catalonia,* Franco assumes this role, and in *The Road to Wigan Pier,* Hitler does. Notice, for instance, how Hitler provides Orwell with an excuse for socialist reform in England. According to Orwell, Hitler is a dire and imminent threat to the security of England, and the only way to marshal the full resources of England is to implement socialism. Though Hitler certainly was a historical figure and did pose a grave threat to England, Orwell still seems to be manipulating Hitler as a symbol here. What specifics does he ever provide about Hitler? Very few, in fact. What does Hitler symbolize for Orwell? Why might Hitler operate better as a symbol if Orwell never directly addresses him in a factual way? By keeping Hitler as a looming threat just offstage, never quite seen, what does Orwell accomplish?

2. **Language use and meaning:** Orwell consistently demonstrates his belief that language choices have very real consequences and that, therefore, people need to be very conscious and precise in their use of language. How does language operate in Orwell's works? Do minor choices in language carry as much meaning and consequence as Orwell suggests?

Orwell addresses the use of language quite explicitly in a number of works. "Why I Write" and "Politics and the English Language" deal almost exclusively with language use and argue that there is such a thing as better and worse language usage. In *Animal Farm,* the greatest advantage the pigs have over the other animals is their ability to read and write. This skill allows them to manipulate language in subtle but important ways and gives them great power over the other animals. In *1984,* the party equates a robust and growing language with a freedom of thought that they wish to eradicate. Their goal with Newspeak is to pare the language down to an absolute minimum, reducing the citizens' ability to think for themselves in the process. In both *The Road to Wigan Pier* and *Down and Out in Paris and London,* Orwell makes the case that speech patterns carry a great deal of meaning as class markers and therefore have great consequences on every aspect of life in England. And in *Homage to Catalonia,* Orwell analyzes the various ways that people speak of the war, noting in particular that people began referring to the war in passive voice, thereby indicating their lack of responsibility for the atrocities occurring. Once they made this linguistic distinction, their obligation to do something positive to end the war diminished. Is Orwell right about the operation of language? Do seemingly minor linguistic choices have major consequences? Or is language more flexible and malleable than that? As long as two people understand what the other means, do the small details not matter? Is there such a thing as "better language" or "corrupted language"? What do the choices we make when we speak mean?

Compare and Contrast Essays

Setting two elements side by side in order to determine their similarities and differences can be surprisingly illuminating. You might choose two elements that seem similar to you and spend some time focusing on their distinguishing characteristics or you might select two elements that seem very different and examine them closely for underlying similarities. You can choose elements within a single work, elements in two or more works by the same author, or even elements in works by different authors. You will want, of course, not only to identify differences and similarities, but to choose the most meaningful ones and interpret them for your reader. This way, your essay will not amount to a list of interesting details but will instead use significant similarities and differences to make a point about the work(s) you are analyzing.

Sample Topics:

1. **Orwell's fiction and nonfiction:** Orwell produced two significant bodies of work, one of fictional works and one of nonfictional pieces. Compare and contrast some of Orwell's fiction and nonfiction. What does each type of work reveal about the other? Does Orwell convey the same ideas in each type of work, or does he use each type for a different purpose?

Although he wrote extensively in both fiction and nonfiction, Orwell claimed that all of his work—at least all written after 1936—was anti-totalitarian and pro-socialism. Looking at one of his nonfiction pieces and one of this fictional ones, do you find that they share the same message? For instance, if you put "The Lion and the Unicorn" side by side with *Animal Farm*, does Orwell seem to advocating the same goals? Or preaching against the same evils? Presumably, when an author writes nonfiction, he is somewhat compelled to give his straightforward views on the issues about which he is writing. When writing fiction, on the other hand, he is a bit more free to try out other ideas, to imbue characters with variations of his own theories and then let them play out in the fictional world. Do you find this to be the case with Orwell, or is he reasonably consistent? Does reading the fiction and nonfiction side by side give you any greater insight into Orwell's ideas?

2. **Orwell and other socially conscious writers:** Orwell belonged to a generation of writers who believed literature was a powerful tool for effecting positive social change. Compare and contrast Orwell's works with works from some of these other activist authors.

The way that Orwell used his writing to warn of the dangers of totalitarianism and to advocate for socialism was a relatively new phenomenon in the literary world. Authors in the generations before Orwell usually thought that art reflected the world, but it did not act upon it. In the early twentieth century, however, writers and other artists became increasingly political and activist and saw in their art the opportunity to influence the rest of the world. Orwell was part of a generation of writers who strove to better the world through their art. Compare and contrast Orwell's work with the work of one of these authors. For instance, you might compare and contrast *1984* with Aldous Huxley's *Brave New World; The Road to Wigan Pier* with Upton Sinclair's *The Jungle; Animal Farm* with *It Can't Happen Here* by Sinclair Lewis; or *Down and Out in Paris and London* with *The Grapes of Wrath* by John Steinbeck.

Bibliography and Online Resources

Bloom, Harold. Bloom's Modern Critical Interpretations. *Animal Farm.* New York: Chelsea House, 1999.

———. *George Orwell's* 1984. Bloom's Notes. New York: Chelsea House, 1996.

———. *George Orwell's Animal Farm.* Bloom's Notes. New York: Chelsea House, 1999.

Brendon, Piers. *The Dark Valley: A Panorama of the 1930s.* New York: Vintage, 2002.

Cannadine, David. *The Class in Britain.* New York: Penguin, 2000.

Carsten, F. L. *The Rise of Fascism.* Los Angeles: U of California P, 1982.

Crick, Bernard. *George Orwell: A Life.* Boston: Little, Brown, 1980.

Fleming, Thomas. *Socialism.* Political Systems of the World. New York: Benchmark, 2008.

Hibbert, Christopher. *The English: A Social History, 1066–1945.* New York: HarperCollins, 1988.

Hollis, Christopher. *A Study of George Orwell.* Chicago: Regnery, 1956.

Internet Modern History Sourcebook. Accessed on 15 Nov. 2009. <http://www.fordham.edu/halsall/mod/modsbook.html>.

Lee, Robert A. *Orwell's Fiction.* Notre Dame, IN: U of Notre Dame P: 1969.

Orwell, George. *1984.* New York: Penguin, 1972.

———. *Animal Farm.* New York: Penguin, 1972.

———. *Down and Out in Paris and London.* New York: Harcourt, 1961.

———. *Homage to Catalonia.* San Diego: Harcourt Brace, 1980.

———. *Keep the Aspidistra Flying.* San Diego: Harcourt, 1956.

———. "The Lion and the Unicorn." *Why I Write.* New York: Penguin, 2005, 11–94.

———. "Politics and the English Language." *Why I Write.* New York: Penguin, 2005, 102–20.

———. *The Road to Wigan Pier.* New York: Penguin, 1985.

————. "Shooting an Elephant." *A Collection of Essays.* New York: Harvest, 1981, 148–55.

————. "Why I Write." *Why I Write.* New York: Penguin, 2005, 1–10.

Patai, Daphne. *The Orwell Mystique: A Study in Male Ideology.* Amherst: U of Massachusetts P, 1984.

Russell, Bertrand. "George Orwell." *World Review* 16 (1950): 5–6.

Shelden, Michael. *Orwell: The Authorized Biography.* New York: Harper Collins, 1991.

1984

READING TO WRITE

PUBLISHED IN 1949, Orwell's classic dystopian novel, *Nineteen Eighty-Four* (or *1984* as it is often published now), has become so well known as to have provided a sort of shorthand for critiques of overly intrusive and heavy-handed government. One need only to apply the epithet of "Big Brother" to a government or organization in order to conjure up the nightmarish oppression so vividly portrayed in Orwell's most famous novel. *1984* depicts a fictional society ruled by an oppressive regime that functions mainly to ensure and to increase its own power and status. To this end, Big Brother demands complete obedience and allows its subjects very little in the way of personal freedom of action or expression. Not for lack of considerable effort, the government has been unsuccessful in wiping out all thoughts of rebellion. Protagonist Winston Smith marshals the courage to engage in a small act that is considered a terrible crime by the party: recording his own thoughts in a private diary. Winston's journal reveals a great deal about the society in which he lives and about his own inner workings as well. Have a look at the scene that describes Winston making an entry in his journal:

> He was a lonely ghost uttering a truth nobody would ever hear. But so long as he uttered it, in some obscure way the continuity was not broken. It was not by making yourself heard but by staying sane that you carried on the human heritage. He went back to the table, dipped his pen, and wrote:
>
> *To the future or to the past, to a time when thought is free, when men are different from one another and do not live alone—to a time when truth exists and what is done cannot be undone:*

From the age of uniformity, from the age of solitude, from the age of Big Brother, from the age of doublethink—greetings! (26–27)

That Winston is concerned about carrying on what he considers to be the "human heritage" makes it clear that he believes that the society he lives in strips its citizens not only of their freedom but of their very humanity. When he writes in his diary, Winston compares his own totalitarian society to an alternative society; though he is not sure if that society is to be found in the "present" or the "past," Winston clearly visualizes an alternative to party society, a fundamentally different world that recognizes and allows for the humanity of its inhabitants.

At this point, you might be wondering how it is that a government can take away the humanity of its citizens and if such a feat is, in fact, possible. To figure this out, think about what Winston sees as the defining qualities of humanity. We can begin to do this by examining his roughly parallel descriptions of his own age of dehumanization and the alternate past or present age he imagines. To begin with, while his own age is one of "uniformity," Winston imagines the other possible society as one in which "thought is free" and "men are different from one another." This comparison makes two points clear: One, that when Winston speaks of uniformity in Oceania, he means that all people are expected to share the same thoughts and opinions and, two, that he thinks it more natural or correct for people to engage in their own thought processes which, when combined with their life's experiences, will lead them to their own personal conclusions and opinions. The expression of those unique thoughts will inevitably create people who are recognizably different from one another. So, we can say that one aspect of humanity, according to Winston, is freedom of thought and the related freedom to create a unique identity based at least in part on those thoughts.

Further, Winston speaks of his age as the age of solitude and of the alternative age as one in which men "do not live alone." He indicates here that one of the ways Oceania divests its citizens of their humanity is by preventing them from establishing relationships with one another. You might note at this point that Oceania's citizens spend a great deal of time with one another at party-mandated events that seem to fill up their every waking hour. While this lifestyle would certainly not be considered solitude in the traditional sense, it is designed to reinforce certain behaviors and ideas that the party wants to cultivate rather than to foster true interpersonal interaction. Winston's indication that people should not "live alone" suggests that he sees true community, true relationships, as something that involves making a choice between sharing and privacy. In other words, the only way to have a true relationship with another person is to choose to trade privacy for spending time with that person, a situation that requires one to have ownership of one's own time in the first place. Winston suggests these kinds of relationships—not directed group activity—to be the kinds of interactions that are vital to the human experience.

Finally, when Winston despairs over Big Brother and doublethink, he imagines an alternative society in which "truth exists" and "what is done cannot be undone." Setting up this comparison, Winston criticizes his own society for being so driven by party ideology that it requires its citizens to engage in complicated mental processes, often denying what they perceive as reality, in order to adapt to the party's self-serving and constantly fluctuating versions of reality and history. Winston wants to live in a society that acknowledges what is real whether or not it serves the goals of the people in power. How, then, is what is "real" determined? Winston seems to believe that truth and history lie in the individual citizen's observations and memories. Were they allowed to express these, presumably they would arrive at some sort of collective interpretation. Further, although all societies have, in some form, competing visions of truth and alternate versions of history, presumably, in the kind of society Winston imagines, an individual who holds a view inconsistent with the mainstream consensus would be allowed to retain that view and even to argue for it to others.

We have now established that Winston views freedom of thought, interpersonal relationships, and the power to participate in the social processes of interpreting "truth" and recording "history" as the fundamental building blocks of humanity that Big Brother strips away. Winston wants to ensure that there is a possibility of achieving an alternative society that respects these needs, and he believes that to keep this possibility alive he must ensure the "continuity" of humanity. But how does one do that in such an oppressive world? Winston has a tentative link to a time before the party; he has memories and dreams of his mother and their life in a different world, but those who were born later, like Julia, do not. All they know is life under party rule. If they cannot remember the fundamental aspects of their humanity, and those who remember cannot pass it on to them in any way, then how will the continuity of humanity be sustained? Winston decides that the way to preserve the human heritage is simply to retain his own sanity, his own humanity. Presumably, Winston is thinking that there are other "lonely ghosts" who remember, or discover, their humanity besides himself and that as long as those people persevere, then when the opportunity for revolution arises, someone will be there to recognize and take advantage of it.

These observations bring up questions you might want to pursue. For one, you might want to think about whether or not Winston is ultimately successful if judged by his own terms. Winston actively engages in actions to preserve what he considers his humanity—engaging in a personal relationship with Julia; expressing his thoughts to her, to O'Brien, and to his diary; and refusing to believe party propaganda when it conflicts with his own personal sense of reality and truth. Winston pursues these things even though he knows that they will result in torture and death. By claiming and holding on to his humanity and his sanity for as long as he is able, do you think Winston has successfully done his part in preserving humanity's heritage? Or do you think the fact that he is ultimately brainwashed nullifies all his efforts? You might also examine Winston's benchmarks of humanity further. Does the rest of the novel bear out the connections he makes in his initial journal entry between humanity and freedom of thought, personal relationships, and the right to participate in the creation of reality by voicing one's own opinions and memories? Do any of these elements come to stand out as more important than the others? Finally, you might also investigate whether Winston's point of view, including his definition of the essence of humanity, is shared by the narrator and endorsed by the book.

In any case, when you decide on a topic you would like to pursue, you should begin by examining the novel for other passages that seem relevant to your line of questioning. Closely read these passages, analyzing the language to see what it reveals to you, and then allow the results to lead you to other passages to examine as well. Once you have come to some insightful conclusion that you would like to serve as your thesis, you will then revisit your analyses, looking for the points that best support your thesis. These points will serve as the evidence supporting your claim in the body paragraphs of your essay. You will certainly not use every observation in your essay. Much of the close-reading work you do will only help you to refine your topic or will end up bringing up interesting but unrelated issues. All of this you will simply ignore in the actual construction of your essay as it has already served its purpose—helping you arrive at an interesting and thoughtful thesis.

TOPICS AND STRATEGIES

1984 is a deeply textured and complex novel that has been the focus of many critical studies in the decades since its publication. Despite the vast interpretive work that has been done so far, the novel's depth, coupled with your personal perspective, provides nearly unlimited perspectives from which to approach the work. The sample topics below will give you an idea of the types of essays that might be written about this novel; they will get you thinking and help you generate your own topic. Alternatively, you might be particularly intrigued by one of the sample topics and choose to focus your essay on the basic question it poses. However, rather than attempting to write an essay that answers each subquestion provided in the sample topic in a linear fashion, you should use those questions as springboards to your own thinking, using them to help guide you back to the novel to find relevant passages to analyze, always recording your thoughts as you do this prewriting. Once you have generated some ideas and insights of your own, you are ready to leave the sample topic behind entirely and craft a thesis that will lay out your particular and distinct perspective on the topic.

Themes

When we talk about themes in literature, what we mean are the central ideas—the big ideas, if you will—that run through a work. One way to get at a work's themes is to ask yourself what a work makes you think about. What ideas does it force you to confront? Orwell's *1984* prompts contemporary American readers to think critically about many fundamental aspects of our lives that we typically take for granted, from the role of the government and its relationship to the populace to our freedom to express love. Thus, there are many themes in this novel that cry out to the modern reader for examination and discussion. The danger of such a rich thematic field is that the writer will try to cover too much ground. When you are thinking about writing an essay on a theme in *1984*, then, your first challenge will be to select the theme, or even one aspect of a particular theme, you want to examine and to push off to the side (perhaps for a later essay) all of the very interesting subtopics and details that intrigue you but that are not solidly connected to the theme you have chosen to investigate. Take government's role in society as an example. This theme could very easily lead you to discussion of the regulation of love or the disintegration of the family, and your essay could quickly get unwieldy as these topics could support essays in their own right. If you choose to focus on government, you will have to make a conscious effort to keep your focus on the party and its relationship to the people; you might certainly mention the loss of romantic love and the disintegration of the family unit as negative consequences of party control, but a discussion of the intricacies of these consequences likely belongs in another essay. One way to make sure you maintain a clear focus is to use the sample topics below to help you arrive at a clear thesis sentence that lays out the main point you want your essay to make. Then, if you make sure that all of the details and discussion in the body of your essay support that thesis sentence, you will know that your essay remains focused on its central point and does not veer off into tangential territory.

Sample Topics:

1. **Government's role in society:** The government is so overwhelming and all-controlling within the world of the novel that all serious consideration of the proper role of government is quashed. As readers, however, we have the opportunity to contrast the party to other forms of government and judge their respective success. What does the novel ultimately want to say about the relationship of government to the people under its control?

   Undoubtedly, *1984* explores the potential consequences of a totalitarian regime on the hearts and minds of the populace. What would you say is the main thrust of its critique? Begin by thinking about what you would consider the ideal relationship between a government and its people. What should the functions of a government be? What fundamental rights should its citizens possess? How should the government and its citizens relate to one another? You might think about the answers to these questions in terms of different forms of government—how, for example, would the ideal democratic government differ from the ideal socialist government? What type of ideology is Oceania's government most similar to? What are the party's goals and motivations? What is the relationship of the party to the people, including party members and Proles? Keeping all this in mind, what would you say is Orwell's main message about the role of government and its relationship to its citizens? Does learning that Orwell was a fierce advocate of socialism affect either your reading of the novel or your concept of socialism?

2. **The essence of humanity:** According to Orwell's *1984*, what defines the human experience? Generally speaking, we tend to think of each human life as unique and precious. Does that hold true in Oceania? What other way is there to conceive of human life and human essence?

After Winston has been caught and tortured, O'Brien tells him that if he is indeed a man, then he must be the last man left. What do you think he means by this? What characteristics or traits are there in Winston that are missing in rank and file party members? What makes him different? Are these same traits present in Julia? You will also want to consider whether Winston ultimately loses his humanity. If you think he does, can you pinpoint the exact moment? What does he become if he ceases to be a man? What are the pros and cons of his life at his most "human"—when he is rebelling against the party—and his life after he emerges from O'Brien's custody as Big Brother's biggest supporter? What is Orwell trying to say about the essence of humanity through Winston's story?

3. **Love:** What does the novel have to say about the nature of love under a repressive regime?

What might Winston and Julia's relationship have been like if they were both Proles? What if Winston had not been married before? Would they have enjoyed a long-term, satisfying romance, or is their connection too wrapped up in their mutual feelings about the party? Winston and Julia definitely see their relationship and the act of having sex as a political act—an act of rebellion against the party. Evaluate the success of this political act: What effect does Winston and Julia's relationship have on the political landscape? What effect might it have had if it had ended another way or if theirs was one of thousands of such liaisons? What possible political consequences could love as an act of rebellion produce? What effect might the politicizing of love have on the nature of love?

You might think about the current debate concerning same-sex marriages in context of this question. What is the government's role in regulating romantic relationships? Does it go too far, or not far enough, in the contemporary United States? Could same-sex relationships in contemporary society be seen as a political act similar to Winston and Julia's relationship in *1984?*

4. **Family ties:** If love is an expression of openness and is an expansive and inclusive human experience, what happens to it when expression is brutally restricted? Can love become an act of rebellion under such circumstances? What kind of commentary is Orwell making about the bonds of family in a totalitarian society?

Describe family life under Big Brother. You might take the Parsons, Winston's neighbors, as an example. How do the parents and children feel about each other? What are their relationships like? Are they an ideal party family? Why or why not? What function does the party see the family unit as playing? How might family relationships bolster or hinder party goals? Are Prole families different from party families? In what ways? What accounts for these differences? You might think as well about Winston's memories of his own family, particularly his mother and sister. How was his family, what little he remembers of it, different from the average party family of the present? Use this comparison to help you figure out how the meaning and function of family changes in the transition from a free to a controlled society.

5. **Hope or despair:** Analyze and evaluate the ending of *1984.* How does Orwell want to leave the reader feeling at the conclusion of the story?

According to Patrick Reilly, *1984* is not intended to prophesize an apocryphal ending for the world and leave its readers bereft of hope. Instead, the novel "paradoxically continues to fight for man even as it depicts the destruction of the last man alive. . . .

Without minimizing the threat or underestimating the danger, we must believe, but not too easily, that we can foil Oceania. That is the human response and surely the one that Orwell sought" (Reilly 127–29). Reread the novel, paying particular attention to the later chapters, particularly the final scenes. Do you see the novel as "fight[ing] for man"? In what way? Do readers believe that Oceania can be foiled? Why or why not? Write an essay in which you disagree with Reilly's argument, agree with and extend it, or modify it to reflect what you have determined to be the novel's message about hope and the human condition.

Character

One interesting way to work toward the central ideas and meanings of a work is through a study of its characters. When doing so, you may opt to study a single character, whether major or minor, and the role he or she plays in the novel, or you may study a class of characters, such as female or male characters. Orwell's *1984* has many characters that would make for interesting character analysis essays. Of course, there is the main character Winston, but there is also Julia, O'Brien, the Proles, and the elusive Big Brother, among others. When writing about character, you will want to be sure to record everything you know about the character you are focusing on, including what he or she says, does, and thinks. You will also want to analyze how you receive that information. Through whom is it being filtered, and how does that affect it? Consider whether the narration seems to align itself with a particular character. Does the novel seem to be critical of or sympathetic to the particular character you are looking at? You will want to examine how the character changes, whether that change is for better or worse, and what prompts that change. Finally, you will want to determine what function the character is playing in terms of the novel's overall themes and messages.

Sample Topics:

1. **Winston:** How you perceive Winston carries great consequence in terms of the final message you take away from the novel. Is Winston a sort of everyman, an unlikely hero who evolves as the novel progresses? Or is he somehow extraordinary from the beginning, a born rebel who finally forsakes his values in the end? Analyze and evaluate main character Winston.

Begin by recording what you would consider Winston's most salient characteristics and the important details of his life. What do you know about his background? His habits? His disappointments? His hopes and dreams? Do you think Winston is a fairly typical party member or is there something unique about him that sparks his rebellion? If so, what might that be? Do you find Winston to be a likeable character? Do you sympathize with him? Why or why not? Finally, consider whether you would label Winston a hero. Granted, his attempt at rebellion fails, but he knew it was going to. He knows exactly how things will end when he first begins to write in his diary. Would you agree that the fact that Winston follows through with his rebellion in the face of certain torture and failure makes him a hero? Why or why not?

2. **Big Brother:** For someone who never appears and who may not even exist, Big Brother plays a pivotal role in Oceania and in the novel. Analyze and evaluate the character Big Brother.

Who is Big Brother? How is he portrayed? What does he look like? Sound like? Is he a real person? Is he a fictitious character? If so, why does the party create him? What does he represent? How does Winston feel about him? How do other party members and Proles feel about him? Think about what the novel would be like without Big Brother. What major function does he serve in the novel's overall messages and themes?

3. **O'Brien:** O'Brien plays the role of the foil to Winston. But is O'Brien a meaningful character beyond his role? Had O'Brien not been there, would someone else have stepped in and behaved identically? Can someone loyal to the party even be a fully-fledged person? Analyze and evaluate the character of O'Brien.

Record everything you know about O'Brien. What are O'Brien's ultimate goals and motivations? Trace Winston's perceptions of him from the beginning of the novel to the end. The novel insinuates that Winston really knows O'Brien's true allegiance from the beginning even though he pretends to himself that O'Brien is part of the rebellion. Why would Winston deceive himself this way? What is it about O'Brien that fascinates him so? What do you think the story would be like if it were told from O'Brien's point of view? What the story be like if it did not include O'Brien at all? What point do you think Orwell is trying to make by including this character in the novel?

4. **The Proles:** Analyze and evaluate the "Proles," the people outside of the party who make up 85 percent of Oceania's population.

Examine the scenes in which Winston observes the Prole woman singing from his room above the junk shop. What does he notice and appreciate about her? What does he appreciate about Proles in general? How are their lives different from the lives of party members? How do party members aside from Winston perceive Proles? Why do they not want these people to be indoctrinated into the party? What function do they serve in Oceania? Why does Winston think that they might hold the key to the party's destruction and the revival of a more authentic society? Do you think Winston is right? Is there any indication that a Prole rebellion against the party is possible or probable? If it were to occur, would it have a chance at success? Why or why not?

5. **Julia:** Analyze and evaluate the character of Julia.

Why does Julia participate so heartily in party activities? What are her true motives? What does Winston initially think of Julia? What does he envision her inner life to be like? What does he envision doing to her? How and why does his opinion change? What views do she and Winston share? Although the two undoubtedly discover a great deal of common ground between them, Julia's view of the party and her relationship to it fundamentally differ from Winston's. How exactly? What do you think accounts for that difference? How do each of them respond to the torture they suffer at the hands of the party? How is a woman's life under the party different from a man's? What do the roles of women and men seem to be in party society?

History and Context

No author writes in a vacuum, and no literary work fails to bear the marks of the times in which it was written. Some novels are intentionally set in earlier historical periods, while others comment very heavily on their contemporary times. As time passes, however, the time period in which the novel was produced shifts for readers from contemporary to historical, and many of the nuances of the work can only be fully appreciated if the reader is willing to do some historical research. *1984* is one of those novels that is closely associated with the period in history in which it was conceived and on which it comments. It would definitely benefit a student of the novel to read about the Russian Revolution and the evolution of communism and fascism that occurred in the first half of the twentieth century. You might start with Rex A. Wade's *The Russian Revolution, 1917* or Shelia Fitzpatrick's *The Russian Revolution.* Then, reread the novel in order to better understand the kinds of social changes that Orwell was reacting to with *1984.* Once you have a stronger sense of cultural context, you might decide to focus your entire essay on a topic having to do with the text's relationship to its own historical moment. You might investigate what society, group of people, or political philosophy Orwell is criticizing in his novel. Or, you might investigate what the novel has to say about Orwell's stance toward women's rights and gender equality, taking care to understand these issues through the lens of Orwell's times, as well as through our own.

Sample Topics:

1. **The Soviet Union, communism, and socialism:** What kind of commentary does *1984* ultimately make on communism and socialism?

   Fredric Warburg writes that the government depicted in *1984* is a caricature of the Soviet Union. He writes:

   > For what is *1984* but a picture of man unmanned, of humanity without a heart, of a people without tolerance or civilization, of a government whose *sole* object is the maintenance of its absolute totalitarian power by every contrivance of cruelty. Here is the Soviet Union to the nth degree, a Stalin who never dies, a secret police with every device of modern technology. (103)

Orwell's own comments suggest that he is not targeting one society specifically but exploring what can happen when a philosophy he does support, socialism, is overtaken by one he does not, communism. He wants to be sure that people understand that his criticism of communism and fascism does not imply a critique of socialism. He writes:

> My recent novel is NOT intended as an attack on Socialism or on the British Labour Party (of which I am a supporter) but as a show-up of the perversions to which a centralized economy is liable and which have already been partly realized in Communism and Fascism. I do not believe that the kind of society I describe necessarily *will* arrive, but I believe (allowing of course for the fact that the book is a satire) that something resembling it *could* arrive. (Orwell, "Letter" 502)

With these thoughts in mind, reread *1984* and do some background reading on the Russian Revolution. Do you agree with Warburg that Orwell's critique is aimed directly at the Soviet Union, or do you believe Orwell's comments that the critique was designed as more of a general warning for the entire world?

2. **Orwell's portrayal of women:** Analyze and evaluate Orwell's portrayal of women in *1984.*

Orwell's *1984* was published in 1949, a time in which both the United States and England were still largely patriarchal countries that afforded women only a modicum of rights and circumscribed social roles. Daphne Patai criticizes Orwell for simply recreating the patriarchal social order of his own society instead of creating a new paradigm and then failing even to explore the ramifications of the patriarchal social order on the women in his story and on the culture of Oceania as a whole. She writes:

> The women in Orwell's narrative by and large appear as caricatures: They are Party secretaries, Party fanatics, Party wives like Katharine or the stereotypically helpless housewife Mrs. Parson. . . .[N]o female Inner Party members are mentioned.

When Winston sees a man and woman in the canteen, he
assumes that the woman is the man's secretary. . . . Although
Orwell reveals male dominance to be a continuing feature of
life in Oceania, he does not treat this as worthy of analysis and
does not raise the issue of its role in a totalitarian society. (243)

Do you agree with Patai's assertion that Oceania is fundamentally a patriarchal society? If so, do you also agree that Orwell,
typically so capable of calling traditional social ideas into
question, simply accepts this as matter of course and remains
uninterested in the gender issues his novel, perhaps unintentionally, raises? Write an essay in which you counter, confirm
and expand, or modify Patai's argument.

Philosophy and Ideas

All works of literature present us with ideological or philosophical elements to explore, but *1984* is especially rich in both. You might choose
to examine the political philosophy of Oceania, called Ingsoc, or English
socialism, for instance, discussing its principles, motivations, and faults.
Or, you might elect to focus on what the novel has to say about the construction of memory and the difference between individual and collective memory. Then, there is also the question of the relationship between
language and reality, and language and thought, which would make for a
fascinating essay, as would a discussion of the concept of doublethink and
its role in party endeavors. Although many of these topics tend to bleed
into one another, you will need to narrow your focus to one of them so
that the scope of your essay does not become unmanageable. Because the
novel is so concerned with ideological and philosophical concerns and
has so much to say about them, you will likely discover that you cannot
even cover everything you'd like to say about your narrowed topic, such
as Ingsoc, for example. Depending on the length of essay you are aim-
ing for, you may have to narrow your topic further and explore a certain
element of it, such as the effects of Ingsoc on family relationships, the
sustainability of a society based on Ingsoc, or Ingsoc's justification of the
methods used to maintain control of Oceania's population, for example.
You will want to make sure that the body of your essay can fully support
the argument you lay out in your thesis. If it cannot without going on too
long, then you likely need to refine your argument further. If you wind up

with an essay that adequately supports your thesis but is too short, then you will also need to work on your argument, covering additional ground or refining your argument, drawing out nuances and complications that need explaining and exploring.

Sample Topics:

1. **Memory:** What kind of commentary is the novel ultimately making about the construction, manipulation, and function of individual and collective memory?

How is memory constructed and maintained in the novel? Look for a minute at the memory of a party member. What happens to his or her memories of being at war with Eastasia when all references to such a war are obliterated by the party? How do party members handle the fact that history, and thus society's collective memory, is being constantly and regularly rewritten? Now think about Winston's memory. How are his memories different from the typical party members' memories, and, perhaps more importantly, why are they different? Does O'Brien ultimately gain control over Winston's memory? How does he manage this? All told, what does the novel have to say about the relationship of individual memory to collective or institutional memory? Is one more important than the other? More authentic? Do these conclusions apply in all societies to some degree or are they limited to the totalitarian world described in *1984?*

2. **The relationship of language to thought and the understanding of reality:** Analyze and evaluate Newspeak.

What is Newspeak? How is it different from regular English, or, as it is referred to in the novel, Oldspeak? Why is the party trying to cut down on the number of possible words in the language? Why is it trying to omit words for certain ideas? What do you think a society that speaks in perfected Newspeak would be like? How would it be different from contemporary American society? How would it be different even from Oceanic society as described in the novel? What is the novel saying about the way our language is connected to the way we understand the world?

What is it saying about the connection of a private, inalienable self to the capacity for varied and unique expression?

3. **Ingsoc, or English socialism:** Analyze and evaluate the political philosophy of Oceania.

What are Ingsoc's basic principles and ideas? How did it develop? What are its goals? What kind of society does it perceive as ideal? What do you perceive as this philosophy's virtues and faults? What kind of a world does it actually create? What real historical society or government do Oceania and its political system most closely resemble? What, if anything, do you think Orwell was trying to say about that society through this novel? Or, do you think *1984* is more of a philosophical exercise? If so, what is Orwell using Ingsoc to say about the nature of government and its relationship to the people under its purview?

4. **Doublethink:** What is the purpose of doublethink, and what effects does it have on Oceania and its inhabitants?

What exactly is doublethink and how does it function? Identify some examples of doublethink in the novel. What purpose does it serve? What qualities are necessary to be a good "doublethinker"? Which characters in the novel are particularly good at it? Why do you think Winston has difficulty with doublethinking? How does doublethink affect Oceania society? How does it affect individuals within that society? Do you think doublethink is a phenomenon isolated to fictional societies? Can you think of any cases in contemporary American society in which doublethink is alive and well?

Form and Genre

There is much to be discovered through an analysis of the form and genre of a particular piece. When an author sits down and begins to craft a new work, he or she is faced with an array of choices regarding the possible forms and genres into which the new work can fit. While occasionally a work is so revolutionary that it creates a new form or genre, for the most part, authors work within the confines of existing traditions. This gives readers something to consider: Why did the author choose this particular form, this particular, genre, for this work? And how does this work fit in with all the previous examples from this genre? Is the author commenting on the form or genre? Trying to change it in some way? Somehow conversing with his or her predecessors? Therefore, thinking about the building blocks of a novel—the basic choices the author makes in the construction of the work—as well as how it relates to other, similar works, can be very illuminating. In the case of *1984*, you might think about several of Orwell's choices, including the style of narration he employs and the fact that he interrupted the narrative flow with excerpts from a book within the fictional universe. You might also examine his work in relationship to other dystopic novels; such an exercise will help you to figure out Orwell's influences as well as to identify the original ideas he brought to the genre.

Sample Topics:

1. **Omniscient narrator:** Analyze and evaluate Orwell's narrator of *1984*.

   Think about the narrating voice that is presenting the story. What kind of information is it privy to? Does it simply portray events as they unfold or does it get inside the thoughts and feelings of some or all of the characters? Does the narrative seem sympathetic to Winston? To Big Brother? What makes you think so? To help you figure out what bias the narrative might have, think about what the novel would be like if the story were told by Winston, or Julia, or Goldstein. What elements might have been left out? What new details might have been included? What would have been told differently?

2. **Goldstein's book:** Why does Orwell incorporate portions of Goldstein's book into the narrative? What pragmatic and/or thematic functions does this method serve?

   What was O'Brien's motive in getting the book to Winston? What function does the book serve for the party? How do Winston and Julia react to Goldstein's book? Rather than just telling readers that Winston is reading such a book and perhaps summarizing what he is learning, Orwell actually includes portions of Goldstein's book as Winston reads it. What does this literary device allow Orwell to accomplish? What information is transmitted to the reader through Goldstein's book? How would it be different if this same information were presented through the narrator instead? What happens to the flow of the narrative and the reading experience when the pieces of Goldstein's text are encountered? What do you think Orwell was trying to accomplish with this technique and do you feel he was successful?

3. **Dystopia:** What kind of commentary is Orwell making about human nature or the nature of government by creating a dystopia like Oceania?

1984 can be categorized with many other works of literature that present some version of a dystopia, characterized as a generally miserable human civilization, the opposite of an ideal society, or utopia. Do some research into literary dystopias—you might begin with Keith M. Booker's *The Dystopian Impulse in Modern Literature* or *Dystopian Literature: A Theory and Research Guide*—and then reread *1984* to see how it fits in. What makes Oceania a dystopia? Are the party members trying to create an ideal society and creating a monstrosity instead, or is idealism not even in their mindset? How is Oceania different from other dystopic realms? What do you think was Orwell's purpose in creating it?

Language, Symbols, and Imagery

Authors can pack a lot of meaning into the language, symbols, and imagery they use. In this way, they convey complicated and nuanced ideas without ever expressly stating them. For this reason, it can be exciting and rewarding to choose a certain element of language or a recurring symbol or image and to analyze it carefully to see what it reveals about the novel's overall themes and meanings. In *1984,* there are many symbols or images you might choose, but two especially interesting ones are the ubiquitous telescreens and Winston's recurring dreams. For either of these topics, you would need to start by identifying key passages that feature these elements and performing close readings on them. You would then use your analysis to draw a conclusion as to what new insight about the novel can be gained through a careful examination of that particular symbol or image. That conclusion would serve as your thesis sentence, which you would then support by presenting the most compelling points from your analysis in the body paragraphs of the essay.

Sample Topics:

1. **Telescreen:** What does the telescreen come to symbolize in the novel?

   How is the telescreen described? What are its functions? How do various characters feel about it? Why do you think inner party members are allowed to turn their screens off for brief periods of time? What do you think the screens come to symbolize or represent in the novel? What would the book be missing without them?

2. **Dreams:** What commentary is the novel ultimately making about the function and power of dreams, particularly in an oppressive society?

   Because Big Brother prevents him from expressing doubt or uncertainty in writing or speech, Winston's questions and disappointments come through in his dreams. What do you think his frequent dreams about his mother and sister signify? How about his dreams of O'Brien? How does Winston interpret his dreams? Does he come to understand their meaning and significance? Do you think Winston is the only party member to experience dreams of this sort? What does the persistence of Winston's dreams have to say about the ability of the party to control its members' thoughts and perception of reality?

Compare and Contrast Essays

Comparing and contrasting can be one of the most fruitful ways to approach writing an essay. Setting an element—a book or character, for example—against another element—a different book by the same or another author, another character, or a possible source for that character in real life—can bring to the forefront meaningful elements that might not have been easy to spot in isolation. Just like any other type of essay, however, a compare and contrast essay requires a great deal of preliminary work, much of which does not show up in the final product. You will spend a fair amount of time exploring the similarities and differences between multiple elements and then examining them for meaningful patterns, and arriving at a significant conclusion that will be the thesis of your essay before you can begin actually writing the essay. For example, a comparison and contrast essay about *1984* and *Brave New World* would not simply list all the ways that the two novels are similar and different. Instead, it would use these similarities or differences to say something new and interesting about one or both of the novels in question. Such an essay might argue, for instance, that the novels demonstrate that the key to controlling people and gaining their total loyalty to the government and its principles is destroying meaningful relationships such as romantic and familial bonds. Such an essay would explore the various ways that the governments orchestrate the loss of these relationships and the effects of this loss on individuals in the society, specifically the main characters Bernard and Winston. It might also discuss what this fact—that the loss of relationships makes humans susceptible to control—says about the nature of human beings and their basic needs. Such an essay would not, however, need to include all of the similarities and differences between the two novels unrelated to the thesis that were noted in the initial prewriting and brainstorming stages.

Sample Topics:

1. ***1984* and *Brave New World*:** Compare and contrast these two visions of a totalitarian society. What do they have in common? What makes each vision distinct?

   How are people controlled in each of the societies? What methods does the government employ to get its citizens to do what it wants them to? What are the governments' overall goals? What type of society is the government trying to create? What are the governments' opinions on family, love, and sex?

   Once you have examined the social and ideological frameworks of the two novels, you will want to focus specifically on their protagonists. Think about the main characters in these two works, Bernard and Winston. What makes them different from the average person in their respective societies? What traits, if any, do they share? Next, you will want to examine the notes you have generated comparing and contrasting *1984* and *Brave New World* to see what patterns or meaningful differences you can find.

2. **Goldstein and Trotsky:** Compare and contrast the fictional Goldstein with Leon Trotsky.

Begin by recording everything you know about Goldstein. What do you know about his history and ideological stance? Read the portions of *1984* that are purported to be selections from Goldstein's book given to Winston by O'Brien. What are the main ideas outlined there? Within the universe of the novel, do you think that this is truly Goldstein's book or is it a fabrication created by the party? Does Goldstein, in fact, exist? Has he ever existed? What function does his legend serve for party members? For those who seek to rebel? Once you've done your examination of Goldstein, you'll want to do some background reading on Leon Trotsky, his role in the Russian Revolution, and his relationship to Lenin. You might start with Ian Thatcher's biography *Trotsky.* What similarities can you find between Goldstein and Trotsky? What significant differences? You might also want to compare and contrast Trotsky's work *The Revolution Betrayed* with the fictional Goldstein's *The Theory and Practice of Oligarchical Collectivism.*

Bibliography and Online Resources for *1984*

Bloom, Harold. *George Orwell's* 1984. Bloom's Notes. New York: Chelsea House, 1996.

———. *George Orwell's Animal Farm.* Bloom's Notes. New York: Chelsea House, 1999.

Booker, Keith M. *The Dystopian Impulse in Modern Literature.* Westport, CT: Greenwood, 1994.

———. *Dystopian Literature: A Theory and Research Guide.* Westport, CT: Greenwood, 1994.

Fitzpatrick, Shelia. *The Russian Revolution.* New York: Oxford UP, 2008.

Hollis, Christopher. *A Study of George Orwell.* Chicago: Regnery, 1956.

Kaplan, Carter. "The Advent of Literary Dystopia." *Extrapolation* 40.3 (1999): 200–12.

Lee, Robert A. *Orwell's Fiction.* Notre Dame, IN: U of Notre Dame P: 1969.

Orwell, George. *1984.* New York: Penguin, 1972.

———. *1984.* Accessed on 15 Nov. 2009. <http://www.netcharles.com/orwell/ books/1984.htm>.

———. "Letter to Francis A. Henson (16 June 1949)." *Collected Essays, Journalism, and Letters of George Orwell.* Vol. 4. Ed. Sonia Orwell and Ian Angus. New York: Harcourt Brace, 1968, 502.

Patai, Daphne. *The Orwell Mystique: A Study in Male Ideology.* Amherst: U of Massachusetts P, 1984.

Rabkin, Eric S., Martin H. Greenberg, and Joseph D. Olander, eds. *No Place Else: Explorations in Utopian and Dystopian Fiction.* Carbondale: Southern Illinois UP, 1983.

Reilly, Patrick. Nineteen Eighty-Four: *Past, Present, and Future.* Boston: Twayne, 1989.

Russell, Bertrand. "George Orwell." *World Review* 16 (1950): 5–6.

Shelden, Michael. *Orwell: The Authorized Biography.* New York: Harper Collins, 1991.

Thatcher, Ian D. *Trotsky.* Routledge Historical Biographies. New York: Routledge, 2002.

Wade, Rex A. *The Russian Revolution, 1917.* New York: Cambridge UP, 2000.

Warburg, Fredric. *All Authors Are Equal.* London: Hutchinson, 1973.

ANIMAL FARM

READING TO WRITE

GEORGE ORWELL'S *Animal Farm,* first published in 1945 in England and 1946 in the United States and now firmly ensconced in the literary canon, is generally accepted to be a satire focused on the 1917 Bolshevik Revolution and its aftermath, in which leaders Lenin and Stalin ultimately destroyed the ideals of equality and self-determination that spawned the socialist revolution by allowing their thirst for power to corrupt them into betraying the very people they had pledged to represent. More generally speaking, *Animal Farm* is a testament to Orwell's passionate hatred for totalitarianism as well as his belief that political knowledge and understanding could be cultivated through art. In Orwell's own words: "Every line of serious work that I have written since 1936 has been written, directly or indirectly, against totalitarianism. . . . *Animal Farm* was the first book in which I tried, with full consciousness of what I was doing, to fuse political purpose and artistic purpose into one whole" ("Why I Write" 8, 10). The success of that fusion and the purchase it had gained on the American consciousness in the decade after its publication is reflected in C. M. Woodhouse's 1954 *Times Literary Supplement* piece; in it, he writes: "it is impossible for anyone who has read *Animal Farm* (as well as for many who have not) to listen to the demagogues' claptrap about equality without also hearing the still, small, voice that adds: 'but some are more equal than others'" (xiii).

The clear, strong antitotalitarian message of the novel notwithstanding, there are some slightly more nuanced themes and meanings that readers can find in the pages of *Animal Farm* as well. Performing close readings of significant passages can help to reveal those nuances and help you to engage the text in a more complex way. In one such passage, the idea of religion is introduced. Orwell writes:

> Moses, who was Mr. Jones's especial pet, was a spy and a tale-bearer, but he was also a clever talker. He claimed to know of the existence of a mysterious country called Sugarcandy Mountain, to which all animals went when they died. It was situated somewhere up in the sky, a little distance beyond the clouds, Moses said. In Sugarcandy Mountain it was Sunday seven days a week, clover was in season all the year round, and lump sugar and linseed cake grew on the hedges. The animals hated Moses because he told tales and did no work, but some of them believed in Sugarcandy Mountain, and the pigs had to argue very hard to persuade them that there was no such place. (27)

This passage introduces the idea of religion, with its invocation of the name "Moses" and its reference to life after death in what, for animals, would surely be paradise, and exploring it may reveal something about the relationship between the political and ideological bent of a society and its attitude toward religion. By introducing Moses, the primary proponent of Sugarcandy Mountain as "Mr. Jones's especial pet" and as a "spy," the passage also suggests the possibility that Mr. Jones may be behind the spreading of the story of Sugarcandy Mountain to the animals. Perhaps he asked Moses to spread it, or perhaps he simply told the story to Moses, knowing that he would likely tell the other animals. At the very least, Moses's strong associations with Mr. Jones and with religion create a secondary link between Mr. Jones and religion. It might prove fruitful to investigate why Moses, the animal most closely associated with human rule, would spread religious ideas while the pigs, proponents of a new society governed by the animals themselves, would be working "very hard to persuade [the animals] that there was no such place" as Sugarcandy Mountain.

Stop for a moment and compare Sugarcandy Mountain to the pigs' idea of paradise, an earthly society run by animals and in which all animals are equal. In both cases, all animals get rewarded equally, no matter how smart they are or how hard they work. Notice the above passage mentions that "all animals," not just the ones who work hard or follow a given set of rules, go to Sugarcandy Mountain when they die. Likewise, in the pigs' conception of paradise on earth, all the animals share equally in the rewards of a just, productive society. The major difference between Sugarcandy Mountain and the pigs' paradise is that in the case of Sugarcandy Mountain the reward is mysterious, off in the future, and out of the animals' control. All they have to do to reach it is to endure whatever this life throws at them until they die; in the pigs' ideal world, stoic acceptance of current conditions is the problem, not the solution. The paradise they offer is one that is tangible, attainable, and totally within their control. In fact, according to the pigs' philosophy, it is this very act of taking their fates into their own hands and refusing to be exploited that is the highest reward. It would make sense, then, for the pigs to discourage belief in Sugarcandy Mountain, since such a belief would distract the animals from their lives in the here and now.

It might also be worth asking why the animals "hated" Moses for telling "tales and [doing] no work." That the animals resent him for not working, coupled with the fact that Sugarcandy Mountain is a place where every day is Sunday, suggests that the animals' ideal situation is one in which they do not have to work. This makes sense if you consider that the animals are used to working solely for the benefit of Mr. Jones and not garnering their own rewards from their labor. This may be another reason for the pigs to work against the Sugarcandy Mountain message—they need to get the animals to think of work in a fresh way—not as something to be forced out of them for the benefit of another but as something that can be pleasurable in itself when done to support themselves and each other.

Perhaps what's most interesting, though—if we think about the trajectory of these ideas throughout the remainder of the book—is that as the pigs begin to assume more power on Animal Farm, they begin to get into the business of sweet promises themselves. The pigs begin to talk of vague rewards and an easier life for all the animals once they have constructed the giant mill. Building the mill is exhausting, all-consuming work, which the pigs supervise. In the same way that the Sugarcandy Mountain story encouraged stoic resignation to poor conditions under Farmer Jones, so do the promises of life on easy street after the completion of the mill. Do these observations allow you to draw any conclusions about Orwell's perception of the role of religion in society? Do they prompt you to ask additional questions about what the novel has to say about motivation and rewards or about psychological manipulation?

Obviously, all the answers to your questions about the novel or even about one aspect of the novel won't be answered by analyzing one passage. But one passage can definitely lead you to some interesting questions, and perhaps even some possible interpretations, and help you to think about the remainder of the text with a slightly different perspective. Eventually, when you have done sufficient brainstorming and close reading and have developed a claim or interpretation of the text that you want to put forth in your essay, the best evidence from your close readings will serve as the vital support that convinces your readers of the validity of your argument.

TOPICS AND STRATEGIES

The following topics and essay ideas are only suggestions. Rather than limit or constrict you, they should spark your imagination. On a related note, do not approach these essay topics as a series of questions to be answered in sequence. Instead, use the questions to help you generate ideas about a given topic. Once you have recorded your ideas and analyzed relevant passages in the novel, you should formulate your claim, the argument you want your essay to make. Then, you will go back to your notes and begin to marshal the evidence for your claim, organizing and arranging your thoughts into a persuasive essay.

Themes

The themes of a work are its most fundamental concerns, the subjects or issues at its core. Most pieces of literature have multiple themes; *Animal Farm,* for instance, concerns itself with the Russian Revolution, power distribution in society, and the notion of social progress and improvement, among others. An investigation into any of these themes has the potential to become a compelling essay. Your first task when beginning an essay on theme is to select the theme you want to work with; your goal is to focus sharply on one theme rather than to create an essay that simply identifies all of the possible themes in the book. Once you have identified your theme, you will want to reread the text with that theme firmly in mind and isolate particular passages that you feel are relevant in order to perform close readings on them. Once you have investigated what the novel has to say about your theme, you will synthesize your notes and your thoughts into a thesis sentence that sums up the argument your essay will make. For example, if you are writing an essay about power distribution in *Animal Farm,* you might, through close reading and analysis, conclude that the central message of *Animal Farm* is hope for equality. The animals, you might say, had a real chance to create a society in which all animals were equal until the pigs ruined it and that, since they recognize the pigs' faults at the novel's end, they are on the verge of another, hopefully wiser, revolution. Alternatively, you might argue that *Animal Farm* illustrates the impossibility of a society in which all beings are equal because societies must have leaders, and leaders inevitably use the power temporarily vested in them for their own benefit instead of for the common good. Neither argument is more correct than the other; what makes a good essay is your ability to articulate a clear position and support that position with persuasive evidence from the text.

Sample Topics:

1. **Revolution:** *Animal Farm* is most often read as a critique of the 1917 Russian Revolution, and the expulsion of the humans by the animals certainly represents a revolutionary act. Explain how the fable can be read as an allegory of the revolution, and as a depiction of revolution in general, and discuss what Orwell sees as its major flaws.

   First, you will want to brush up on your Russian history. You might begin with Rex A. Wade's *The Russian Revolution, 1917* or Shelia Fitzpatrick's *The Russian Revolution.* Then, reread the novel with an eye toward matching up the figures and events in the story with those of the revolution. What similarities can you find? What significant differences? Use this comparison and contrast to help you think about what Orwell most wants to say about the revolution. What does he emphasize and what does he downplay? Which characters come off worst? Which seem most sympathetic? In your view, does Orwell condemn the revolution entirely, or is his wrath directed at certain characters or events? Furthermore, what is Orwell saying about revolution in general? Does he seem to be suggesting the ultimate futility of revolutionary ideals, or is he suggesting that the animals somehow got the revolution wrong, that it could have succeeded had they approached it differently somehow?

2. **Power distribution in society:** What is Orwell saying about the nature of power? Is it inevitable that people grapple for as much power and control as they can get? Is it inevitable that they should use that power and control for their own benefit?

What are the animals' goals in terms of power sharing at the start of the revolution? How are decisions to be made? How do the pigs wind up in charge of the other animals? What makes this possible? How do they increase their control? Stop and think for a moment about why the pigs desire control in the first place. Was this their goal from the start? What are they, Napoleon in particular, truly after? Spend some time analyzing Napoleon's character and his relationship with Snowball to discern his motives and his major flaws. According to the overall viewpoint of the book, is Napoleon to blame for the failure of the revolution to uphold the principle that all animals are equal? Is Orwell saying that a philosophy of equality cannot be upheld, or did the animals make an error that they might have avoided? It may be tempting to see Napoleon as the bad guy and Snowball as the good guy, but, looking closely at the text, are there signs that Snowball, had he not been run off, would have been vying for power in the same ways that Napoleon was?

3. **Progress:** What does Orwell ultimately have to say about the nature of progress and the human ability to measure and track it, whether our own or others'?

The animals begin planning the revolution because they want to see some progress, some improvement in their lives, and during the course of the novel, they struggle to determine whether their lot has improved or, in fact, degenerated. As you begin planning this essay, reread the novel and chart the quality of the animals' lives from beginning to end. First, you will want to think about what makes a good life for the animals—enough food? Rest? Control over their own lives? And then you will want to figure out when life is best and when it is worst for the animals. Once you have figured this out, think about progress from various perspectives. The narration seems to suggest that the quality of the animals' lives increases briefly after the departure of Mr. Jones and then decreases after the pigs establish their tyranny. Is this a correct assessment in your view? Next, consider how the animals themselves perceive and measure the quality of their lives. Do they share the narrator's impression? If not, how does their own perception differ? What role do the pigs, Squealer in particular, play in these determinations? According to the novel, how is progress determined? Is it, after all, a meaningful concept?

Character

When writing about character, it is helpful to start with a list of salient features of any particular character you are exploring and by doing close readings of those passages that seem to you to provide the most insight into the internal workings of that character. You will want to note how the character sees himself and how others see him. You will need to study his actions, his dialogue, and any internal life that the narrative makes you privy to. It is also helpful to examine your character for any change, as oftentimes characters will develop throughout the course of the story as they respond to unfolding events. Because *Animal Farm* is a clear commentary on the Russian Revolution, you will also want to figure out which historical figures the characters are meant to represent and then spend some time thinking about what Orwell's novel is trying to say about these figures by means of his fictional characters.

Sample Topics:

1. **Squealer:** As a powerful propagandist, Squealer plays an important role in maintaining the pigs' place at the top of the farm's hierarchy while keeping the other animals from becoming discontent with their own respective stations. Is Squealer simply a mouthpiece for Napoleon, or is he a full-fledged player in the pigs' plot for domination? Is he even a full-fledged character in his own right?

   Begin by recording what you know about Squealer. What are his particular talents? What role does he play on *Animal Farm?* Squealer obviously serves as a "middleman" between the pigs in charge and the other animals. Why is such a middleman needed? Does Squealer simply convey messages from the pigs to other animals, or does his job require more of him? Does he ever create his own message or modify the content of the messages he conveys? What would you say are his major duties? To whom is Squealer loyal? In your view, does Squealer tell the truth? Where would you rank him in terms of the farm's

hierarchy of power and control? Does Squealer have a historical counterpart? Who might it be?

2. **Boxer:** Boxer is the physical backbone of Animal Farm, but he
   seems unable to act without guidance from someone else. Who
   or what does Boxer represent? Analyze and evaluate the character of Boxer.

   What are Boxer's major strengths? What role does he play in
   the *Animal Farm* community? What are Boxer's weaknesses?
   Why do you think Boxer's answer to everything is to work
   harder? Does this philosophy result in solving problems or
   making life better? For whom does Boxer's hard work reap
   rewards? What do you think of Boxer's other maxim—that
   Napoleon is always right? How is this maxim established in
   Boxer's mind? What good does it do him? Why does he hang
   onto it? How do you think the novel would be different if Boxer
   did not appear in it? What role does he fill in the story?

3. **Snowball:** In some ways, Snowball's character and his contributions to Animal Farm remain a mystery because he is chased
   away relatively early in the development of the new community.
   What do we know about him, and what can we reasonably predict his behavior may have been like had he been allowed to
   remain?

   What is Snowball like? What are his contributions to the
   establishment of Animal Farm? How and why is he forced off
   the farm? How is he used as a scapegoat by Napoleon and the
   other pigs? What does the treatment of Snowball tell us about
   other characters, such as Napoleon? Look closely at how he
   and his actions are described in the narration. Can you make
   some projections about the type of leader he would have been
   had Napoleon not run him off?
       According to some critics, Snowball is said to represent
   Trotsky, Lenin's second in the Russian October Revolution. Do
   some background reading on Trotsky and his relationship to
   Lenin and the Russian Revolution. What connections can you

draw between Snowball and Trotsky, and how do such connections help you to better understand the novel?

4. **Napoleon:** In some ways, Napoleon is the main character in the novel. Certainly, he comes to dominate the farm. Was this domination preordained, or did Napoleon grow and change as his circumstances changed? Is he a static character—a mere symbol—or does he undergo genuine character development over the course of the novel?

   What would you say are Napoleon's defining characteristics? What are his strengths and foibles? What are his goals and his motivations? Analyze Napoleon's development through the course of the novel. How does he change and what precipitates those changes?
   It is generally accepted that Napoleon was created by Orwell to represent Lenin or Stalin, the leaders of the revolution in Russia. Do some research into the Russian Revolution and Lenin's and Stalin's roles. What might Orwell have been trying to say about Lenin or Stalin by crafting the character Napoleon?

5. **Old Major:** Though he appears only briefly, Old Major has a significant role in *Animal Farm*. Discuss the significance of this interesting character.

   What do you know about Old Major's life? What messages does he offer the animals before he dies? How would you describe his philosophy of life? Why do the animals all listen to what he has to say? Are the principles that Old Major elucidates upheld when the actual animal revolution occurs? When, if ever, do they begin to become corrupted? Do some background reading on Karl Marx and his ideas about communism. How closely does Old Major's commentary resemble Marx's ideas?

6. **Benjamin:** Analyze and evaluate Benjamin's character.

   What would you say are Benjamin's most salient characteristics? What are his strengths and weaknesses? How does he process all of the events that occur on Animal Farm; what does he think of them? What makes Benjamin unique? Imagine the events unfolding without him as part of the cast of characters. What would be different? Use this line of thinking to help you figure out the significance of Benjamin's character to the novel's overall themes and meanings. Critics have often suggested that Benjamin's wry skepticism makes him the most obvious stand-in for Orwell himself. Do you think Benjamin might represent Orwell? If so, what is Orwell revealing about himself through this character?

You might apply the same questions to other characters in the novel, including Clover, Moses the raven, and Mollie the mare, among others.

History and Context

Considering history and context is always very important to developing a clear understanding of a piece of literature. In the case of a work such as *Animal Farm*, it is absolutely essential, as Orwell fully intended to engage the events and ideas unfolding in his world through this novel. Understanding what prompted Orwell to pen the piece, the historical happenings taking place as he was writing it and attempting to have it published, and the critical reception of the work can bring the novel's social and political meanings into much sharper focus. Doing some background reading, perhaps beginning with Michael Shelden's *Orwell: The Authorized Biography*, will help you get a handle on the cultural and historical context in which the novel was written. This aspect of the work is so interesting that you might choose to investigate part of this context further and to make it the central focus point of your essay. You might, for instance, decide to go past the standard interpretation that the novel is a direct critique of the Russian Revolution and probe its stance for yourself. The novel is certainly criticizing the revolution, but what elements of it is he condemning? Its goals? Methods? Results? Alternatively, you might investigate the novel's journey through the publication process. Was it easy for Orwell to get such a topically relevant and politically sensitive book as *Animal Farm* published? Did he get the reaction that he hoped for? You may also want to look at the political climate in which Orwell produced this novel. Were the critiques he was making in line with mainstream political thought, or was he saying something radical in the context of British culture at the time?

Sample Topics:

1. **Socialism:** What attitude does Orwell display toward socialism in *Animal Farm?*

Literacy critic Michael Shelden notes that *"Animal Farm* caught the popular imagination just when the Cold War was beginning to make itself felt. For many years 'anticommunists' enjoyed using it as a propaganda weapon in that war, but this was a gross misrepresentation of the book and a violation of the spirit in which Orwell wrote it" (369). Shelden writes that Orwell was not actually an enemy of socialism or of the Soviet Union but of the movement's leaders who ultimately betrayed the people they were supposed to represent. He notes that the idea for *Animal Farm* actually occurred to Orwell in connection with the workers revolution in Barcelona and Stalin's ultimate betrayal of them. In actuality, Shelden argues, *"Animal Farm* affirms the values of Orwell's ideal version of socialism, making it clear that before the barnyard revolt was subjected to the treachery of the pigs, 'the animals were happy as they had never conceived it possible to be'" (369–70).

You might want to think first about how Orwell's "ideal version of socialism" is similar to and different from socialism, or communism, as it manifested in postrevolutionary Russia. Some background reading to start with might include Shelden's *Orwell: The Authorized Biography,* Rex A. Wade's *The Russian Revolution, 1917,* and Shelia Fitzpatrick's *The Russian Revolution.* Once you have done your reading, you will want to revisit the novel and ask yourself exactly what Orwell is criticizing. Could the animals have remained in the happy state they enjoyed for a brief period after the rebellion? Why or why not? Does Orwell's judgment fall on the entire animal revolution, or is he really blaming the pigs for the failure of a grand idea? Write an essay in which you support, contradict, extend, or modify Shelden's conclusions.

2. **Timing of publication:** What effect did the timing of the publication of *Animal Farm* have on its reception?

According to Orwell biographer Michael Shelden, Orwell had a bit of difficulty publishing *Animal Farm* because "[m]any influential people in Britain did not want to risk giving serious offense to the Soviet dictator at this crucial period in [World War II]" considering that Britain was dependent on the Soviet Union in its fight against Hitler's regime (366). Orwell's book was, in fact, rejected by four houses before it was picked up by Fredric Warburg, who had also published Orwell's *Homage to Catalonia* and "The Lion and the Unicorn." Warburg informed Orwell that he could not publish the book immediately due to paper shortages, and as a result, the book did not appear "until after Hitler had been defeated and Stalin's usefulness as Britain's ally was at an end. That delay, deliberate or not, took some of the sting out of the book's effect on its first readers. If it had appeared in the summer of 1944, there might have been a much greater outcry over its publication, which would have pleased Orwell" (Shelden 368–69). When it was finally released, sales of the book were brisk. It came out in Britain in August 1945 and in America in 1946. The British edition sold more than 25,000 copies in its first five years, and its American counterpart sold 590,000 copies in just the first four years (Shelden 369).

Do some research into the political and social climate in Britain and the United States in 1944 and 1945. How did the general population feel about Russia and communism? *Communism: A History,* by Richard Pipes, gives some good overviews of how the West felt about Russian communism and would be a good starting point for your research. Research also the critical reception of *Animal Farm.* A good place to start is Michael Shelden's *Orwell: The Authorized Biography.* Why do you think Shelden writes that if the book had sparked a greater outcry, Orwell would have been pleased? What kind of a reception was he looking for? Were Orwell's hopes out of line with those of his potential publishers? What do you think the publishers were afraid of; do you think the four publishers who rejected the book were justified in their concerns?

PHILOSOPHY AND IDEAS

Thinking about philosophy and ideas in a piece of literature is similar to thinking about theme: You are asking, what is this piece really about? But you will need to think a bit more broadly this time. What universal human concerns or significant social ideas does this work comment on? Because of the inherently broad scope of this sort of inquiry, it is necessary to narrow your focus once you have selected an idea or philosophy you would like to investigate. Although *Animal Farm* certainly has no shortage of philosophy and ideas to consider, a couple of the most interesting are religion and false consciousness. If you choose to write about either of these, you will want to reread the novel with this topic in mind and select some passages to closely read. Your goal is not simply to illustrate that the novel is concerned with your topic but to figure out and articulate for your reader what exactly the novel has to say about this topic. Take the case of religion, for example. You want to learn more about what the novel has to say about the goals of religion and its effects on society. To do this, you will examine the character of Moses and his ideas of Sugarcandy Mountain. You might end up concluding that the novel suggests that religion is incompatible with a socialist society, as its focus on a future that fulfills their every desire encourages the animals to think about their own rather than the collective good and takes their focus off the work that needs doing in the here and now. Or, you might argue that the novel suggests that by suppressing religion, the pigs missed out on a potentially useful tool; they might get even more work out of the animals if the animals believed that the reward of Sugarcandy Mountain would only be theirs if they worked tirelessly and selflessly till their deaths. The important point is that the conclusion you reach and present as the thesis of your essay must be based on evidence you have gained from careful analysis of pertinent passages and consideration of how these passages fit into the scheme of the novel as a whole.

Sample Topics:

1. **Religion:** What kind of commentary does Orwell make about religion and its role in social and political ideology?

   Look carefully at the role of Moses the raven. You might start with a close reading of the passage quoted at the beginning of this chapter in which Moses's tales about Sugarcandy Mountain are described. What do you make of Moses's Sugarcandy Mountain? How is life there different from life on the farm? How is Sugarcandy Mountain similar to and different from the Christian notion of heaven? Is Moses's Sugarcandy Mountain story connected to the belief that he is a spy for Mr. Jones? Would Mr. Jones benefit from Moses telling this story to his animals? What do you think motivates Moses to tell all of the other animals about Sugarcandy Mountain? What is he trying to achieve? What effects, if any, do his stories have on the animals' behavior and perception of the world and their place in it? Why do you think the pigs work so hard to convince the animals that Moses's tales of Sugarcandy Mountain were lies? Track Moses's comings and goings; is there a pattern to his appearances?

2. **Marxism and false consciousness:** Does the society of *Animal Farm* hold true to the principles it espouses or do the animals only think that it does? Do they suffer from what Marx called "false consciousness"?

The fundamental principle of Marxism is that social and economic circumstances define one's life and, to a large extent, one's identity. In the words of Karl Marx: "It is not the consciousness of men that determines their existence, but their social existence that determines their consciousness" (qtd in Bertens 81). Marxist critics argue, for instance, that capitalism, an economic system in which wealth is inequitably divided and in which the wealthy possess more social power than the poor, has the unintended consequence of "turn[ing] people into things" or "*reifi[ing]* them." Further, they argue that it "generates a view of the world—focused on profit—in which ultimately all of us function as objects and become alienated from ourselves" (Bertens 83). If this is the case, you might expect people in a capitalistic society to rebel. Ultimately, they do not because of the ideology that capitalism insists it is based on, that each member of its society is completely free to determine his or her own identity and place in the world. According to Marxist thought, if we believe these ideas, which are contrary to our own reality, we live in a state of "false consciousness."

Turn a Marxist eye on the society created in *Animal Farm.* What are its basic principles, those it claims as fundamental and those embraced by all of the animals? Would you classify their system as capitalism? As socialism? As communism? Think about whether the reality of the animals' condition is different from their perception of it. Do the animals suffer from a state of "false consciousness"? Is Orwell suggesting that false consciousness is inevitable? Why or why not?

Form and Genre

Asking questions about the genres and forms the piece seems to be working within can result in some interesting lines of inquiry. Instead of simply accepting that *Animal Farm* is a beast, or animal, fable, for example, you might decide to explore how exactly the novel interacts with that form. What elements of the animal fable does it possess? What other animal fables is it like? What, if anything, makes it stand out from other animal fables? Why do you think Orwell selected this form with which to tell his story? How does the form relate to the message of the text? Does it ask us to look at the subject matter in a way that other forms might not? Similarly, you might cast a questioning glance at another label often applied to *Animal Farm,* and that is satire. Instead of merely applying the label and moving on, you might make *Animal Farm*'s use of satire into the primary focus of your paper. You might examine how Orwell employs satire in the novel and whether satire and the animal fable are often combined. Does Orwell use these elements in a common way, or does he introduce a spin of his own? What are the effects of his choice to employ satire to get his message across in *Animal Farm?* Finally, you might investigate how the narration affects the meaning of the story.

Sample Topics:

1. **Animal fable:** Typically, we tend to group fables in with other genres like fairy tales and nursery rhymes, works we think of as being for small children. Why then would Orwell choose this genre to criticize totalitarianism in the real world? Is it counterproductive to use a fable to make a serious political critique?

Analyze and evaluate Orwell's use of the animal fable to convey his political sentiments.

You will want to begin by listing some other well-known animal fables. What subject matter do they generally cover? What sorts of lessons do they teach? How is Orwell's novel similar to and different from other animal fables you know? Christopher Hollis writes: "The animal fable, if it is to succeed at all, ought clearly to carry with it a gay and light-hearted message. It must be full of comedy and laughter. The form is too far removed from reality to tolerate sustained bitterness . . . the trouble with Orwell was that the lesson he wished to teach was not ultimately a gay lesson" (147). What do you make of Hollis's argument? Do you think that the animal fable suits Orwell's subject matter or do you agree that Orwell's message is too dark to be properly conveyed in this format? Presumably, Orwell realized that his subject matter was incongruent with the traditional fable story lines; why then do you think he chose to fashion his novel into a fable? What might he be saying about fables, as well as about his subject matter?

2. **Ending:** Analyze and evaluate the novel's final scene to determine what it says about the overall message of the book. Is it apocalyptic, or is there a ray of hope present by the final words?

   Animal Farm ends with a meeting between the pigs and the neighboring farmers at which a fight breaks out over cards. Orwell writes: "Twelve voices were shouting in anger, and they were all alike. No question, now, what had happened to the faces of the pigs. The creatures outside looked from pig to man, and from man to pig, and from pig to man again; but already it was impossible to say which was which" (128). Would you argue that this ending is a hopeful or despairing one? Is Orwell implying that the pigs are now irrevocably in charge and that the animals are doomed to be under someone else's domain? What is the evidence for this interpretation? Or, do you think Orwell offers us a more hopeful view, emphasizing that the creatures are having the veils pulled from their eyes and recognizing the pigs' tyranny? What might such a realization accomplish?

3. **Satire:** Analyze and evaluate Orwell's use of satire in *Animal Farm.*

Begin by establishing a working definition of satire. Think about some other satirical pieces you have read, such as Joseph Heller's *Catch-22* or Sinclair Lewis's *Main Street* or *Babbitt.* What do all of these works have in common? How is *Animal Farm* different from these other satirical standards? Think about other rhetorical devices or formats that Orwell might have used to convey the same messages he does in *Animal Farm.* How would the reading experience and the critical and popular reception have been different had he chosen one of these other possibilities? Do you think social commentary is more readily digested and accepted by the public when it is couched in satire instead of news pieces or nonfiction? Why or why not?

Using one or more Orwell biographies, do some research into the reception of *Animal Farm;* how did the public react? Did they pick up on the satire right away? Did the novel accomplish what Orwell wanted it to? All told, how effective is Orwell's use of satire in *Animal Farm?*

4. **Narration:** Discuss the effect of the narrator on the meaning of the novel.

What type of narration does Orwell employ in *Animal Farm?* What information is the narrator privy to? Can he or she access the thoughts or feelings of the characters? Is the narrator objective, or does he or she seem to see things from a certain perspective? What events does the narrator linger over? Are there any events that he seems to gloss over? Are there obvious questions that he doesn't answer? One useful way to ascertain the stance of the narrator and his influence on readers' perceptions is to imagine what the novel would be like if it were told by someone else. Imagine that *Animal Farm* were told by Snowball, Napoleon, Boxer, or Benjamin. How would the story be different?

Language, Symbols, and Imagery

Precise word choice, symbols, and images are the fundamental building blocks of literature; they are the elements that enable stories to develop layers of complex meaning. In the case of Orwell's *Animal Farm*, there are many symbols that can be used as entryways into the various themes and meanings of the novel. You might study the possible meanings of the windmill that the animals devote endless hours of labor to building, or you might focus on "The Beast of England," the song that holds special meaning to the animals and that is incorporated into their social rituals. Or, you might investigate what the novel has to say about the function of language and communication in the animal community. How does language, oral and written, play into the animals' fates? Is the command of language connected to intelligence? To power or privilege? How do the book's messages about language complement or complicate its other major themes?

Sample Topics:

1. **Language:** What does the novel have to say about the significance of language in the social order?

   Robert A. Lee makes an interesting argument that the basic problem of the *Animal Farm* universe is not the greed of the pigs but "the corruption of language." He argues that

   > the basis of this society's evil is the inability of its inhabitants to ascertain truth and that this is demonstrated through the theme of the corruption of language. So long as the animals cannot remember the past, because it is continually altered, they have no control over the present and hence over the future. A society which cannot control its language is, says Orwell, doomed to be oppressed in terms which deny it the very most elemental aspects of humanity. (127)

   Reread the novel with special attention to language and literacy. Which animals can read? Which cannot? What might have been different if more of the animals were literate? How do the pigs manipulate the other animals through the use of language? How do the pigs' use of language confuse the other animals' ideas of past and present reality?

2. **Beast of England song:** Analyze the role that "The Beast of England" and other songs and chants play in the novel.

Think about the words to "The Beast of England." What message does it convey? When is it sung and by whom? What effect does it have on the animals when they sing it? What role does the song play in the animals' psychology and in their communal lives? How do they incorporate it into their weekly routines and rituals? Trace the way that the use and meaning of the song change throughout the novel: How does it help the animals before the revolution and during the initial days and weeks of their independence? What does it come to mean later, after the pigs have taken control of the farm and all of its inhabitants? Why do you think Napoleon eventually forbids the animals to keep singing it?

You might take this inquiry even further and ask yourself what other songs or chants are important in the novel. What about the sheeps' chanting of "Two legs bad. Four legs good," to take one example? What effect does this have on the animal community? When you consider all of the songs and chants, what does the novel ultimately have to say about the power and potential uses of this mode of communication?

3. **The windmill:** Discuss the symbolic meanings of the construction and destruction of the windmill.

Begin by thinking about how the idea for the windmill comes about. Whose idea is this enormous and ambitious project? What are the animals' motivations for building it? What is it supposed to accomplish? Who builds it? What happens to the animals' morale when it is destroyed? Once the windmill is finally built, what is it used for? Who benefits most from its use? Thinking in terms of the Russian Revolution, what might the windmill stand for? What point is Orwell using it to make?

Compare and Contrast Essays

Comparing and contrasting is a useful method for helping ourselves see distinctions or shades of meaning that might not come to light if we were looking at one element in isolation. When considering Orwell's use of satire, for example, in *Animal Farm,* we would certainly be justified in concluding that Orwell possessed a terribly misanthropic worldview. What happens, though, when we compare it with another famous satire, such as Swift's *Gulliver's Travels?* Can we see some element of kindness or hope in Orwell's *Animal Farm* that we might have missed before? Perhaps the most important consideration in writing a compare and contrast essay is to make sure that the essay does not simply identify interesting points of comparison and/or contrast, no matter what powers of perception on your part such a list would evidence. You want to make such a list, of course, but then you will want to use it to help you to say something meaningful about one or more of the elements you are comparing/contrasting.

Sample Topics:

1. ***Animal Farm* and *Gulliver's Travels:*** Compare and contrast *Animal Farm* with another famous satire, Jonathan Swift's *Gulliver's Travels.*

   According to Bertrand Russell: "while Swift's satire expresses universal and indiscriminating hate, Orwell's has always an undercurrent of kindliness; he hates the enemies of those he loves, whereas Swift could only love (and that faintly) the enemies of those he hated. Swift's misanthropy, moreover, sprang mainly from thwarted ambition, while Orwell's sprang from the betrayal of generous ideals by the nominal advocates" (6). You will want to reread *Gulliver's Travels* and *Animal Farm* and do a bit of background reading on Swift and Orwell as you are thinking about this question. Further, you might want to read the remainder of Russell's piece, called "George Orwell," in order to fully contextualize the above quotation. Once you have done your research, what would you say are the most significant similarities and differences in these two satires? Do you agree with Russell that Orwell's satire is fundamentally kinder than Swift's? What evidence can you find for this argument? Is there another distinction between the two that you find more striking or meaningful?

2. ***Animal Farm* versus *1984:*** Compare and contrast these two Orwellian works and use them to discuss Orwell's estimation

of the potential within humankind to create governing systems that work for the benefit of the community while respecting the will of the individual.

Compare and contrast Orwell's two most famous works, *Animal Farm* and *1984*. What are the major similarities and most meaningful differences between the two novels? What elements of society do the books critique? What does each book say about Orwell's estimation of the human condition? Does he see humanity as fundamentally flawed? In what ways? Would you argue that one of the works presents a more hopeful vision of humanity's potential? Which, and why?

Bibliography and Online Resources for *Animal Farm*

Bloom, Harold. Bloom's Modern Critical Interpretations. *Animal Farm.* New York: Chelsea House, 1999.

———. *George Orwell's Animal Farm.* Bloom's Notes. New York: Chelsea House, 1999.

Fitzpatrick, Shelia. *The Russian Revolution.* New York: Oxford UP, 2008.

Hollis, Christopher. *A Study of George Orwell.* Chicago: Regnery, 1956.

Internet Modern History Sourcebook. Accessed on 15 Nov. 2009. <http://www.fordham.edu/halsall/mod/modsbook.html>.

Lee, Robert A. *Orwell's Fiction.* Notre Dame, IN: U of Notre Dame P: 1969.

Letemendia, V. C. "Revolution on Animal Farm: Orwell's Neglected Commentary." *Journal of Modern Literature* 18.1 (1992): 127.

Miller, Martin A. *The Russian Revolution: The Essential Readings.* Hoboken, NJ: Wiley-Blackwell, 2001.

Orwell, George. *Animal Farm.* New York: Penguin, 1972.

———. *Animal Farm.* Accessed on 15 Nov. 2009. <http://www.netcharles.com/orwell/books/animalfarm.htm>.

———. "Why I Write." *Why I Write.* New York: Penguin, 2005, 1–10.

Patai, Daphne. "Political Fiction and Patriarchal Fantasy." *The Orwell Mystique: A Study in Male Ideology.* Amherst: U of Massachusetts P, 1984, 201–18.

Russell, Bertrand. "George Orwell." *World Review* 16 (1950): 5–6.

Shelden, Michael. *Orwell: The Authorized Biography.* New York: Harper Collins, 1991.

Wade, Rex A. *The Russian Revolution, 1917.* New York: Cambridge UP, 2000.

HOMAGE TO CATALONIA

READING TO WRITE

FROM JUNE 1936 to July 1937, George Orwell volunteered as a soldier in Spain with the Partido Obrero Unificación Marxista (POUM) militia, one of the groups united in the fight against Francisco Franco during the Spanish civil war. Entering the war idealistic and naïve, particularly when it came to the complexities of the political situation in Spain, Orwell did not understand that while many groups, including his own, the anarchists, and the Partit Socialista Unificat de Catalunya (PSUC)—the Spanish government—shared the goal of defeating Franco, not all shared the same vision for Spain's future. Although initially claiming otherwise, the government did not share the anarchists' and the POUM's goal of a workers' revolution and the development of a socialist state. Ultimately, the infighting between the groups grew, and the government destroyed the POUM's reputation and had them outlawed. Orwell had to escape Spain under very real threat of imprisonment and death. Upon his return to England, Orwell felt that the world had not been told the truth about what was really happening in Spain. No one outside of Spain seemed to be aware that while the country was fighting a war against Franco, it was concurrently fighting a full-scale civil war. He wrote *Homage to Catalonia* at least in part to correct this misinterpretation and to spark discussion over the ideological and political conflicts at the heart of the very complex situation he discovered after spending some time in a country he dearly loved.

Some of the major themes of the book come across clearly in a scene described at length on the first page. Orwell describes a young Italian militiaman he saw in the Lenin Barracks in Barcelona soon after his arrival in Spain:

> He was a tough-looking youth of twenty-five or six, with reddish-yellow hair and powerful shoulders. His peaked leather cap was pulled fiercely over one eye. He was standing in profile to me, his chin on his breast, gazing with a puzzled frown at a map which one of the officers had on the table. Something in his face deeply moved me. It was the face of a man who would commit murder and throw away his life for a friend—the kind of face you would expect in an Anarchist, though likely as not he was a Communist. There were both candour and ferocity in it; also the pathetic reverence that illiterate people have for their supposed superiors. Obviously he could not make head or tail of the map; obviously he regarded map-reading as a stupendous intellectual feat. I hardly know why, but I have seldom seen anyone—any man, I mean—to whom I have taken such an immediate liking. While they were talking round the table some remark brought it out that I was a foreigner. The Italian raised his head and said quickly:
> "Italiano?"
> I answered in my bad Spanish: "No, Inglés. Y tú?"
> "Italiano." (3)

One of the first things that might strike you as you are analyzing this passage is the sense of ambiguity or contrast pervading it. To begin with, there is certainly a tension between appearance and reality here. Initially, Orwell describes the militiaman not as "tough" but as "tough-looking," explicitly emphasizing his appearance and perhaps hinting that it may not correspond with reality. Other details support this "tough-looking" image, including his "powerful shoulders," the "ferocity" in his face, and the way his cap "was pulled fiercely over one eye," with the latter detail certainly suggesting the possibility that the young man is posturing, that he is trying to look tougher than he is. Further support for that theory comes when Orwell finds in his face "the pathetic reverence that illiterate people have for their supposed superiors." This look covers the man's face because he obviously, to Orwell, cannot read the map he is poring over. "Pathetic reverence" for those who can understand what he cannot suggests vulnerability, not toughness or power, and the fact that the young man cannot read a map has a pretty strong symbolic significance—he is lost or disoriented in a fundamental way. Finally, when someone brings up the fact that Orwell is a foreigner, the "Italian raised his head quickly" and asked "Italiano?" This response indicates the young man's isolation and his desperation to find a kindred spirit. Clearly, the Italian's "tough-looking" appearance does not reveal the true, or the whole, picture of who he is.

On another level, Orwell's reference to the officer as the young man's "supposed superiors" indicates another sense in which appearance and reality are not the same. While the officer has a higher rank than the young man and can read maps that the young man cannot, the young man is described as having a face filled with both "candour and ferocity"; indeed, he seems the kind of man "who would commit murder and throw away his life for a friend." These aspects of the man "deeply move" Orwell, and this emotional reaction, coupled with his reference to the officer as a "supposed superior," suggests his belief that a man's loyalty and bravery are better indicators of his worth than his rank or ability to read a map. In Orwell's estimation, even though it would not seem so to the casual observer, the Italian is superior to the map-reading officer, not the other way around. Finally, Orwell notes that the man had the "kind of face you would expect in an Anarchist, though as likely as not he was a Communist." With this sentence, he brings himself and the reader into the appearance versus reality conflict, asking us to consider our own judgments based on appearance by insisting that what we "expect" does not necessarily conform to reality. This particular instance of the blurriness between appearance and reality also introduces the reader to the vast complexities inherent in the political alliances during the Spanish civil war.

The Italian militiaman is not the only lost person in this scene; in a way, Orwell as narrator here is trying with difficulty to read a metaphorical map of his own. He is trying to interpret the scene before him without all the necessary tools, including linguistic and cultural knowledge, just as the Italian soldier does with the map. This is part of what gives the passage that sense of conflict and tension that we discussed earlier. Orwell seems to be figuring out what he thinks as the paragraph progresses. Although Orwell tries to determine what group the young man belongs to, whether he is an Anarchist or a Communist, he cannot tell. It is on a more basic level, human being to human being, outsider to outsider, that they make a connection. Knowing almost nothing about the man except what he believes he can read about his character on his face, Orwell declares that "I have seldom seen anyone—any man, I mean—to whom I have taken such an immediate liking." This is evidence of another type of contrast that the passage highlights: ideology versus individual humanity. Orwell joined the militia because of his ideology; this passage poses an interesting question: Does it remain the fundamental driving force for him?

You might take either of these basic concepts, appearance versus reality or ideology versus individual humanity, and explore how it plays out in the remainder of the text. You might even investigate how the two concepts relate to one another. In Orwell's perception, you might ask, what is ultimately more real, ideology or individual humanity? To do this, you will want to identify other passages that deal with these issues and analyze them like we've done here. Allow a close study of Orwell's choice of language to help you figure out the answers to your questions. Keep in mind that you can perform close readings on passages in this volume just as you would with a work of fiction. Even though Orwell is basing the book on his actual experiences, he is still crafting a work of literature, and as such, the choices he makes in what to present and how to present it are fair game and great fodder for literary analysis.

TOPICS AND STRATEGIES

The topics listed below are designed to illustrate how many different approaches you might take to writing an essay about *Homage to Catalonia* and to help you decide on the angle you want to pursue. After reading through the topics, you may also think of one of your own that is not on the list. Or, you might decide to modify a suggested topic or to combine two or more topics to form another one that suits your interests. Finally, you might discover in the following pages a topic that seems intriguing and promising, one you want to pursue for your essay. In this case, you should feel free to use the initial question and the subquestions to help you do your preliminary thinking. You should not feel compelled to answer all of the questions included in the topic, nor should you consider yourself restricted by them. Remember that the topic is not an essay question on an exam; rather, it is a prompt created to help you begin to probe an issue for yourself. You should use the questions and suggestions to help you arrive at a thesis that will serve as the fundamental claim or argument of your essay. If you begin with one topic and set of questions and find that they lead you to a promising idea about a different topic entirely, you should feel absolutely free to pursue those new ideas and to leave the topic behind you. In short, the topics that follow will be much more helpful for you if you keep firmly in mind that they are designed to help spark your own thinking and to arrive at a thesis that will support an interesting and insightful essay.

Themes

The major themes of *Homage to Catalonia* are fairly clearly spelled out. The book is certainly concerned with the personal experience of war, the role of the press in war, and the move from innocence to experience. There are certainly other themes present in the book that you might examine, and you can use the sample topics below as a model for how you might approach those as well. Whether you choose one of the three topics suggested for you or identify one of your own, you will want to go back through the text to locate and examine passages that comment on or are relevant in some way to the theme you have elected to work with. Doing close readings of those passages will likely lead you to think about the topic in new ways and to identify other passages that now seem more important to your topic than they may have before. Once you study these passages, you will begin to organize and synthesize your thoughts into one central claim you want to make about the theme you are examining, and this will function as the thesis of your essay. This preliminary work will help to make sure that your essay does its job—that it provides its readers with a fresh way of looking at or new insight into *Homage to Catalonia* that they would not have gotten by simply reading the work for themselves.

Sample Topics:

1. **War:** As an Englishman, Orwell certainly was in no way compelled to fight in Spain. Driven by his political ideals, he volunteered to face the brutal realities of war firsthand. How do the actualities of war impact Orwell over the course of the book? Analyze and evaluate Orwell's thoughts on the day-to-day existence of a soldier and the larger purpose of war.

   Analyze the following passage and any other relevant scenes you identify as revealing Orwell's ideas about war in his early days at the front:

> In secret I was frightened. I knew the line was quiet at pres-
> ent, but unlike most of the men about me I was old enough to
> remember the Great War, though not old enough to have fought
> in it. War, to me, meant roaring projectiles and skipping shards
> of steel; above all it meant mud, lice, hunger, and cold. (19)

What was the day-to-day reality of war like? Is it like what Orwell imagined? Does his attitude toward war—not politics, but war itself—change during his time in Spain? If so, describe how and what prompted the change. How did Orwell himself change due to the time he spent in the war? In what ways was he mentally, physically, psychologically, or emotionally different when he left Spain? What particular events caused those changes? Did Orwell perceive his own experience of the war to be fairly common or unusual? What does Orwell want to express to readers about the effects of war on the psychological and emotional states of human beings by taking us through his very personal wartime experience?

2. **Power of the press/propaganda:** What kind of commentary is Orwell ultimately trying to make about the power and purpose of the press, especially in times of war?

In *Homage to Catalonia*, Orwell writes:

> The thing that had happened in Spain was, in fact, not merely
> a civil war, but the beginning of a revolution. It is this fact
> that the anti-Fascist press outside Spain has made it its spe-
> cial business to obscure. The issue has been narrowed down
> to "Fascism versus democracy" and the revolutionary aspect
> concealed as much as possible. (50)

Orwell proceeds to explain the reasons that the war was portrayed this way, and throughout the rest of the text, he provides concrete examples of news stories that contradict the
reality that he observed in the service of sustaining this illusion. Identify and analyze those passages to determine what
exactly Orwell wants to say about the relationship between
press, propaganda, and war.

One passage you will definitely want to examine is the following: "The fact is that every war suffers a kind of progressive degradation with every month that it continues, because such things as individual liberty and a truthful press are simply not compatible with military efficiency" (180). Does Orwell honestly think that a free press is impossible in times of war? Do you agree with him? What exactly does he mean when he suggests that the lack of a free press and individual liberty causes a "progressive degradation" of war? What exactly does he think is degrading? What, finally, would you say is Orwell's opinion of the press and its relationship to war and politics? Does he make a convincing case? Do you think he would make a similar argument today? Why or why not?

3. **Innocence to experience:** Analyze and evaluate Orwell's depiction of his slow transition from innocence and idealism to experience and understanding.

Instead of applying the deep understanding of Spanish politics that he painstakingly gained during his war experience retroactively to his first weeks in the militia, Orwell takes great pains to take the reader on the educational journey with him. During his time in Spain, Orwell's increasing knowledge of politics corresponded with a loss of idealism. Trace his burgeoning understanding of the true nature of events in Spain through the course of the narrative. What did he believe he was fighting for when he first entered the militia? Which group was he most ideologically attracted to? When did he learn that his initial understanding was false or, at the very least, incomplete, and how did his ideological views change? In what ways did Orwell lose his initial idealism? What was this idealism replaced with? Was the exchange a profitable one for Orwell, or did he come away changed for the worse?

Why do you think Orwell carefully presents his growing understanding and changing perspective instead of writing the entire book from his later, more mature perspective? How does this choice affect readers' experiences and interpretations of the text?

Character

Nonfiction works like this one sometimes make it difficult to talk about character and characterization. Keep in mind, however, that it is simply impossible to portray a person as he or she truly is; it would require virtually an infinite number of pages even to attempt to paint the entire picture of a living person. Therefore, authors, even of nonfiction, must make calculating decisions about how to depict the characters populating their works, choosing which details to include and emphasize and which to leave out altogether. The characters in *Homage to Catalonia* are all based on real people, but they are still literary constructions. Consider them as you would fictional characters. What traits do they possess? What do you know of their backgrounds? How do other characters, especially the narrator, perceive them? How and why do they change through the course of the narrative? You can write about characters in *Homage to Catalonia*—their function in the narrative—by studying only their portrayal in the text. Because the text is grounded in reality, however, if you wish, you can step outside of the text and do some background research on the figure(s) you're studying. Then you can compare and contrast the real person with the fictional representation. How authentic is Orwell's depiction? What did he emphasize and deemphasize about this person's characteristics and deeds? Why did he portray the person in the precise way that he did; what does this character add to the overall themes and meanings of the work?

Sample Topics:

1. **George Orwell:** Even when writing in first person, Orwell has to make many literary decisions about how to portray himself, both as the narrator and as a character taking part in the action of the book. Analyze and evaluate Orwell as a character in his own story.

   Think about what the work would be like if it were written about Orwell's experiences but by someone other than Orwell. What would be different? What events do you imagine would have been given more or less weight than Orwell gives them? What else do you think might be different? Next, think about the way that Orwell presents himself. It might help to imagine that he is a fictional character. How is he described? How are his actions presented? Does Orwell come across as sympathetic? Likeable? Is he heroic? In what way(s)?

2. **The Spanish people:** Not all characters have to be a single person. Orwell reflects and comments frequently on the Spanish people as a whole, as if they act in concert, sharing certain characteristics, goals, and ideals. Analyze and evaluate the Spanish people as a character in *Homage to Catalonia*.

Orwell draws a lot of conclusions about the character of the Spanish people. How does he characterize them? On what are these characterizations based? Do they come across as objective or biased in some way? Look for instances in which Orwell characterizes other groups, particularly the English, and compare his depiction of that group to his portrayal of the Spaniards. What does he see as the major differences between them? Which does he see as superior and why? What can Orwell's depictions of these groups tell us about his own values and priorities?

3. **Bill Smillie:** Analyze and evaluate the character Bill Smillie.

What do you know about Bill Smillie? What kind of person is he? How does Orwell feel about him? What happens to Smillie, as far as Orwell can ascertain? Analyze the following passage to help you determine why Smillie is so important to Orwell and what the fate of this young soldier comes to represent for him:

> Smillie's death is not a thing I can easily forgive. Here was this brave and gifted boy, who had thrown up his career at Glasgow University in order to come and fight against Fascism, and who, as I saw for myself, had done his job at the front with faultless courage and willingness; and all they could find to do with him was to fling him into jail and let him die like a neglected animal. I know that in the middle of a huge and bloody war it is no use making too much fuss over an individual death. One aeroplane bomb in a crowded street causes more suffering than quite a lot of political persecution. But what angers one about a death like this is its utter pointlessness. To be killed in battle—yes, that is what one expects; but to be flung into jail, not even for any imaginary offence, but simply owing to dull blind spite, and then left to die in solitude—that is a different matter. I fail to see how this

kind of thing—and it is not as though Smillie's case were exceptional—brought victory any nearer. (217)

Orwell was surrounded by death in his time at the front. What was it about Smillie's death in particular that was so meaningful for Orwell? Surely Orwell knew other "brave and gifted" soldiers who died and others who died through friendly fire, senseless accidents, and in prison. What was different about Smillie?

4. **Kopps:** Analyze and evaluate Orwell's relationship to Kopps.

Take some time to record what you know about the relationship between Orwell and Kopps. What is it about Kopps that Orwell admires? How would you describe the relationship between the two? Now, read the information about Kopps in Michael Shelden's *Orwell: The Authorized Biography,* which asserts that Kopps definitely had feelings for, and possibly had an affair with, Orwell's wife Eileen. Does this information change the way you interpret any of the events presented in *Homage to Catalonia?* Does Orwell's failure to realize his friend's motives call any of his other observations into question? Why or why not?

History and Context

Literature that is inextricably tied up with actual historical events can offer challenges to its readers. Reading *Homage to Catalonia* will give you an insider's perspective on the political situation in revolutionary Spain, but that political situation is likely to be one with which you are completely unfamiliar. Understanding Orwell's work, then, requires some attention to the historical details. You might do some background reading, beginning with Stanley Payne's *The Spanish Civil War, the Soviet Union, and Communism* or Paul Preston's *The Spanish Civil War: Reaction, Revolution, and Revenge* in order to put Orwell's book into a broader perspective. If the political and historical aspects of the book pique your interest, you might decide to focus your study on Orwell's descriptions of the various political factions in Spain and their motives. You might speculate on why Orwell feels it important to record these details so precisely. Why did he feel that a true, insider's account of politics in Spain in this time period was necessary? What function did he imagine it serving? Alternatively, you might focus your attention on another interesting aspect of the creation of this work—its journey through the publication and review process—which can also be illuminating of the social currents of the time.

Sample Topics:

1. **Politics of the Spanish civil war:** What kind of commentary does Orwell ultimately make about the civil unrest in Spain and its impact on the struggle against Franco and the fascists?

   Orwell describes the complicated political struggles occurring in Spain in the following way:

   > As a militiaman one was a soldier against Franco, but one was also a pawn in an enormous struggle that was being fought out between two political theories. . . . Franco was not strictly comparable with Hitler or Mussolini. His rising was a military mutiny backed up by the aristocracy and the Church, and in the main, especially at the beginning, it was an attempt not so much to impose Fascism as to restore feudalism. This meant that Franco had against him not only the working class but also various sections of the liberal bourgeoisie—the very people who are the supporters of Fascism when it appears in a more modern form. More important than this was the fact that the Spanish working class did not as we might conceivably do in England, resist Franco in the 'democracy' and the *status quo*; their resistance was accompanied by—one might almost say it consisted of—a definite revolutionary outbreak. (47–49)

   In Chapter V, or Appendix 1 in later editions, Orwell explains further that while the communist government (PSUC) and the socialist revolutionaries (POUM, anarchists) were united, for a time, at least, in fighting off Franco and fascism, the rifts between the ultimate goals of these two groups—the PSUC was trying to ward off the socialist revolution sought by both the POUM and the anarchists—ultimately resulted in the PSUC denouncing and outlawing the POUM and persecuting its members.

   Reread chapters 5 and 11, or the appendixes if you have the later edition, recording the distinctions between the various groups in play. When and how does Orwell come to understand their distinctions and the importance of these distinctions? Why was he unaware of them when he initially enlisted? What role did the fighting in Barcelona among the PSUC, POUM, and anarchists play in his increasing understanding of the political subtleties underlying the war he had volunteered to fight in? With what group did Orwell align himself politically? Did his ideological affiliation change as time passed? You will also want to think about how the infighting among the groups who were in theory united in the fight against the fascists ultimately impacted the outcome of the war.

Finally, think about why Orwell takes the time to delineate the nuances of the politics involved in the war. What larger point is he trying to make?

2. **Publication/reception:** What can the publication process and the critical reception of *Homage to Catalonia* reveal about attitudes in the Western world toward Spain and Russia in the late 1930s through the 1950s?

Orwell was hoping that he could sell 3,000 to 4,000 copies of *Homage to Catalonia* and that the book would spark a real discussion about the complicated political situation in Spain. However, in its first four months, the book sold just 700 out of the 1,500 copies the publisher, Warburg, printed. In fact, Warburg still had copies of the book in 1951, and the book did not see print in America until 1952. So what went wrong? Biographer Michael Shelden argues that it was a question of timing. He writes that "[a]lthough Orwell could hardly have worked any faster to bring it out, it was published at a time when the subject had already been examined in several noteworthy books and the public's attention was moving away from it to other topics" (294). Orwell himself, however, blamed the poor reception at least in part on the publishing industry. According to Shelden, "[t]he commercial failure of *Homage to Catalonia* made Orwell's opinion of the book trade sink even lower. He liked to say that it was a 'financial racket' that favored heavily advertised books, regardless of their quality, and that exerted a certain influence over the reviewers' opinions in the big Sunday papers" (294).

Do some background reading on the publication of *Homage to Catalonia*. Start with one or more of Orwell's biographers. In addition to Shelden's biography of Orwell, Bernard Crick's *George Orwell: A Life* and Jeffrey Meyers's *Orwell: Wintry Conscience of a Generation* will be particularly helpful with this topic. Write an essay in which you investigate and interpret the poor sales of Orwell's book. Was its fate sealed by poor timing, lack of advertising, or something else entirely?

Philosophy and Ideas

Though *Homage to Catalonia* is in some ways the memoirs of a soldier, Orwell was no ordinary soldier. In fact, it was in large part his intellectual engagement in the problems of the world that convinced him to enlist in the POUM in revolutionary Spain. He wrote *Homage to Catalonia* to spark lively discussions about the political situation in Spain, which he felt was being misrepresented around the world. Not surprisingly, then, there are many essays to be written about philosophy and ideas in *Homage to Catalonia.* Much of the text has to do with socialism, and you might consider it from several angles. First of all, you might investigate Orwell's thoughts on the plausibility of creating and sustaining a true socialist society after living for a brief time in a society that fully embraced socialist principles. Or, you might narrow your focus to Orwell's portrayal of an army operating with socialist principles and a belief in the equality of all enlisted. Can an army of this sort be successful? If one believes in a socialist society, then must all elements of it, including its armies, operate under these same principles? Finally, you might elect to focus your study on gender roles, specifically on the way that the roles of women in Spain seemed to Orwell to change as the revolution progressed. What factors determine the way that women are perceived and treated in a given society?

Sample Topics:

1. **Socialism and equality in practice:** Analyze and evaluate Orwell's thoughts on the actualization of socialist ideals.

   Orwell writes about seeing socialist principles put into action on the Aragon Front:

> In theory it was perfect equality, and even in practice it was not
> far from it. . . . Many of the normal motives of civilized life—
> snobbishness, money-grubbing, fear of the boss, etc.—had
> simply ceased to exist. The ordinary class-division of society
> had disappeared to an extent that is almost unthinkable in the
> money-tainted air of England; there was no one there except the
> peasants and ourselves, and no one owned anyone else as his
> master. Of course such a state of affairs could not last. (104)

What was daily life like in this society Orwell describes? What
details does Orwell provide to substantiate his claim that this
society he lived in was "not far from" achieving "perfect equality"? Why does he say that "of course such a state of affairs could
not last"? Why could it not last? What happened to bring an end
to it? Is he saying that it is impossible to sustain a socialist state?

2. **Socialist ideals in the military:** Analyze and evaluate what
   Orwell has to say about socialism in the military.

Orwell was surprised by the extent to which social equality
existed in the militias. He observed that the socialist troops
related to one another in a very different way from American
or British military groups, which depended on a rigid hierarchy to function. Orwell describes the POUM militia as follows:

> It was understood that orders had to be obeyed, but it was also
> understood that when you gave an order you gave it as com-
> rade to comrade and not as superior to inferior. . . . They had
> attempted to produce within the militias a sort of temporary
> working model of the classless society. Of course there was not
> perfect equality, but there was nearer an approach to it than I
> had ever seen or than I would have thought conceivable in time
> of war. But I admit that at first sight the state of affairs at the
> front horrified me. How on earth could the war be won by an
> army of this type? (27)

Were Orwell's fears well founded? How well, in fact, did the
army function? Ultimately, did Orwell see the equality of its

members as a flaw or an asset? Did his observations of equality in the army teach him anything about the way socialist theory might play out in civilian life?

3. **Gender roles in revolutionary and socialist societies:** What kind of commentary does Orwell's book make about the role of women in a socialist society?

You might begin by thinking about a hypothetical, perfect socialist society; what would the relationship between men and women be like? Would each gender have distinct social roles? If so, what would they be? Next, consider passages such as the following, in which Orwell comments on the role of women in a revolutionary or socialist society:

> In the early battles they had fought side by side with the men as a matter of course. It is a thing that seems natural in time of revolution. Ideas were changing already, however. The militiamen had to be kept out of the riding-school while the women were drilling there, because they laughed at the women and put them off. A few months earlier no one would have seen anything comic in a woman handling a gun. (7)

Why do you think women's roles were so volatile in Spain during the revolutionary period, and why do you think they changed the way they did?

Form and Genre

Studying form and genre means taking a look at how a particular work, such as *Homage to Catalonia,* compares to similar works and thinking about what distinguishes it from other titles like it. It also has to do with examining the choices that authors and editors make as they create a work of literature and prepare it for publication. In the case of *Homage to Catalonia,* you might begin by asking yourself what kind of book it is—a memoir, a piece of journalism, or history? What are the most salient characteristics of the book that allow you to place it in a given category? Is it easily categorizable? Why or why not? What makes it distinctive among the other titles in this category? You will also want to examine the choices that Orwell made as he was crafting the book. Why, for example, did he decide to include an epigraph? And why did he choose the one he did? What effect does this choice have on the readers' experience of the book as a whole? You might also investigate the fate of the political sections, which were originally published as chapters 5 and 11 but which were moved to appendices in an edition published after Orwell's death. Why did the editors decide to make such a change? Did it alter the book for better or worse? When you evaluate Orwell's choice of epigraph, the placement of the political information, or other elements, such as Orwell's choice of title or point of view, you will need to keep in mind that you do not simply want to evaluate whether or not Orwell made, to your mind, a good aesthetic choice. Instead, you want to use your analysis of the element(s) you're evaluating to help you arrive at a fresh insight into or interpretation of *Homage to Catalonia* that you can put forth as the main claim, or thesis, of your essay.

Sample Topics:

1. **Genre:** Discuss what genre *Homage to Catalonia* belongs to and its impact on that genre.

   Begin by thinking about what sort of book *Homage to Catalonia* is. What other sorts of books is it like? Would you consider it a history book, a piece of journalism, or a memoir? Something else entirely? What makes you place the book in the category you do? How is it similar to and different from books in the same category that were published before and after it? How did it adhere to and depart from the expected conventions of the genre?

2. **Movement of political chapters to appendices:** Discuss the effect that the location of the political material—initially in chapters 5 and 11 and later in appendices—has on the overall impact and significance of *Homage to Catalonia.*

   In the initial edition of *Homage to Catalonia,* Orwell includes detailed discussions of the political factions vying for power in Spain in chapters 5 and 11, but some of his remarks, such as this one which appears near the beginning of chapter 5, reveal his uncertainly about including lengthy explanations of the political forces involved in the war:

At the beginning I had ignored the political side of the war, and it was only about this time that it began to force itself upon my attention. If you are not interested in the horrors of party politics, please skip; I am trying to keep the political parts of this narrative in separate chapters for precisely that purpose. But at the same time it would be quite impossible to write about the Spanish war from a purely military angle. It was above all things a political war. (46)

Biographer Michael Shelden argues that these chapters, while they may be necessary to provide background knowledge, disrupt the narrative flow of the main story. He writes:

From a literary standpoint, the weakest parts of his book are those in which he tries to sort out the points of dispute among the left-wing parties. . . . [I]n any case the objection is neatly dealt with in the Complete Works edition of 1986, which places Chapters 5 and 11—the two most political chapters—at the back of the book in two appendixes. It was done in accordance with suggestions for revision that Orwell made near the end of his life. (283)

Spend some time thinking about what the book is like with the political information as part of the main narrative and then with this information plucked out and moved to the back as appendices. How does the placement of this information affect the experience of the reader? Would you argue that the new edition is essentially the same as the original? Or does the editorial tweaking result in a significantly different literary experience? If you think it does, is the difference, in your view, a positive or negative one?

3. **Epigraph:** Analyze and evaluate the epigraph that Orwell uses to open *Homage to Catalonia.*

The epigraph, from Proverbs, reads:

Answer not a fool according to his folly, lest thou be like unto him. Answer a fool according to his folly, lest he be wise in his own conceit. Proverbs XXVI 5–6.

What does this quotation mean? How does it help you to understand the text that follows? How is the readers' experience of the
book different because of this epigraph? What would the book
be like without it? In terms of the story that ultimately unfolds,
who do you think is the "fool" referred to in the epigraph?

4. **Title:** Discuss the significance of the book's title: *Homage to
Catalonia.*

Think about Orwell's selection of a title for this volume and
what it can tell you about the themes and meanings of the
work. Does this title indicate what the book is actually about?
If Orwell had wanted a purely descriptive title, what might he
have chosen? What kind of feel does that descriptive title have
in comparison to *Homage to Catalonia?* Why do you think
Orwell used the word "homage"? What are the connotations
of this word? How about Catalonia? Why not Spain?

5. **Point of view:** Analyze and evaluate Orwell's use of first-person
point of view.

Why do you think Orwell chooses to use first person? What would
the book be like had he written it in third person instead? Does
the book seem less objective because of the personal element that
a first-person narration creates? Why or why not? Think specifically about the sections in which Orwell delves into the complexities of Spanish politics. How is this type of information typically
presented? What are the ramifications of Orwell's decision to
write these in first person? Overall, does the book seem more or
less journalistic based on Orwell's choice? In your estimation, is
this a positive or negative characteristic of the book?

Language, Symbols, and Imagery

Language, symbols, and imagery are important to conveying meaning
in works of nonfiction just as they are in fiction. Granted, in *Homage to
Catalonia*, Orwell is describing his own personal experiences and reporting events that actually occurred rather than creating characters and a
plot from scratch. Still, the final result is a crafted piece of writing. Orwell

made the same kinds of decisions for this work as he did creating *1984* and *Animal Farm*. He had to decide on a point of view and a structure; he had to determine what events to cover and how to present them. He had to decide which scenes to describe in detail and which to omit, which thoughts to record and which to pass over. Finally, as he actually wrote the book, he had to decide exactly what words to use to tell his story. The good news is that you can examine each of these decisions that Orwell made as he crafted this book, using them to help you analyze the themes and meanings of the work. Take the early passage describing an Italian militiaman in great detail, for example. Orwell's account of his experience in the war would not have been any less factually correct had he mentioned that militiaman simply in passing. Instead, he elects to devote an extended passage to describing this person who does not end up becoming in any way a central character in the text. Recognizing and investigating the considered choice Orwell made here can alert you to the themes he wishes to emphasize. Additionally, Orwell himself points out that the language people use to talk about something can reveal a great deal about their perceptions of it; this is true of Orwell's own language as well. He notes that people in Barcelona began to talk about the war in passive voice, as though it were something happening to them, and that this shift in language conveyed the sense of powerlessness they felt. In the same way that Orwell analyzes this use of language, you can analyze his word choices. How does Orwell talk about the war? Does the language he uses to discuss it convey his own biases? How so? If you keep in mind that even a work of nonfiction is a piece of crafted writing requiring many of the same decisions and choices that fictional writing does, you will likely discover other images and symbols and language use patterns that you might investigate as the topic for an essay.

Sample Topics:

1. **Italian militiaman:** Analyze and evaluate the image of the Italian militiaman in the opening scenes of the novel.

The image of the Italian militiaman that shows up on the first page of *Homage to Catalonia* is definitely a powerful one for Orwell. Analyze the following passage to determine why this image resonates so deeply for him:

> He was a tough-looking youth of twenty-five or six, with red-
> dish-yellow hair and powerful shoulders. His peaked leather
> cap was pulled fiercely over one eye. He was standing in profile
> to me, his chin on his breast, gazing with a puzzled frown at a
> map which one of the officers had on the table. Something in
> his face deeply moved me. It was the face of a man who would
> commit murder and throw away his life for a friend—the kind
> of face you would expect in an Anarchist, though likely as not
> he was a Communist. There were both candour and ferocity
> in it; also the pathetic reverence that illiterate people have for
> their supposed superiors. (3)

What is it about this militiaman that Orwell finds so striking?
How does this image, appearing so early in the text, affect how
you interpret what comes after? What does it tell you about
Orwell's priorities? Can you identify any echoes of this passage later in the text?

2. **Language and perception:** Analyze and evaluate the rhetoric
   that people use when they talk about the war and how it reflects
   on their understanding of it.

Orwell writes the following about the fighting in Barcelona:

> on every side you heard the same anxious questions: 'Do you
> think it's stopped? Do you think it's going to start again?' 'It'—
> the fighting—was now thought of as some kind of natural
> calamity, like a hurricane or an earthquake, which was happen-
> ing to us all alike and which we had no power of stopping. (139)

Orwell makes an interesting point here: By speaking in passive
voice, the city's residents were avoiding attributing responsibility
for the fighting to any particular group. He notes that the result
of this was feeling a lack of control and general powerlessness.
Reread the entire text, paying careful attention to the language
used to describe the fighting. Pay attention to Orwell's reports of
others' speech as well as his own narrative characterizations. All

told, what does the language used to talk about the war have to say about the attitudes of the speakers?

Compare and Contrast Essays

Comparing and contrasting often helps put things in perspective and helps you see patterns and distinctions that may escape notice in isolation. In the case of *Homage to Catalonia,* as in most literary works, the potential for comparisons and contrasts are almost infinite. You can compare and contrast Orwell to any of the other soldiers, Madrid to Barcelona, or the PSUC to the POUM, for instance. Or, you might find it more instructive to compare *Homage to Catalonia* to other works, such as Hemingway's *For Whom the Bell Tolls,* that also examine a soldier's experience in the Spanish civil war, albeit from a fictional perspective. Alternatively, you might compare *Homage to Catalonia* to another of Orwell's works, such as the fictional *1984,* which describes a totalitarian society that has some things in common with wartime Spain. In any case, no matter what you decide to compare and contrast, you will want to make sure that your essay does not devolve into a mere list of interesting similarities and differences. This is what you might come up with initially, as you are brainstorming, but ultimately you want to use your observations in the service of a fresh interpretation of or perspective of the elements you are studying.

Sample Topics:

1. **Orwell's *Homage to Catalonia* versus Hemingway's *For Whom the Bell Tolls:*** Compare and contrast these two works that deal with the Spanish civil war. What new insights about the war or either of these works does such a comparison allow you to make?

   Read or reread *Homage to Catalonia* and *For Whom the Bell Tolls.* Compare and contrast the main characters of each work, Orwell himself in *Homage to Catalonia* and Robert Jordan in *For Whom the Bell Tolls.* What would you say are the authors' opinions on socialism, communism, the Spanish people, and war in a more general sense? Taken together, what do these two powerful works of literature, one a novel and the other a work of nonfiction, have to tell us about the Spanish civil war?

2. Orwell's *Homage to Catalonia* **versus his novel** *1984:* Compare and contrast Orwell's nonfiction book describing his experiences in the Spanish war with *1984*, which describes the experiences of citizens under a totalitarian state.

Read or reread *Homage to Catalonia* and *1984*. What similarities can you find in these two books? Consider, in particular, the function of the press in war-torn revolutionary Spain and in Big Brother's Oceania. How are events reported in each of these societies? Who gets to decide what is truth and what gets recorded as history?

Bibliography and Online Resources for *Homage to Catalonia*

Crick, Bernard. *George Orwell: A Life.* Boston: Little, Brown, 1980.

Fitzpatrick, Shelia. *The Russian Revolution.* New York: Oxford UP, 2008.

Graham, Helen. *The Spanish Republic at War, 1936–1939.* Cambridge: Cambridge UP, 2002.

Hollis, Christopher. *A Study of George Orwell.* Chicago: Regnery, 1956.

Lee, Robert A. *Orwell's Fiction.* Notre Dame, IN: U of Notre Dame P: 1969.

Letemendia, V. C. "Revolution on Animal Farm: Orwell's Neglected Commentary." *Journal of Modern Literature* 18.1 (1992): 127.

Miller, Martin A. The *Russian Revolution: The Essential Readings.* Hoboken, NJ: Wiley-Blackwell, 2001.

Newsinger, John. "Orwell and the Spanish Revolution." *International Socialism Journal* 62 (1994). <http://pubs.socialistreviewindex.org.uk/isj62/contents.htm>.

Orwell, George. *Homage to Catalonia.* San Diego: Harcourt Brace, 1980.

Patai, Daphne. "Political Fiction and Patriarchal Fantasy." The *Orwell Mystique: A Study in Male Ideology.* Amherst: U of Massachusetts P, 1984, 201–18.

Payne, Stanley. *The Spanish Civil War, the Soviet Union, and Communism.* New Haven: Yale UP, 2004.

Preston, Paul. *The Spanish Civil War: Reaction, Revolution, and Revenge.* New York: Norton, 2007.

Russell, Bertrand. "George Orwell." *World Review* 16 (1950): 5–6.

Shelden, Michael. *Orwell: The Authorized Biography.* New York: Harper Collins, 1991.

Wade, Rex A. *The Russian Revolution, 1917.* New York: Cambridge UP, 2000.

"SHOOTING
AN ELEPHANT"
AND OTHER ESSAYS

READING TO WRITE

ORWELL IS perhaps as well known for his insightful and often politically charged essays as he is for his novels. Among the most well known of these essays, "The Lion and the Unicorn" (1941) was originally the "first in a new series called Searchlight Books, which . . . were advertised as 'popular but serious works' that would 'serve as an arsenal for the manufacture of mental and spiritual weapons needed for the crusade against Nazism'" (Shelden 336). In this piece, Orwell forcefully and convincingly argues that England must have a socialist revolution in order to defeat Hitler. Since its initial publication, scholars have debated Orwell's ideas and speculated on what he got right and wrong in his predictions of England's future. Two other popular and acclaimed Orwell essays have to do with the power and potential of writing. In "Politics and the English Language" (1946), Orwell enumerates the faults of political rhetoric and ruminates on the consequences of such sloppy discourse. In "Why I Write" (1946), he muses on the various motivations of writers before analyzing his own reasons for pursuing the craft, explaining his love for both literature as art and literature as political weapon:

> What I have most wanted to do throughout the past ten years is to make political writing into an art. My starting point is always a feeling of partisanship, a sense of injustice. When I sit down to write a book, I do not say

to myself, 'I am going to produce a work of art.' I write it because there is some lie that I want to expose, some fact to which I want to draw attention, and my initial concern is to get a hearing. (8)

"Shooting an Elephant," one of Orwell's earlier pieces, first published in 1936 in John Lehmann's *New Writing*, exemplifies this dual purpose. The essay tells the story of an officer in the Imperial Guard in Burma who feels compelled to shoot an elephant that has gotten out of control when he would really rather spare the animal. He describes his dilemma as follows:

> Here was I, the white man with his gun, standing in front of the unarmed native crowd—seemingly the leading actor of the piece; but in reality I was only an absurd puppet pushed to and fro by the will of those yellow faces behind. I perceived in this moment that when the white man turns tyrant it is his own freedom that he destroys. He becomes a sort of hollow, posing dummy, the conventionalized figure of a sahib. For it is the condition of his rule that he shall spend his life in trying to impress the "natives," and so in every crisis he has got to do what the "natives" expect of him. He wears a mask, and his face grows to fit it.

One of the first things that may strike you about this passage is imagery of the theater running throughout. There are references to the "leading actor of the piece," "an absurd puppet," "a hollow, posing dummy," and to "wear[ing] a mask." Obviously, the narrator feels as though he is playing a part in some sort of scene. The narrator's complaint about his lack of self-agency seems valid since, even if he were "the lead actor of the piece," he would still not really be in control of his own actions, since all actors, leading or not, play out a scene as it was written. Following this line of thinking, however, take a moment to consider the "natives." If they are part of the colonial scene that that narrator imagines himself in, then they too have been handed their lines. And if this is true, then it seems unfair for them to bear the brunt of the blame for the narrator's untenable position. If we agree with the narrator, then we must agree too that both the narrator and the "natives" are being directed by roles and relationships that existed long before they stepped into them, the roles of the colonizer and the colonized.

In an effort to emphasize his lack of culpability, the narrator insists he is not the leading actor in the piece, but rather an "absurd puppet," an object animated by an outside force, and then escalates the imagery to a "hollow, posing dummy," a completely inert object. Then, just when he has removed all agency from himself, the passage takes a sort of turn. The narrator's imagery shifts again; he claims that he "wears a mask and his face grows to fit it." Envisioning himself as a person wearing a mask that his face "grows to fit" counters the previous image of the narrator as inert object manipulated by outside forces with the idea that, given enough time, the narrator, or others in his position, actually transforms into the role he has stepped into. His identity becomes indistinguishable from this role. If this is so, then does he again become responsible for his actions? Also, if the narrator's face grows to fit the mask he wears, what does this say about the "natives" who are also playing roles or wearing masks? Are their true identities being changed by the roles they have been assigned as well? What are the ramifications of such an idea?

Orwell's "Shooting an Elephant" blends his love of the literary with his political motivations. The essay makes for a compelling read and its imagery is powerful, but it also has a strong political component as well. Take the analysis of the above passage a few steps further and analyze other, similar passages in the essay. Do not simply take Orwell's statements at face value. He writes that white men sacrifice their own freedom when they take away the freedom of others, and the essay definitely supports this idea. But what else does it have to say about the relationship between colonizers and the colonized? Who is really in control? Is anyone? What happens to the actual human beings involved in a relationship of this kind? How does filling the role of colonizer or colonized affect a person's identity and potential? Who, if anyone, is to blame for the situation in the story? Who, if anyone, has the power to change it?

TOPICS AND STRATEGIES

Use the topics provided below to give you ideas for how you might approach writing an essay in response to one of Orwell's essays. The prompts should serve as springboards for your own ideas; do not allow them to constrain you in any way. You certainly do not have to answer all of the questions posed or limit yourself to those particular questions.

In fact, after reading through some of the suggested topics, you might decide to modify one of them or even to create your own. Given the number of excellent essays by Orwell that are not directly addressed in this chapter, you may even decide to read an Orwell essay not covered in this chapter and to create a topic for it. Whatever topic you choose, remember that your job is to do enough brainstorming and thinking to generate a thesis sentence, a main point of argument or interpretation that you want to make about a certain piece of Orwell's writing.

Themes

Writing about the theme of an essay is much like writing about the theme of a short story or novel. You are trying to get at what the essay is fundamentally concerned with. First, you will want to read the piece you are studying carefully, noting what you consider to be its primary concerns. These may or may not be obvious from the essay's title or the main topics it purports to discuss. You might also think about what themes occur in more than one of Orwell's essays. Then, once you have selected the theme you want to work with and the work(s) you want to study, reread the works carefully, highlighting passages that have to do with your theme so that you can go back and analyze them. Remember that a good essay does not just point out the themes present in a work; it must make an interpretive argument about that theme. For instance, you would not want to assert simply that war is a recurring theme in Orwell's essays. Rather, you want to delve into what Orwell is saying about war and its place in human civilization, not sticking to surface-level meanings but really exploring the subtleties and undercurrents so that you can help the reader of your essay gain a fresh insight into the essay that they would not have arrived at from their own initial reading of the piece.

Sample Topics:

1. **War as agent of social change:** In Part III of "The Lion and the Unicorn," Orwell claims that war is "the greatest of all agents of change" (71). Write an essay in which you respond to this assertion. Remember, as you work on your prewriting, to consider the distinct possibility that Orwell does not necessarily mean this statement to be taken at face value. And, even if he does, should we assume that he condones war as the best way to effect social change?

In Part III of "The Lion and the Unicorn," Orwell writes:

> War is the greatest of all agents of change. It speeds up all processes, wipes out minor distractions, brings realities to the surface. Above all, war brings it home to the individual. That he is *not* altogether an individual. It is only because they are aware of this that men will die on the field of battle. (71)

What is the context for this quotation? What kind of change is Orwell hoping will happen, and how does he imagine war helping to bring about that change? Does war, in fact, make people feel like part of a unit in a way that they otherwise cannot feel? Is it the most likely impetus for major social change? You can answer this question in a number of ways. You might evaluate the claim based solely on Orwell's own evidence and rhetoric. Or, you might do some historical research to decide for yourself whether what he says was true before he wrote it and whether it has been true since. Finally, you might use this quotation and question as a springboard to your own thoughts about the world today. What wars are happening now, and how, to your mind, are they affecting people's sense of unity and inspiring change?

2. **Writing and moral choice in "Politics and the English Language":** In this essay, which was first published in *Horizon* in April 1946, Orwell "makes the case that bad writing is morally wrong, as well as politically and aesthetically wrong" (Shelden 393). Write an essay in which you support and extend, modify, or argue against his thesis.

How does Orwell make the case that bad writing is not only politically and aesthetically, but morally, wrong? What is his evidence, and is his case convincing? Biographer Michael Shelden notes the connection between this essay and the novel *1984.* He writes:

> Newspeak is a perfect language for a society of bad writers because it reduces the number of choices available to them. . . .

> Big Brother likes it because it deprives people of their freedom
> to make choices. Before it corrupts politically, Newspeak cor-
> rupts morally, since it allows writers to cheat themselves and
> their readers with ready-made prose. (394)

Reread both *1984* and "Politics and the English Language" and
consider Shelden's remarks. What is the connection between
morality, the freedom to make choices, and language? Write
an essay in which you discuss how the arguments Orwell
makes in the essay regarding language and morality are sup-
ported (or not) in his novel.

3. **Motivations for writing:** In "Why I Write" Orwell discusses
   what motivates all writers to write as well as his own personal
   motivations for writing. Discuss Orwell's perception of himself
   as a writer, the competing impulses he contends with, and how
   those impulses show up in his work.

According to Orwell, why do writers write? What are their
major impulses? What motivates Orwell himself to write?
When did he first begin to define himself as a writer, and how
did his perception of his authorial persona evolve?

    In "Why I Write," Orwell lists the following as motivations
of writers: "Sheer egoism," "Aesthetic enthusiasm," "Historical
Impulse," and "Political purpose," and he goes on to write: "I
am a person in whom the first three motives would outweigh
the fourth. In a peaceful age I might have written ornate or
merely descriptive books, and might have remained almost
unaware of my political loyalties. As it is I have been forced
into becoming a sort of pamphleteer" (6). What did Orwell
feel forced him in this direction? Did he manage to incorporate some of the other motivations into his political writing?
Orwell biographer Michael Shelden claims that Orwell made
the right choice in opting to write works with a clear political
element. Did Orwell believe so? Do you? Why or why not? How
do you think Orwell's concern with the politics of his time
has affected his literary reputation and his place in the canon
of modern literature? You might take a particular case, such

as *Homage to Catalonia,* which Orwell discusses in "Why I Write," as a case study. What motivations were at work in the creation of this book? How did those motivations complement and compete with one another?

4. **The nature of political writing:** In "Politics and the English Language," Orwell argues that "political writing is bad writing" because it is so prone to a "lifeless, imitative style" and the use of exhausted phrases, euphemisms, and vagueness. Analyze and evaluate Orwell's take on the nature of political rhetoric. Has political writing always been this way? Is it still? Must it be so?

Orwell writes:

> In our time, political speech and writing are largely the defense of the indefensible. Things like the continuance of the British rule in India, the Russian purges and deportations, the dropping of the atom bombs on Japan, can indeed be defended, but only by arguments which are too brutal for most people to face, and which do not square with the professed aims of political parties. Thus political language has to consist largely of euphemisms, question-begging and sheer cloudy vagueness. . . . Millions of peasants are robbed of their farms and sent trudging along the roads with no more than they can carry: this is called *transfer of population* or *rectification of frontiers*. People are imprisoned for years without trial, or shot in the back of the neck or sent to die of scurvy in Arctic lumber camps: this is called *elimination of unreliable elements*. Such phraseology is needed if one wants to name things without calling up mental pictures of them. (114–15)

Do you agree with Orwell's assessment that rhetorical sleights of hand are often used to make political points? Is one group or nation guiltier of this than others, or is it a universal fault? Is it an inevitable fault? What do you think Orwell would have to say about current political rhetoric? Is it any clearer, or does it suffer from the same problems he saw in the writing of his era? What do Orwell's remarks have to tell us about the power and limitations of language?

Character

When writing about essays, you will need to expand your notion of character. Think of all of the people involved in an essay such as "Shooting an Elephant" as characters because, even though this essay is, at least according to some scholars, based on events that really occurred in Orwell's life, their manifestations on the page are creations of Orwell's. Through his authorial decisions, including how he describes them and what he includes and omits, he has shaped these people into characters you can study as you would characters in a fictional work. You can study the first-person narrator—whether you perceive this narrator to be based on Orwell or not—and ask yourself how Orwell presents this character and to what effect. You can also consider the Burmese people and even the elephant as characters. What motivations does Orwell assign them? How does he craft this tale to make a point, and what exactly is the point he wants to make? Does the Orwell character of the piece evolve any from its beginning to its end? You can also think of Orwell's presentation of a certain group as a type of character. For example, you might examine Orwell's portrayal of the English people in "The Lion and the Unicorn," asking the same types of questions in your brainstorming as you would if you were studying a single character or group of characters in a fictional work. What are the characters' most salient characteristics? What are their strengths and weaknesses? What questions about the characters remain unanswered? What details or facts does Orwell leave out that you would like to know?

Sample Topics:

1. **The English:** In "The Lion and the Unicorn," specifically in Part I, "England, Your England," Orwell asserts that national identity is a real phenomenon and that the people of a given nation have a certain identifiable character. He goes on at length about the character of the English; how does he describe them? Does his assessment come across as objective and true or biased in some way?

   According to Orwell's observations, what do most English citizens have in common? What are the things that make them recognizably English? What would you say is Orwell's opinion of the English? In his mind, would they compare favorably to, say, Americans or Spaniards? Why or why not? What would he say are the English citizens' best qualities? Their worst? How does he anticipate England being changed in his lifetime, particularly by World War II?

Keep in mind that another writer, even one of the same time period and circumstances, would likely describe the English in very different terms than Orwell. This helps demonstrate the way that the people of England are constructed as characters playing on the world stage inside Orwell's mind. Think, then, about how Orwell came to view, and create, the English as he did. Do some reading on Orwell's background. How might his background and his formative experiences have affected the way he perceives the English?

2. **Cultures as characters in "Shooting an Elephant":** Much of the action in this story comes as a result of the interplay between an English police officer and the Burmese population. What characteristics does Orwell attribute to these two sides? How does their interplay result in the killing of the elephant?

Orwell uses characterization in an interesting way in this essay. On the one hand, he has a single character, himself, stand in for the entire culture of England; he represents every Englishman scattered throughout the far-flung British Empire. On the other hand, while there are literally thousands of Burmese who show up to watch the elephant get shot, Orwell reduces them to a single entity, a group who stand in for some simple, stereotypical assumptions about the Burmese culture. In fact, there is no sense of loss that a man had been trampled to death. Quite the contrary, Orwell says, "I was very glad that the coolie had been killed; it put me legally in the right and it gave me a sufficient pretext for shooting the elephant." What is going on with this method of characterization? Orwell's explicit point is that imperialists end up losing control of their own wills in their efforts to impress their colonial subjects, but does this character scheme support or undercut that assertion? How would the story have been different had individual

Burmese characters been given names and voices? What if another Englishman had accompanied Orwell?

3. **Orwell as a character:** In all of these essays, George Orwell himself presumably is the first-person narrator; however, in "Shooting an Elephant" and "Why I Write," he is both narrator and subject matter. Who is this person presented in these essays? Is this the "real" Orwell? Is it a polished version of himself, created for public consumption? Is it a more-or-less fictional character who shares some experiences with the writer?

Many scholars assume that the account detailed in "Shooting an Elephant" is based on an event that happened to Orwell, though others have argued that, while Orwell was a member of the Imperial Guard in Burma, he in fact never shot an elephant. In any case, whether you believe the first-person narrator is based on Orwell, is modeled on someone else he knew, or is simply a figment of his imagination, you will ask the same questions about the character. What type of person is he? Is he sympathetic? Does he change from the beginning of the essay to the end? What does Orwell's creation of this character that has at least some degree of similarity to himself tell us about Orwell's own feelings about his past and the events he took part in in Burma? Likewise, in "Why I Write," what is it we are really learning about the writer? Why is it important that we know about the history of a writer's experiences with the written word? Orwell claims that it is impossible to "assess a writer's motives without knowing something of his early development" (4). What do you think we are supposed to assess about Orwell's motives for writing about his own writing? Is this character created in order to tell us how to read Orwell's works?

History and Context

Some background reading is very helpful in fully appreciating and understanding the significance of Orwell's essays. You would do well to read up on politics in England during World War II, including the history of the English Labour Party and the evolution of the English class structure, particularly the changing role of the upper class, as you prepare to write on "Politics and the English Language" or "The Lion and the Unicorn." If you are planning to write an essay on "Shooting an Elephant," you will probably want to do some background reading on England's relationship to Burma and on Orwell's stint in the Imperial Guard, beginning with Emma Larking's *Finding George Orwell in Burma* and Michael Shelden's *Orwell: The Authorized Biography.* Doing this type of research helps you to understand the context in which Orwell was writing so that you are better able to appreciate his motivations and perspective. In addition to serving as background knowledge, your research into the historical and cultural context of Orwell's pieces could function as a springboard to an essay topic.

Sample Topics:

1. **English class structure:** In "The Lion and the Unicorn: England, Your England," Orwell devotes a great deal of attention to the evolution of the English upper class; how does he believe it has changed? Is this change for the better or worse? What is his ultimate estimation of this group? Do you agree?

   You might start with an analysis of Orwell's argument that the upper class is "morally sound" but "unteachable":

   > One thing that has shown that the English ruling class are *morally* sound, is that in time of war they are ready enough to get themselves killed. Several dukes, earls and whatnots were killed in the recent campaign in Flanders. That could not happen if these people were the cynical scoundrels that they are sometimes declared to be. It is important not to misunderstand their motives, or one cannot predict their actions. What is to be expected of them is not treachery, or physical cowardice, but stupidity, unconscious sabotage, an infallible instinct for doing the wrong thing. They are not wicked, or altogether wicked; they are merely unteachable. Only when their money and power are gone will the younger among them begin to grasp what century they are living in. (37)

First of all, do you agree with Orwell that because some members of the upper class are willing to die in battle, it means that they are morally sound? Why or why not? How does this prove they are not "the cynical scoundrels that they are sometimes declared to be"? By declaring the upper classes not "altogether wicked," but "unteachable," is Orwell saying that people should not be held accountable for what he identifies as their "stupidity, unconscious sabotage, [and] an infallible instinct for doing the wrong thing"? Does Orwell make a convincing case that it is only when their money and power are gone that upper-class people will be able to appreciate the changes that have taken place in the world and stop their "unconscious sabotage"? What is it that Orwell believes they are sabotaging? What is it that they cannot be taught?

How has the class hierarchy changed in England since Orwell's essay was published? Does the upper class still exist? Do its members seem "morally sound" or like "cynical scoundrels"? How and why has the ruling class in particular changed since the 1940s? What do you think Orwell would make of these changes?

2. **The war and the revolution in "The Lion and the Unicorn, Part III: The English Revolution":** Analyze and evaluate Orwell's commentary on the connection between the war against Hitler and a potential socialist revolution in "The English Revolution."

Considering the need for a fundamental cultural change in England in order to defeat Hitler, Orwell writes:

> The war and the revolution are inseparable. We cannot establish anything that a western nation would regard as Socialism without defeating Hitler; on the other hand we cannot defeat Hitler while we remain economically and socially in the nineteenth century. The past is fighting the future and we have two years, a year, possibly only a few months, to see to it that the future wins. (65)

Taking into account the remainder of the essay, analyze Orwell's argument here. Is it a convincing case? Why or why not? What are the connections between the reigning political system and military success? Clearly, one way to assess just how astute Orwell's pronouncements were in this case is to look at just how far toward the direction of socialism did England move in its efforts to defeat Hitler. Was England able to remain, more or less, the same economically or socially? Did any social changes made during the course of World War II remain in place following the war, or did the country revert to its previous state once Hitler was defeated?

3. **The Labour Party in "The Lion and the Unicorn: Part III: The English Revolution"**: Orwell claims that "In England there is only one Socialist party that has ever seriously mattered, the Labour Party." Does he think the party can make the kind of substantial move toward socialism in England that Orwell wants to see? Why or why not? What does he see as the Labour Party's primary goals and motivations? What is its biggest challenges and pitfalls? What is Orwell's final estimation of this group and its efforts, and do you agree with his assessment?

Do some research into the evolution of the Labour Party in England. You might start with Matthew Worley's *The Foundations of the British Labour Party*. To your mind, was Orwell's estimation of this party correct? What role did it ultimately play in the defeat of Hitler? How has the party changed since this essay was published? In ways Orwell would have foreseen? Why or why not?

Philosophy and Ideas

Orwell's essays take philosophies and ideas as their central subjects. Of course, he writes about capitalism and socialism in "The Lion and the Unicorn," but he also considers other ideas in that piece, including national identity. In "Shooting an Elephant," one of his major concerns is the relationship between an oppressor and the oppressed and the effects of that relationship on both parties. In "Why I Write," Orwell discusses the major motivations that writers have for indulging in their craft and his own personal drive to write, but he also makes the striking argument that all art is in some way political. If your aim is to write an easy about the philosophy and/or ideas at the heart of one or more of Orwell's essays, any of the aforementioned subjects would make a good potential topic, and there are many more that you might identify for yourself. Remember that for this type of essay some background reading is typically very helpful so that you are reading the piece with the richest sense of cultural and social context possible. This will not only help you to make a more astute and sensitive argument, but it will also help you avoid a potential stumbling block for this type of essay: evaluating Orwell's philosophies and ideas with your own, twenty-first-century, American standards.

Sample Topics:

1. **Socialism, fascism, and capitalism in "The Lion and the Unicorn, Part II: Shopkeepers at War":** Orwell does not just bandy about these terms. He uses them in quite specific ways. Look up each of these terms in a dictionary to get an accurate sense of their accepted meanings and then discuss Orwell's particular take on these terms as expressed in "Shopkeepers at War."

   What is the difference between socialism and fascism as outlined by Orwell? How do both of these differ (or not) from capitalism? How does Orwell describe Hitler's state? According to Orwell, how does British capitalism compare to socialism and fascism?

2. **The nature of freedom under colonialism in "Shooting an Elephant":** In this short essay, Orwell makes some striking comments on the consequences that tyranny brings to bear on the tyrants who exert it. Write an essay in which you support, modify, or argue against Orwell's claim that a person or country relinquishes its own freedom when it takes control of someone else.

   Orwell writes about what it was like to be a British officer in Burma during the 1920s. Specifically, he describes an experience in which he feels compelled to shoot an elephant because the populace expects him to. He writes:

I perceived in this moment that when the white man turns tyrant it is his own freedom that he destroys. He becomes a sort of hollow, posing dummy, the conventionalized figure of a sahib. For it is the condition of his rule that he shall spend his life in trying to impress the 'natives,' and so in every crisis he has got to do what the 'natives' expect of him. He wears a mask, and his face grows to fit it. I had got to shoot the elephant. I had committed myself to it when I sent for the rifle. A sahib has got to act like a sahib; he has got to appear resolute, to know his own mind and do definite things. To come all that way, rifle in hand, with two thousand people marching at my heels, and then to trail feebly away, having done nothing—no, that was impossible. The crowd would laugh at me. And my whole life, every white man's life in the East, was one long struggle not to be laughed at. (3)

Analyze the paragraph above as well as any others you find relevant in the text. How is it that in "turn[ing] tyrant" the white man destroys his freedom? Does Orwell make a convincing case that oppressors are changed just as the oppressed are by their interrelationship? What do you make of his statement that his life and "every white man's life in the East, was one long struggle not to be laughed at"? What would happen if Orwell were to be laughed at? What would happen if he had simply walked away from the elephant? What would he be losing, and is the keeping of it worth his shooting the elephant, an act he finds distasteful and disturbing?

3. **Art and politics in "Why I Write":** Orwell asserts that all art is fundamentally political in "Why I Write." Write an essay in which you explore Orwell's views on the relationship between art and politics as expressed in this essay.

Orwell lists the four reasons he believes that writers write: "Sheer egoism," "Aesthetic enthusiasm," "Historical impulse," and "Political Purpose." As he elaborates on political purpose, Orwell indicates that he is "using the word 'political' in the widest possible sense. Desire to push the world in a certain direction, to alter other people's idea of the kind of society that they should strive after" (5). He claims that "no book is genuinely free from political bias" and asserts that "[t]he opinion that art should have nothing to do with politics is itself a political attitude" (5). What do you make of this argument? Are there any literary works that are in fact free from political bias, and do these works hold more or less literary merit than overtly political works?

Orwell also writes in this essay: "And the more one is conscious of one's political bias, the more chance one has of acting politically without sacrificing one's aesthetic and intellectual integrity" (8). What does he mean here? Do all writers, all people even, have political biases even if they are unaware of them? His statement that "The opinion that art should have nothing to do with politics is itself a political attitude" seems to suggest so. What is the difference between a political attitude and a political bias? How does each of them typically play into a writer's motives and the writing he or she ultimately produces?

4. **National identity in "The Lion and the Unicorn, Part I: England, Your England":** Orwell writes: "Till recently it was thought proper to pretend that all human beings are very much like, but in fact anyone able to use his eyes knows that the average of human behavior differs enormously from country to country. Things that could happen in one country could not happen in another" (12). Write an essay in which you support and extend or contradict Orwell's statement regarding the concept of national identity.

Why is it "thought proper to pretend that all human beings are very much alike"? Where did this impulse come from? Do you agree with Orwell that "human behavior differs enormously from country to country"? In what ways? What example does Orwell give of things "that could happen in one country" that "could not happen in another"? Do you agree with his assessment? Can you think of additional, and current, examples? Would you argue that citizens of different nations are fundamentally more alike or dissimilar?

Form and Genre

Form and genre have to do with the foundations, or building blocks, of a piece of literature. Take "Shooting an Elephant," for example. You might consider Orwell's source material for this essay—is it in fact autobiographical, as it seems to be, or it is based on the experiences of someone else? Did Orwell invent the incident entirely? And why does this matter? How does it affect the way that the reader experiences the text or color his or her interpretation of it? You might also consider what genre "Shooting an Elephant" might be considered. Is it more like a short story? An essay? What makes it so? If you consider it an essay, what type of essay is it? What are Orwell's goals in writing it? These kinds of questions are not merely academic. Or they should not be. You ask them and pursue them in hopes that your investigation will produce some fresh insight into the themes and meanings of the work that you might not have arrived at via other angles of entry.

Sample Topics:

1. **"Shooting an Elephant"—fact or fiction:** No one seems to know for certain whether the experience recounted in "Shooting an Elephant" actually happened to Orwell, although most readers assume the account is autobiographical. How would readers' interpretation and experiences of this essay be different be if they believed that Orwell did not, in fact, ever shoot an elephant?

   Although many have assumed that the first-person narrator in "Shooting an Elephant" is actually Orwell himself, biographer Bernard Crick, author of *George Orwell: A Life*, brings up the possibility that the story is more fiction than fact because he is unable to find a record of an incident in which Orwell shoots an elephant. Read the appropriate sections in Crick's biography and any other information you can gather about the veracity of this story.

   Can you determine with any degree of certainty whether or not the account is autobiographical? Spend some time thinking about the significance of whether or not this experience actually happened to Orwell. Did he lead people to believe it did, or did readers simply assume the "I" to be the authorial persona? Does the meaning or significance of the account change depending on whether Orwell shot the elephant himself or simply knew someone who did? How exactly?

2. **Genre of "Shooting an Elephant":** What type of writing do you consider "Shooting an Elephant" to be, and how does this decision affect the way you read and understand the piece?

In what genre would you place "Shooting an Elephant"? Would you classify it as a story or an essay? Why? On what do you base this decision? If you have called it an essay, what type of essay would you say it is: expository, argumentative, descriptive, or narrative? Some combination of these? What would you argue is Orwell's main motivation for writing this piece? Does he achieve what he aims to? In your view, is the genre he selects the best vehicle for his message? Why or why not?

Language, Symbols, and Imagery

Examining the multitude of images and symbols within the texts is a good way to enter into Orwell's texts and probe some aspects of them more deeply. For instance, instead of simply appreciating that Orwell feels powerless in "Shooting an Elephant" because he describes himself as a puppet, you might stop and analyze that image and similar images in the text. You might ask yourself, who is controlling this puppet? How did Orwell come to be this puppet? What has happened to his own agency and will? You could also think about why he describes himself not only as a puppet, but as an "absurd puppet." What would make a puppet absurd? Absurd to whom? Finally, you could examine similar images, such as Orwell's remark that he was "seemingly the leading actor of the piece." Why does Orwell see this experience in terms of a production and himself as either an actor or a puppet? Who is directing the play? In a similar manner, you can analyze symbols such as the parade step of the military and the English hanging judge that Orwell describes in "The Lion and the Unicorn." In these cases, Orwell quickly explains what he feels these symbols represent; your job is to investigate those connections at length. Orwell writes, for example, that a military's parade step can say a great deal about the character of that nation. Explore that idea to determine whether it is true, what it can tell you about the characters of various nations at various times, and Orwell's motivations for pointing out this particular symbol to his readers.

Sample Topics:

1. **Puppet image in "Shooting an Elephant":** In "Shooting an Elephant," an essay in which Orwell recounts a traumatic experience of shooting an elephant while a British officer in Burma, Orwell creates an image of himself as a puppet being manipulated by a crowd of 2,000 Burmese. What can Orwell's imagery tell us about his relationship with the Burmese people and his perception of his own role as an officer?

   Orwell writes:

   > And it was at this moment, as I stood there with the rifle in my hands, that I first grasped the hollowness, the futility of the white man's dominion in the East. Here was I, the white man with his gun, standing in front of the unarmed native crowd— seemingly the leading actor of the piece; but in reality I was only an absurd puppet pushed to and fro by the will of those yellow faces behind. (3)

   Analyze the imagery Orwell uses here. Why does he view himself as a "puppet," especially an "absurd puppet"? Who does he imagine is controlling him and how are they exerting that control? Orwell compares the puppet he believes he truly is to the "leading actor of the piece" that he seems to be. Why do you think he describes the whole event in terms of some kind of artistic production—as a play or a puppet show? What does this say about Orwell's perception of England's rule of Burma and his own role in that rule?

2. **The hanging judge in "The Lion and The Unicorn Part I: England, Your England":** Here, Orwell presents us with what he feels is the perfect symbol of England's relationship to the law, the hanging judge. Discuss what his selection of the judge as symbol and his explanation of the symbol's meaning can tell

us about England as well as about Orwell's own feelings toward his home country.

Orwell finds the "hanging judge" an apt symbol for England. He explains:

> The hanging judge, that evil old man in scarlet robe and horse-hair wig, whom nothing short of dynamite will ever teach what century he is living in, but who will at any rate interpret the law according to the books and will in no circumstances take a money bribe, is one of the symbolic figures of England. He is a symbol of the strange mixture of reality and illusion, democracy and privilege, humbug and decency, the subtle network of compromises, by which the nation keeps itself in its familiar shape. (22)

Take some time to think about how the judge can be a symbol of all of the paradoxes Orwell numbers: reality and illusion, democracy and privilege, humbug and decency, and "the subtle network of compromises by which the nation keeps itself in its familiar shape." Does the symbol, to your mind, evoke all these things? Which does it call to mind most strongly? What other ideas does this symbolic figure evoke? What other figure(s) might Orwell have chosen to symbolize one or more of these ideas?

3. **Parade step of the army in "The Lion and the Unicorn":** Orwell argues that "[o]ne rapid but fairly sure guide to the social atmosphere of a country is the parade-step of its army" (20). How, according to Orwell, does the parade step function in this manner, and what do the various steps used by different armies have to say about the countries they represent?

According to Orwell, "[a] military parade is really a kind of ritual dance, something like a ballet, expressing a certain philosophy of life" (20). He uses the goose step as his primary example:

The goose-step, for instance, is one of the most horrible sights in the world, far more terrifying than a dive-bomber. It is simply an affirmation of naked power; contained in it, quite consciously and intentionally, is the vision of a boot crushing down on a face. Its ugliness is part of its essence, for what it is saying is 'Yes, I *am* ugly, and you daren't laugh at me', like the bully who makes faces at his victim. (20)

Would you agree with Orwell's analysis of the goose step? That it is more "terrifying than a dive-bomber"? That "contained in it, quite consciously and intentionally, is the vision of a boot crushing down on a face"? Do you agree with Orwell that the symbolism he points out is conscious and intentional? Why or why not? What type of parade march can be seen in other militaries? Do these steps also reveal something about the character of the nations these armies represent?

4. **England as a family:** "In the Lion and the Unicorn," Orwell writes that "England is a family with the wrong members in control" (54). What does that image evoke? What can it tell us about Orwell's perception of power dynamics in England?

As you think about these questions, consider also Orwell's elaboration of this image. He reveals that the "wrong members" of which he speaks are "the rich" and "people who step into positions of command by right of birth" and complains that "the rule of money sees to it that we shall be governed largely by the old—that is, by people, utterly unable to grasp what age they are living in or what enemy they are fighting" (54–55). What are the defining characteristics of a family? What makes England like a family? How is power distribution decided in families? How do money and age figure into these dynamics? What, if anything, can cause a family's power dynamics to shift? With all this in mind, what exactly do you think Orwell means when he compares England to a "family with the wrong members in control"?

5. Rhetorical strategy in "Politics and the English Language":
Orwell engages in an unusual rhetorical strategy in this essay—
pointing out flaws of writing, exhorting for clear and vigilant
thinking and writing, and then admitting that this very article
is likely swarming with the very errors he cites. What kind of
rhetorical strategy is Orwell using here and, to your mind, how
effective is it?

In "Politics and the English Language," Orwell takes writers
to task for several faults, including using hackneyed phrases,
unnecessarily complicated vocabulary, extraneous words,
passive voice, and unnecessary foreign phrases. He claims
that these flaws make writing unclear and sometimes meaningless and that they signal lazy writing. Then, surprisingly,
Orwell includes this line: "Look back through this essay and
for certain you will find that I have again and again committed the very faults I am protesting against." Why do you think
he would not examine his own writing for the faults he numbers and eradicate them? What point is Orwell trying to make
here? Is he intending for readers to examine his work only
to discover that he has not, in fact, really committed these
errors? Read through the essay looking for them; how many
can you find?

Compare and Contrast Essays

Comparing and contrasting elements within works, across works, or
entire works themselves can help you to gain a fuller perspective of those
works and the issues they explore. For example, you might compare and
contrast two of Orwell's essays, "Politics and the English Language" and
"The Prevention of Literature," to get a more complete picture of Orwell's
thoughts about the powers and limitations of political rhetoric. To probe
his thinking on the relationship between oppressors and the oppressed,
you might compare and contrast two pieces Orwell worked on simultaneously, "Shooting an Elephant" and *The Road to Wigan Pier*. Or to examine this same point from a different angle, you might contrast Orwell's
"Shooting an Elephant" with a similar work by a different author, such

as Kipling's "The Killing of Hatim Tai." Such an endeavor will, ideally, help you to achieve a greater understanding of the common threads that run through Orwell's and Kipling's works as well as to develop a greater understanding of what makes their individual perspectives distinctive.

Sample Topics:

1. **The essay "Shooting an Elephant" and the book *The Road to Wigan Pier*:** Compare and contrast these two Orwell pieces, looking particularly at what each has to say about the relationship between oppressed people and their oppressors.

   Orwell was working on these pieces at the same time. Biographer Michael Shelden writes that the story "Shooting an Elephant" "is not unconnected to the work he was doing in *The Road to Wigan Pier*. Part 2 of that latter work includes a long passage on his life in Burma, providing a context for his interest in the struggle between the oppressed and their oppressors" (244). Reread both of these works, paying particular attention to what they each have to say about the effects of tyranny on the oppressed but also on the tyrants themselves, or their agents. How does such a relationship change everyone involved?

2. **"Politics and the English Language" and "The Prevention of Literature":** "Politics and the English Language" concerns what Orwell sees as the degeneration of English, especially when it comes to political speech and writing, which he says is so riddled with euphemisms and vagueness that it basically precludes clear, honest conversations about vital national matters. In "The Prevention of Literature," Orwell explores and condemns some of the barriers to freedom of expression in literary and journalistic circles, particularly concerning the topic of Soviet Russia. Compare and contrast these two essays, both published in 1946.

   What basic theme(s) do these two essays share? Do they contradict each other in any way? Does reading one essay help you to better understand the other? How? Based on your careful reading of both of these pieces, how would you explain

Orwell's perception of the connections between truth, freedom of expression and use of language?

3. **Orwell's "Shooting an Elephant" and Kipling's "The Killing of Hatim Tai":** Read or reread both of these pieces about shooting an elephant. What can a comparison and contrast of these two works tell us about what each has to say about the relationship between oppressors and the oppressed?

Read both "Shooting an Elephant" and "The Killing of Hatim Tai." What similarities do you note? How are the main characters in the two texts similar? How are the native people portrayed in each text? What differences in the two pieces stand out to you as most meaningful? D. H. Stewart, in an essay titled "Shooting Elephants Right," claims that the "major difference between Orwell's and Kipling's stories is that Orwell's is humorless" (87). Would you agree with this assessment? How does this one element make the two pieces different? Does it change their tone? Their meaning?

Bibliography for "Shooting an Elephant" and Other Essays

Crick, Bernard. *George Orwell: A Life.* New York: Little, Brown, 1981.

Hollis, Christopher. *A Study of George Orwell.* Chicago: Regnery, 1956.

Larkin, Emma. *Finding George Orwell in Burma.* New York: Penguin, 2005.

Orwell, George. "The Lion and the Unicorn." *Why I Write.* New York: Penguin, 2005, 11–94.

———. "Politics and the English Language." *Why I Write.* New York: Penguin, 2005, 102–20.

———. "Shooting an Elephant." *A Collection of Essays.* New York: Harvest, 1981, 148–55.

———. "Why I Write." *Why I Write.* New York: Penguin, 2005, 1–10.

Russell, Bertrand. "George Orwell." *World Review* 16 (1950): 5–6.

Shelden, Michael. *Orwell: The Authorized Biography.* New York: Harper Collins, 1991.

Stewart, D. H. "Shooting Elephants Right." *The Southern Review* 22: (1986): 86–92.

Worley, Matthew. *The Foundations of the British Labour Party.* Burlington, VT: Ashgate, 2009.

DOWN AND OUT IN PARIS AND LONDON

READING TO WRITE

*D*OWN AND *Out in Paris and London* (1933), George Orwell's first full-length work, is based on the time he spent among the working poor and the homeless in Paris and London. Although Orwell could perhaps never have been considered truly down and out, for he had family and contacts who would have helped him had he asked, he chose to live as one of the poor to understand more deeply their lives and then to write about them. The book is based on Orwell's actual experiences, and the first-person narrator is certainly supposed to invoke Orwell, but it is almost certain that Orwell took artistic liberties as he put his experiences into written form. Despite the fact that Orwell always had a way out of his self-inflicted poverty and that he fictionalized some of his experiences, the book that resulted from this time in his life offers some significant insights into the nature of poverty and into the relationships between rich and poor and the different cultures of poverty in France and England. It can be enlightening to take a close look at some of Orwell's observations on poverty, examining and appreciating his insights while also paying attention to how his own particular point of view might be shaping those insights. Orwell writes:

> It is altogether curious, your first contact with poverty. You have
> thought so much about poverty—it is the thing you have feared all
> your life, the thing you knew would happen to you sooner or later; and

it is all so utterly and prosaically different. You thought it would be quite simple; it is extraordinarily complicated. You thought it would be terrible; it is merely squalid and boring. It is the peculiar *lowness* of poverty that you discover first; the shifts that it puts you to, the complicating meanness, the crust-wiping. . . . These three weeks were squalid and uncomfortable, and evidently there was worse coming, for my rent would be due before long. Nevertheless, things were not a quarter as bad as I had expected. For, when you are approaching poverty, you make one discovery which outweighs some of the others. You discover boredom and mean complications and the beginnings of hunger, but you also discover the great redeeming feature of poverty: the fact that it annihilates the future. Within certain limits, it is actually true that the less money you have, the less you worry. . . . And there is another feeling that is a great consolation in poverty. I believe everyone who has been hard up has experienced it. It is a feeling of relief, almost of pleasure, at knowing yourself at last genuinely down and out. You have talked so often of going to the dogs—and well, here are the dogs, and you have reached them, and you can stand it. It takes off a lot of anxiety. (17–21)

In these passages, Orwell writes that poverty is not the great tragedy he had always imagined from his position in the middle class but simply a different kind of ordinary human experience. Where he had expected something "simple" and "terrible," this romantic notion of poverty gives way to a much more realistic vision of it as "complicated," "squalid," and "boring." With these observations and the supporting details he provides through the course of the book, Orwell succeeds at humanizing the poor, which surely was part of the point of his efforts.

What is especially interesting and potentially problematic is that, having chosen to enter the world of poverty so that he may describe it, Orwell occasionally equates himself with the poor in a general way. In the passage above, for instance, Orwell assumes his own experience to be universal when, referring to the sense of relief he feels upon entering poverty, he states his belief that "everyone who has been hard up has experienced it." This general statement should give us pause. Is it truly likely that *everyone* who is or has been poor has experienced a "feeling of relief, almost of pleasure, at knowing [themselves] at last genuinely down and out"? It certainly is not likely that people who grew up being poor have experienced such a feeling.

But Orwell does not seem to be considering those people, for his next line reads, "You have talked so often of going to the dogs—and well, here are the dogs, and you have reached them, and you can stand it." This statement indicates that Orwell is in truth generalizing not really about all people who have experienced poverty but those who have first known something else, those who are having, as he indicates earlier in the passage, their "first contact with poverty." The fact that the line between the always-poor and the newly-poor is blurred in this instance should cause us to investigate further. For whom exactly is Orwell speaking?

It might be tempting to assume that, while Orwell can't speak for all people who have ever been poor, he might be able, at least, to generalize about those who have newly entered the world of poverty, since this is the experience he himself is living. Let us test this theory. Orwell's "you," the person who has just had his first "contact with poverty" and who learns that that poverty is not some grand tragedy but rather another form of human experience, is also someone who has "feared" poverty "all [his] life" because it is "the thing [he] knew would happen to him sooner or later." He is also the person who has "talked so often of going to the dogs" and who feels a sense of relief and pride that he can handle it when the dogs come. Do you think it fair to assume that all people who find themselves newly impoverished have had the same kind of obsession with poverty and the same kind of desire to test themselves against it as Orwell confesses to here? It is more likely that Orwell is ascribing his own personal predilections to a group who may or may not share them.

Orwell's misleading statement that "everyone who has been hard up" feels a sense of relief as well as his use of the second-person "you" to describe what are likely his own very personal reactions to being newly poor indicate that Orwell's observations and insights are not as unbiased and universal as they initially seem. This discovery should inspire you to read the text in a more critical way, to ask yourself as you progress through its pages how Orwell's reportage is colored by his own frame of mind. You might even decide to devote your essay to studying the subtle and not-so-subtle ways that Orwell's bias and personal point of view shape his observations and assessments of the life of the poor in Paris and London. In what ways do his previous middle-class status, his intellectual bent, and his preoccupation with the plight of the poor affect his interpretation of events? Can Orwell ever truly be one of "them"? More importantly, does he think he is? As you reread the book with these ideas in mind, watch carefully for other passages in which Orwell discusses the condition of those who are new to poverty. For instance, much later in the volume, Orwell claims that "it is such nonsense to pretend that those who have 'come down in the world' are to be pitied above all others. The man who really merits pity is the man who has been down from the start" (180). How does this fit in with the statements made in the passage above? Is Orwell's reasoning consistent or not?

Finally, you might consider whether Orwell's extensive use of the second person in the above passage does not reflect Orwell's confusion about how universal his own perspective is but rather points up a specific audience for the book. Is it possible these second-person references indicate that the text is aimed at those who, while they may not have the courage to venture into poverty as Orwell did, have the same peculiar obsession with a life of poverty and how they would measure up to it as Orwell had? In other words, can the text, which is usually assumed to be about helping people to understand poverty, actually be read as an extended fantasy for their voyeuristic pleasure? If nothing else, this line of questioning should get you thinking about Orwell's motives in crafting this book. Who is the intended audience? How does he want them to feel, or what does he want them to do, upon completing the book?

TOPICS AND STRATEGIES

The topic suggestions that follow are designed to illustrate the many different ways that you can approach writing an essay about Orwell's *Down and Out in Paris and London.* Feel free to use any of them to get you started or to help you come up with an entirely different topic of your own. If you decide to use of the options provided here, be sure to treat it as a prompt to spark your own thinking. You do not need to answer all of the subquestions included under the topic and you should not restrict yourself to these questions or the particular passages suggested for analysis. Rather, use the guidance provided under the topic to jump-start your own investigation. You will find that as you begin to answer the questions and analyze the passages suggested, you will come up with additional questions that you want to pursue and additional passages you want to analyze. By all means follow these instincts and leave the topic behind. If it has gotten you interested in a particular aspect of *Down and Out in Paris and London* and helped you to make your way to a thesis that will help your reader to understand the book in a new, more complex way, then it has done its job and can safely be jettisoned.

Themes

Down and Out in Paris and London definitely has a great deal to say about the nature of work, the experience of poverty, and about appearance versus reality. Any of these themes would be an appropriate focal point for an essay. Keep in mind that most works of literature concern themselves with multiple themes. If you choose to write about a theme, you are not committing yourself to covering all of them. You should select one theme to investigate in your essay. Furthermore, some themes figure so prominently in a work that you will need to focus on only one element or aspect of that theme. Take for example, the theme of work in *Down and Out in Paris and London.* You might, if your essay is long enough, be able to do justice to the general theme of work. It is more likely, though, that narrowing your focus will be necessary. You might, for instance, write about what the book has to say about the relationship of work and profit. You can consider questions like: How is the value of work measured? Does society really attribute moral value to work based on how much money that work generates? What are the ramifications of this? Alternatively, you can turn your attention to the social usefulness of various kinds of work. In particular, you can analyze and evaluate Orwell's idea that the lower classes are made to work incredibly long hours doing jobs that provide nothing necessary for society—only luxuries for the rich—because this keeps them "in their place," so to speak. In other words, it keeps them from becoming a threat to the upper classes. Analyzing this argument and its ramifications can certainly provide enough material for an essay.

Sample Topics:

1. **Work and monetary profit:** The life Orwell leads in Paris revolves around the frantic search for work, however exhausting and unprofitable it is. In London, Orwell's life among the poor takes on a different direction. According to Orwell, the "tramps" do work—usually harder than the middle classes—but what they do is not valued and is therefore not even deemed to

be work. What is the connection between work and profit? Why are some forms of work valued so much more greatly than others? What is the connection between work and identity?

Orwell suggests that the worth of a particular kind of work is ultimately determined by the profit it earns. Speaking specifically of beggars, he writes:

> In practice nobody cares whether work is useful or useless, productive or parasitic; the sole thing demanded is that it shall be profitable. In all the modern talk about energy, efficiency, social service and the rest of it, what meaning is there except "Get money, get it legally, and get a lot of it"? Money has become the grand test of virtue. If one could earn even ten pounds a week at begging, it would become a respectable profession immediately. A beggar, looked at realistically, is simply a business man, getting his living, like other business men, in the way that comes to hand. He has not, more than most modern people, sold his honour; he has merely made the mistake of choosing a trade at which it is impossible to grow rich. (174)

Examine the remainder of *Down and Out in Paris and London* carefully, paying particular attention to the value assigned by society to various types of jobs. Does the text as a whole support or contradict the rather bold statement Orwell makes here? One important claim that Orwell presents is that society somehow defines what work is and excludes certain activities from the category of work. How should work be defined? Certainly, the homeless men Orwell lived with in London spent many hours each day physically exerting themselves in order to have a roof over their heads and something in their stomachs. Why is this not work? What other sorts of activities do people put a great deal of energy into that we refuse to consider work? Why?

Depending on the type of essay you intend to write, you might also want to think about contemporary American society in terms of Orwell's argument. Are jobs that allow one to earn a great deal of money considered more "respectable"?

More "virtuous"? Why or why not? How has the worth of different types of work changed between Orwell's time and our own? What do you think accounts for that change?

2. **Work and social value:** In this work, Orwell has a lot to say about the nature of work and its worth. Some of the questions he poses include: Who decides what type of work gets done? Why are some kinds of work done even if they are not useful to society? What answers does he ultimately come to, and do you agree with those conclusions?

Orwell uses the case of a *plongeur*, a dishwasher, to examine some of these questions. He writes:

> Is a *plongeur's* work really necessary to civilization? We have a feeling that it must be "honest" work because it is hard and disagreeable, and we have made a sort of fetish of manual work. We see a man cutting down a tree, and we make sure that he is filling a social need, just because he uses his muscles; it does not occur to us that he may only be cutting down a beautiful tree to make room for a hideous statue. I believe it is the same with a *plongeur*. He earns his bread in the sweat of his brow, but it does not follow that he is doing anything useful; he may be only supplying a luxury which, very often, is not a luxury (117)

Orwell goes on to make the argument that the work of a *plongeur* is actually useless to the overall good of society. After studying his argument, does it convince you that the work of a *plongeur* serves no real purpose? Why or why not? Whether or not you agree, let us suppose, for a moment, with Orwell, that "it is granted that a *plongeur's* work is more or less useless" and consider Orwell's theory of why such useless work continues to be done:

> Then the question follows, Why does anyone want him to go on working? I am trying to go beyond the immediate economic cause, and to consider what pleasure it can give anyone to think of men swabbing dishes for life. For there is no doubt

that people—comfortably situated people—do find a pleasure
in such thoughts. A slave, Marcus Cato said, should be working when he is not sleeping. It does not matter whether his
work is needed or not, he must work, because work in itself
is good—for slaves, at least. . . . I believe that this instinct to
perpetuate useless work, is, at bottom, simply a fear of the
mob. . . . (118–19)

According to Orwell, how do we judge what work is valuable?
Why do people do work that is ultimately useless to society?
Do you agree with his conclusions? Think for a minute about
what these *plongeurs* he writes about would be doing if there
were no dishes to wash? Is the creation of work, even if that
work is to provide luxury services to the wealthy, not a service
to society since it provides the poor with a means to support
themselves? How might Orwell answer this argument?

3. **Appearance versus reality:** In the world Orwell describes
   in *Down and Out in Paris and London,* many things are not
   what they seem. The experiences recounted seem to be autobiographical, but some of the material, at least, has been
   fictionalized. The tramps that Orwell consorts with seem,
   to mainstream society, to be lazy; yet Orwell takes pains to
   describe the work they must do—the pains they must take—
   to survive. Taking all of this into account, what would you
   say is the book's main message about the prevailing theme of
   appearance versus reality?

Locate and examine instances throughout the book in which
appearances are deceiving. You might want to start with the
remarkable example of *boulot,* in which appearance is designed
to mimic reality. Orwell writes:

The customer pays, as he sees it, for good service; the employee
is paid, as he sees it, for the *boulot*—meaning, as a rule, an
imitation of good service. The result is that, though hotels are
miracles of punctuality, they are worse than the worse private
houses in the things that matter. (79)

What are the "things that matter" that Orwell refers to here? What is the difference between good service and the imitation of good service? Why do you think that such a distinction exists? What purpose does it serve? What other instances of "imitation" can you locate in the book? What other appearance/reality relationships exist in the book? Are there cases in which appearance and reality are actually opposite? Cases in which appearance is intentionally falsified to hide or obscure reality? Would you say that, in the world of this book, appearance and reality are more often in harmony or not, and how does this affect the overall themes and meanings of the book?

4. **Poverty:** What would you say is the major message regarding poverty that Orwell's memoir sends?

Reread *Down and Out*, thinking specifically about what it has to say about what it means to be poor. Are there different levels and types of poverty explored in this work? Think, for instance, simply about the difference between Orwell's experiences in Paris and London. Does it seem that being poor means something different in France than it does in England? What does Orwell find surprising about poverty? How does being poor change him? How are the goals, motivations, and obstacles of someone who lives in poverty different from those who don't? Are there any "silver linings" to a life of poverty?

Character

Perhaps the most important question to ask when studying character is how a particular character evolves over time. The changes that occur to a character's perspective or personality, coupled with whether those changes are portrayed as positive or negative, can give you insights into the main messages and themes of a work of literature. You might, for example, ask these questions of the narrator in *Down and Out in Paris and London.* Because the narrator is based on Orwell himself, you might also wish to do some investigation into Orwell's biography to determine just how similar the narrator is to Orwell himself. Any individual character might be analyzed, but you might also consider groups of people as characters; so, for example, you might decide to look at how the text portrays waiters, the police, or the homeless as a group.

Sample Topics:

1. **Orwell:** Because the book is based on Orwell's actual experiences, the narrator of *Down and Out in Paris and London* has a great deal in common with Orwell himself. Orwell fictionalized his adventures to some degree so that the "I" of the piece cannot be said to be Orwell exactly. He might be considered a version of Orwell, one that you can examine like you would any other, wholly fictional, literary character. Analyze this character and his strengths and weaknesses in your essay.

   Ask yourself the following questions: How does the narrator describe himself? How do others seem to see him? How does he interact with others? What does he think about? How does he view the world? You will also want to determine whether the character comes across as sympathetic and likeable. What are his positive and negative qualities? Would he be someone readers would want to emulate? Note too whether the character evolves through the course of the story. If so, how, and what prompts the change? It is important when dealing with this particular character to ask yourself the same kinds of questions you would about any narrator: How reliable is he? Does he present events objectively or is there a discernable bias? Think about whether, given the basic facts presented in the text, an entirely different book could have been written. This narrator, for instance, is obviously very sympathetic to the poor people of both France and England. Could the stories he tells, however, be interpreted in a manner much more critical of the poor? What does the way he chooses to interpret his material tell you about the narrator?

2. **Waiters:** For someone who is imploring his reader to see the poor as individual human beings, Orwell makes some interesting generalizations about the personalities of many groups of people, including waiters. How accurate are these generalizations and what can they tell us about Orwell?

Orwell writes:

> Sometimes when you sit in a restaurant, still stuffing yourself
> half an hour after closing time, you feel that the tired waiter at
> your side must surely be despising you. But he is not. He is not
> thinking as he looks at you, "What an overfed lout"; he is think-
> ing, "One day, when I have saved enough money, I shall be able
> to imitate that man." He is ministering to a kind of pleasure he
> thoroughly understands and admires. And that is why waiters
> are seldom Socialists, have no effective trade union, and will
> work twelve hours a day—they work fifteen hours, seven days
> a week, in many cafes. They are snobs, and they find the servile
> nature of their work rather congenial. (77)

What evidence does Orwell offer for the conclusions he presents
in the preceding paragraph? Why would waiters, in particular,
be disposed to this kind of thinking and not, say, *plongeurs*?
How is the waiter's attitude incompatible with socialism? How
accurate do you think this observation is? What can the fact that
Orwell makes this observation tell us about his own manner of
seeing the world? Keep in mind that Orwell was not working as
a waiter but rather as a dishwasher, a worker much further down
the social hierarchy than waiters. Do you think his assessment
of waiters would have been different had he been one himself?
How do you suppose someone above the waiters, the patron for
instance, would characterize the waiters as a group?

3. **Charlie:** One of the very first characters to appear in the
   narrative is a young man named Charlie, who has a habit of
   declaiming strange stories in the bistro. After one particularly
   horrifying appearance, he does not appear again in the book.
   Why does Orwell include him? What does Charlie mean to the
   overall story?

Orwell describes "Charlie" as "one of the local curiosities." He
quotes Charlie talking at length about an experience in which
he robs his brother and then pays 1,000 francs in order to rape
a young woman in a cellar decked out in red from floor to

ceiling. Charlie describes himself violently assaulting the girl and concludes, "And so, just for one instant, I captured the supreme happiness, the highest and most refined emotion to which human beings can attain. . . . That is Love. That was the happiest day of my life" (15).

After this incredibly disturbing speech, Orwell simply remarks: "He was a curious specimen, Charlie. I describe him, just to show what diverse characters could be found flourishing in the Coq d'Or quarter" (15). What sort of character is Charlie? What do you think motivates him? You will want to spend some time thinking about Orwell's perspective as well. Does it surprise you that Orwell does not condemn Charlie's actions and remarks? Why do you think Orwell includes him in the book? Is it simply to show "what diverse characters" he found in Paris? Could there be another reason? How does the casual inclusion of Charlie's story by Orwell make you feel toward the narrator/observer? Is Orwell trying to prove something about himself as a narrator by including Charlie's story without any editorial commentary?

4. **Boris:** Boris and Orwell become dependent on each other for a time, helping each other through their roughest spots. What do you think Boris's greatest strengths are? What did he have to teach Orwell, and vice versa?

Begin by recording what you know about Boris. What would you say are his greatest strengths and weaknesses? Then, examine his relationship with Orwell. What did they teach each other? At times, each of the men makes bad decisions, and they both have to share the consequences of that decision. Does one man seem to be the stronger partner, one who carries the two of them through the roughest times? Why does Orwell align himself with Boris and then stick with him through the really tough times?

History and Context

Down and Out in Paris and London is all about history and context. Orwell put himself through some difficult times and then wrote this memoir to illustrate to others what life was like for the poor in London and Paris.

Conducting some research into this time period will help you to get a sense of Orwell's motivations and accomplishments. Your first goal will be to determine whether the descriptions and histories of Paris and London in the 1920s that you can find, aside from Orwell's, match what Orwell presents in *Down and Out in Paris and London*. If they do not, why not? Is Orwell describing a portion of society and a way of life largely ignored by others? If so, why might this be, and what does it mean for our ability to evaluate Orwell's perceptions and claims? Can and should Orwell's observations and analysis be perceived as reliable and accurate? Why or why not? This is a lot to consider; if you are interested in the historical aspects of *Down and Out*, you might decide to select one portion of the book to focus on, examining Orwell's description of either Paris or London.

Sample Topics:

1. **London in the 1920s:** How accurately has Orwell portrayed 1920s London, particularly London as seen from the perspective of the poor?

   Read up on Orwell's actual experiences in London. You might start with the "London and Paris" chapter of *Orwell: The Authorized Biography*. Compare Shelden's description of Orwell's time in London to Orwell's own depiction of that time in the London segment of *Down and Out*.

   You will also want to do some background reading on 1920s London. You might start with Noreen Branson's *Britain in the Nineteen Twenties* or *Twenties London: A City in the Jazz Age* by Cathy Ross. What impression of the city during this time period do you glean from these works? Does it match Orwell's depiction of the city? Describe how. If you find the depictions incongruous, why might that be? Pay attention to how Orwell's first-person portrayal compares, not only in content but also in intent, to the more official histories you read. Why did Orwell choose not to include more research in his book? He could have presented overviews of the city's economic and social structures but chose instead to stick to the viewpoint of a single, impoverished individual. Why? What would this book have been like had he tried to include more official data and research in it?

2. **Paris in the 1920s:** What was the social and cultural climate like in Paris in the 1920s, and how accurately does *Down and Out* portray it?

Begin by reading the sections in Shelden's biography *Orwell: The Authorized Biography* that discuss the time that Orwell spent in Paris. How is Shelden's account of Orwell's experiences different from Orwell's own description of his time there? What do you think accounts for these differences?

You will also want to have a look at Hemingway's *A Moveable Feast,* which offers a different perspective on Paris during the 1920s. In his Paris, poor artists had a grand time on meager incomes. You might also peruse the following: *Geniuses Together: American Writers in Paris in the 1920s* by Humphrey Carpenter or *Sylvia Beach and the Lost Generation: A History of Literary Paris in the Twenties and Thirties* by Noel Riley Fitch. Compare and contrast the vision of Paris offered in one or more of these texts with Orwell's vision of Paris. Are both visions accurate? Did they at all overlap? What is the significance of the differences?

Philosophy and Ideas

One interesting way to approach a piece of literature is to write about the larger ideas with which it grapples. There are fundamental questions that all societies and eras strive to answer, questions dealing with topics such as the nature of good and evil or the existence of free will. Also, writers are often interested in questions of ideology. When writing about philosophy and ideas, first identify what question, topic, or ideology the work engages. Simply identifying the ideas will not lead to a very good essay, however; you must determine what the work actually says about the ideas. In *Down and Out,* for instance, you might discover some explicit references to socialism and, with further close reading, quite a few implicit references as well. However, determining what Orwell is saying about socialism in this particular work is not quite so simple. It will require a great deal of analysis on your part to comprehend fully, and then explain to the reader of your essay, what stance *Down and Out* is taking regarding socialism.

Sample Topics:

1. **The rich and the poor:** What are the fundamental differences
between rich and poor as Orwell sees them? How does he come
to understand these two categories of people and their relationship to each other?

Analyze passages such as the following to get you started:

> Fear of the mob is a superstitious fear. It is based on the idea that
> there is some mysterious, fundamental difference between rich
> and poor, as though they were two different races, like negroes
> and white men. But in reality there is no such difference. The
> mass of the rich and the poor are differentiated by their incomes
> and nothing else, and the average millionaire is only the aver-
> age dishwasher dressed in a new suit. Change places, and handy
> dandy, which is the justice, which the thief? (120)

Orwell argues that there is no real difference between the rich
and the poor and that the reason this is not known is because
the "intelligent, cultivated people, the very people who might
be expected to have liberal opinions, never do mix with the
poor" (120). Does Orwell's own experience "mixing with the
poor" as related in *Down and Out* bear out his argument that
there is no fundamental difference between rich and poor?
And what do you think Orwell means by "fundamental difference"? What types of differences do exist between the rich and
the poor? What similarities?

Even more fundamentally, does Orwell either recognize or
refute the idea that society requires both rich and poor people,
that it would be impossible to have a society free of these economic distinctions? What can we tell about this foundational
question from the ending of his memoir?

> I can point to one or two things I have definitely learned by
> being hard up. I shall never again think that all tramps are
> drunken scoundrels, nor expect a beggar to be grateful when
> I give him a penny, nor be surprised if men out of work lack
> energy, nor subscribe to the Salvation Army, nor pawn my

clothes, nor refuse a handbill, nor enjoy a meal at a smart res-
taurant. That is a beginning. (213)

What are these small recognitions "a beginning" of? This does
not sound like a call to revolution or the dream of a utopian
society. Is this evidence that Orwell accedes to the necessity of
poverty? Or is something else going on here?

2. **Socialism:** Orwell is perhaps best known for producing works
   that somehow focus on socialism and/or communism. Would
   you say that *Down and Out* is an exception, or does Orwell
   deliver his message in a more subtle way in this particular
   case?

Orwell rarely mentions socialism directly, the following passage being the main case where he does:

> The moral is, never be sorry for a waiter. Sometimes when
> you sit in a restaurant, still stuffing yourself half an hour after
> closing time, you feel that the tired waiter at your side must
> surely be despising you. But he is not. He is not thinking as he
> looks at you, 'What an overfed lout'; he is thinking, 'One day,
> when I have saved enough money, I shall be able to imitate that
> man.' He is ministering to a kind of pleasure he thoroughly
> understands and admires. And that is why waiters are seldom
> Socialists, have no effective trade union, and will work twelve
> hours a day—they work fifteen hours, seven days a week, in
> many cafes. They are snobs, and they find the servile nature of
> their work rather congenial.

What does this remark about waiters imply about socialism?
Are the waiters' attitudes commendable as Orwell presents
them, or is he being critical of them? How can you tell?

Although Orwell does not mention socialism again directly,
he talks a great deal about the nature of work, the way different types of work are valued, and the usefulness (or useless-
ness) of certain kinds of work. Examine Orwell's commentary
on work in Paris and London. Can these comments be read as

criticism of capitalism? How? Would the issues that Orwell points out be present in a socialist society? Why or why not? Considering how avidly Orwell campaigned for socialism in his other works, why do you think he chose not to in *Down and Out?* How would it change your feelings about the narrator and about the work as a whole if he devoted parts of the narrative to proselytizing on behalf of socialism? How would it affect the rest of the narrative?

Form and Genre

Studying form and genre can be an interesting way to approach a work of literature. When studying form, you are considering the nuts and bolts of a piece, the way the author put it together. One major element of form worth studying in *Down and Out in Paris and London* is its structure. You can look at the book's constituent parts and how they all fit together to form a whole. How is this particular book built? How does its structure contribute to or detract from its themes? If you are thinking about genre, you want to consider how a particular piece of work relates to others. What category can it be placed in? Is it easily categorized? Why or why not? What makes this work distinct within the category(ies) to which it belongs? In the case of *Down and Out,* for example, you might begin your study of genre by asking yourself whether this piece is fact or fiction. Would you consider it autobiographical? A memoir? Or simply a work of fiction inspired by Orwell's own life? Why does it matter what category the book is placed in? How might such a fact affect readers' interactions with and interpretation of the book?

Sample Topics:

1. **Fact or fiction:** Much of Orwell's work is situated somewhere between autobiography and fiction, and *Down and Out in Paris and London* is no exception. Where on the spectrum does this book belong, and what does that placement mean in terms of how we read it?

   According to biographer Michael Shelden:

   > [T]he book cannot be read as literal autobiography, but all the events reflect something of the world in which he had

immersed himself. He was robbed and he did starve, but how he was robbed (by a young Italian? by a French "trollope"?) and why he starved (by necessity? by choice?) are matters he felt free to alter for the sake of his story. (133)

What do you think are the main effects of this writing strategy of Orwell's—of basing works of literature on his own experiences but taking so much liberty in presenting the story that it can rightly be said to have moved into the realm of fiction? How can one tell what is true and what Orwell has invented? Does it matter? Why or why not?

2. **Structure:** How an author chooses to arrange and present the content of a book carries meaning in itself. How do the choices that Orwell made affect the way we read and understand this work?

Reread *Down and Out in Paris and London,* paying particular attention to the way it is structured. You might find it helpful to make an outline as you make your way through the text. How would you describe the structure? Can you imagine what it would be like if Orwell had arranged the work in a different way? How else might he have constructed it?

Biographer Michael Shelden finds the structure of *Down and Out* its primary flaw. He writes: "It is not a coherent narrative, but a series of sketches, some much better than others. This circumstance is further complicated by the fact that the Paris sketches have little in common with the London sketches" (165). Do you agree with Shelden's assessment? Do you find that the book is actually "a series of sketches," or do you perceive it as a coherent narrative? What are your reasons? Do you agree that the Paris and London sections have too little to do with each other? Do you think that Orwell would have done better to focus on either one or the other, or do you see the two sections as necessary to the overall work? What do you think about Orwell's decision occasionally to break into the chronological narrative to include commentary, as he does in chapter 32 when he introduces the reader to the slang and swear words used in London? Are these chapters distracting or elucidating? Why do you think he chose to include them?

Compare and Contrast Essays

Comparing and contrasting two elements within a single work, such as London and Paris in Orwell's memoir, or two distinct works, such as *Down and Out in Paris and London* and *The Road to Wigan Pier,* can allow you to see meaningful patterns and significant differences that escape notice when you are focusing on these individual elements in isolation. When comparing and contrasting, the key strategy to remember is to use your observations about the similarities and differences in the two elements you are comparing in the service of a larger argument. In other words, you do not want your thesis simply to state the ways that two elements are alike and different. You will want to have used that list of significant similarities and differences to help you develop a thesis that helps your readers understand the elements you are comparing in a new or deeper way. The points of comparison that you used to arrive at your thesis will then serve as evidence in the body of your essay.

Sample Topics:

1. ***Down and Out in Paris and London* and *The Road to Wigan Pier:*** Compare and contrast two of Orwell's similarly themed, memoir-based books.

   Read or reread these two works by Orwell. What do the two of them have in common? How are they different? Think about the material each book covers, Orwell's purposes for writing it, and its structure. Which book do you think is more successful? Why? In *Down and Out,* Orwell is a direct participant in the scene he is describing; though he could presumably use his contacts to get out of a tight spot, he is living very poorly. In *Wigan Pier,* however, Orwell is more of an objective observer. He does, of course, live among the coal miners for a short time, but he never attempts to mine coal for a living. How is the level of Orwell's immersion in his subject matter reflected in the two books? Do they aim at, and accomplish, different goals because of this? Is one more effective than the other?

2. ***Down and Out in Paris and London* and Jack London's *The People of the Abyss*:** Compare and contrast these two firsthand treatments of the London poor in the early decades of the twentieth century.

Read or reread these two works. Are London's and Orwell's motives the same? What is the same and different about how they go about their projects? How do the results of each project compare? Is one more successful than the other? Which and why? One important difference between the two works is that London lived among the poor of London in 1902, while Orwell did so in the late 1920s. In the intervening years, World War I had changed the political and social landscape of London. Looking at these books side by side, how had life changed for the impoverished? Had it grown worse, better, or simply different? Or is it surprisingly the same? Orwell was very influenced by *The People of the Abyss;* how did he pick up Jack London's previous work and make it his own? What new feature did he bring to the genre?

3. **Poverty in Paris and London:** One of the criticisms of *Down and Out* is that Orwell's experiences in Paris and London were so distinct, but he does little to reconcile or provide any continuity between the two sets of experiences. How are these experiences different, and what conclusions can be drawn from these differences?

The structure of *Down and Out in Paris and London* practically demands readers to compare and contrast the life of a poor person in Paris versus his life in London. Spend some time doing this. How are Orwell's experiences different in Paris and London? How are his relationships different? His opportunities? His obstacles? What can this comparison and contrast tell us about the character of Paris and London and their citizenry?

Bibliography and Online Resources for *Down and Out in Paris and London*

Branson, Noreen. *Britain in the Nineteen Twenties.* Minneapolis: University of Minnesota Press, 1976.

Carpenter, Humphrey. *Geniuses Together: American Writers in Paris in the 1920s.* New York: HarperCollins, 1989.

Fitch, Noel Riley. *Sylvia Beach and the Lost Generation: A History of Literary Paris in the Twenties and Thirties.* New York: Norton, 1985.

Hemingway, Ernest. *A Moveable Feast.* New York: Scribner, 1996.

Hollis, Christopher. *A Study of George Orwell.* Chicago: Regnery, 1956.

Lee, Robert A. *Orwell's Fiction.* Notre Dame, IN: U of Notre Dame P: 1969.

London Museums Hub. Exploring 20th Century London. Accessed on 15 Nov. 2009. <http://www.20thcenturylondon.org.uk/server.php?show=nav.40>.

Museum of London. 1920s: The Decade that Changed London. 2003. Accessed on 15 Nov. 2009. <http://www.museumoflondon.org.uk/archive/exhibits/1920s/pages/home.asp>.

Orwell, George. *Down and Out in Paris and London.* New York: Harcourt, 1961.

———. *Down and Out in Paris and London.* Accessed on 15 Nov. 2009. <http://www.netcharles.com/orwell/books/downandout.htm>.

Patai, Daphne. "Political Fiction and Patriarchal Fantasy." *The Orwell Mystique: A Study in Male Ideology.* Amherst: U of Massachusetts P, 1984, 201–18.

Ross, Cathy. *Twenties London: A City in the Jazz Age.* New York: Philip Wilson, 2003.

Russell, Bertrand. "George Orwell." *World Review* 16 (1950): 5–6.

Shelden, Michael. *Orwell: The Authorized Biography.* New York: HarperCollins, 1991.

KEEP THE
ASPIDISTRA FLYING

READING TO WRITE

*K*EEP THE *Aspidistra Flying* (1936) has been, from the moment of its publication, considered a bitter and dark work, and many readers have somewhat unfairly conflated the protagonist's dreary outlook with Orwell's own worldview. Contemporary critics even suggested that "the writer of *Keep the Aspidistra Flying* hates London and everything there" (Shelden 238). Set in 1930s London, *Keep the Aspidistra Flying* tells the story of Gordon Comstock, a young man from a lower-middle-class family who rejects all opportunities to "make good" on principle, trying instead to live outside of the corrupt commercial society he was born into. When we first meet him, Gordon is working at a bookstore, and we are given the following description of its merchandise:

> In the shelves to your left as you came out of the library the new and nearly-new books were kept—a patch of bright colour that was meant to catch the eye of anyone glancing through the glass door. Their sleek unspotted backs seemed to yearn at you from the shelves. "Buy me, buy me!" they seemed to be saying. Novels fresh from the press—still unravished brides—pining for the paperknife to deflower them—and review copies, like youthful widows, blooming still though virgin no longer, and here and there, in sets of half a dozen, those pathetic spinster-things, "remainders," still guarding hopefully their long preserv'd virginity. (7)

One of the first things you will notice about this passage is that the books in the shop are being compared to women, and particularly to women who are looking for a husband, who are, so to speak, being traded on the marriage market. Setting aside for the moment the objectification of women inherent in that comparison, we should begin by examining the passage to see what it has to say about what makes a particular book, or woman, valuable. It seems that purity is key—the books that have "unspotted" backs and the books listed first, presumably the most valuable, are "still unravished brides." Virginity, however, appears not to be the only significant indicator of value, since the "youthful widows, blooming still though virgin no longer" seem to be more valuable than the still virginal, yet aging, "spinster-things." Presumably, what makes the youthful widows more valuable than the spinsters is that they are "blooming still." Youth, vitality, and attractiveness seem to be the real indicators of value. According to this passage, then, women and literature are judged not by their inherent value but by their power to attract a "buyer." This could definitely be read as a critique of a consumerist society's tendency to focus on surface over substance and an implied criticism of the consumer's desire to purchase and own the newest and most attractive "products."

What happens to this critique, though, when we consider how the passage portrays the books as deliberately seducing potential buyers? The volumes "seemed to yearn at you from the shelves," to shout "Buy me," and "pin[ed] for the paperknife to deflower them." Does the fact that the objects to be purchased or consumed actively try to sell themselves diminish the culpability of the buyer? Think strictly in terms of women for a moment. The depiction of women as objects on the marriage market to be selected and purchased by men dehumanizes women and suggests that men wield the purchasing power and thus bear the responsibility for the entire situation. However, when the women are depicted as actively trying to seduce men and desperately wanting to sell themselves, it is possible to shift some of the burden for their position on their shoulders. Presuming that this passage of narration reflects Gordon's own beliefs, do you think that Gordon's way of thinking about books and women as masters of seduction is a way to assuage his own guilt for participating in a commercial society he considers fundamentally corrupt?

Return now to a consideration of the basic comparison, books and women, that this passage is built on. Such a comparison blatantly treats women as objects to be bought and sold. Clearly, the passage is meant to criticize the way that books are marketed and sold pretty much without regard to the worth of the literature inside them. The question to ask next is whether, by making his point through a comparison with women, Gordon is intentionally pointing up the way that women are treated as commodities as well, or is he uncritically accepting of this element of his society? An analysis of this passage alone may not provide the answer. You might need to explore additional passages that comment on Gordon's perception of women and his relationship with women in the text, particularly Rosemary, to figure out exactly where he stands.

While closely reading one interesting passage is not likely to reveal everything you want to know about a piece of literature, it can certainly bring to light some issues that you can investigate further. For example, after examining this particular passage from *Keep the Aspidistra Flying*, you might be inspired to look for additional passages that talk about how literature functions as a commodity in Gordon's world and how he does, or does not, come to terms with that. For instance, how does his work at the New Albion compare to his poetry? In his mind and in the eyes of society? Everyone seems to want him to return to writing advertisements, but how do people react when he tells them he is a poet? Is there any difference between the money he makes writing for the New Albion and the check he receives for his poem? Or, you might focus on Gordon's ideas about women and their roles as commodities in his society. What does his transaction with Dora and Barbara reveal about this? Finally, you might investigate how Gordon sees his own role in the corrupt, commercial society he was born into. Is everyone who lives in that society, himself included, equally responsible for its problems? Whether you pursue one of these lines of thought or choose a topic from the suggestions below, you'll want to examine multiple passages that seem relevant to your topic, using your analysis of Orwell's choice of words to help you arrive at answers to your questions and, ultimately, at a thesis on which to base your essay.

TOPICS AND STRATEGIES

Use these topics to get a sense of the wide variety of possibilities open to you. You might be inspired by these suggestions to create a topic of your own. If you use one listed here, remember to treat it as a prompt and not as a series of test questions. In other words, use the questions and subquestions to spark your thinking; do not feel that you have to answer all of them in your essay. You should use your answers to the questions to guide you to new questions, and you should spend a significant amount of time analyzing key passages, those suggested in the topic as well as those you identify on your own. You want to keep asking and answering questions and examining passages until you arrive at a central idea that you feel says something important about the novel, something that will help readers understand or appreciate the novel in a new way. Once you have that central idea, you will use it to write your thesis sentence, which will become the foundation of your essay. At this point, you will leave the topic behind entirely, because you have now created a focal point for your essay that is all yours. You will sift through your notes and select the best evidence to include in your essay to support your thesis. Many of your notes and observations will not be incorporated into your essay, but do not be disheartened by this. All of this work was necessary to help you arrive at your thesis and will show itself indirectly in the sharp, thoughtful argument you craft in your essay.

Themes

When we think about themes in literature, what we are looking at are the really big ideas in the work, often universal and timeless ideas. *Keep the Aspidistra Flying* has some definite recurring themes, among them money, literature, and romance and sex. If you decide to write about any of these themes or another that you have identified, you will want to locate passages that deal with the theme you have selected and analyze them carefully. Once you have analyzed multiple key passages, you will undertake perhaps the most vital task in composing an essay: synthesizing your findings into a thesis that outlines an argument that enables your readers to understand the work in a new way. Use some of the work you did analyzing the key passages as support for your thesis in the body of your essay. When you are writing about theme, remember to choose only one theme to focus on, even though the novel has several. You may even find that one theme is too much to handle in the scope of the essay you intend to write. For example, money is perhaps the most important and recurring theme in the book. According to Gordon, everything always comes back to money. This means that there is probably far too much material to handle in a short essay. In a case like this, you need to narrow your focus to one part of the theme you have selected. Focusing only on how money affects romantic relationships, for instance, might narrow the topic down to a manageable size. Remember also that your essay will need to be more than just the identification of a theme; your task, rather, is to interpret what Orwell is saying about that theme. What is he adding to the conversation among the countless other works that have also commented on that particular theme?

Sample Topics:

1. **Money:** Obviously, money is one of the fundamental concerns of *Keep the Aspidistra Flying*. What are Gordon's objections to the role that money plays in the capitalist society he lives in? What does he do to try to prevent himself from being totally controlled by money—the need for it, having to go to work to make it, being convinced by advertisers to spend it in a certain way—the way he believes most people are? Why is Gordon unable to win his battle against money? Is Orwell saying the battle cannot be won?

   Analyze passages such as the following conversation between Rosemary and Gordon to help you answer these questions:

   > "Do you think there's anything to be ashamed of in having no money?"
   >
   > "Of course there is! It's the only thing in the world there *is* to be ashamed of."
   >
   > "But what's it got to do with you and me making love, anyway? I don't understand you. First you want to and then you don't want to. What's money got to do with it?"
   >
   > "Everything."
   >
   > He wound her arm in his and started down the road. She would never understand. Nevertheless he had got to explain.
   >
   > "Don't you understand that one isn't a full human being—that one doesn't *feel* a human being—unless one's got money in one's pocket?" (146)

   Why do you think Gordon is ashamed of having no money when it is his own principles keeping him from making money? Why is he not proud to have no money? Secondly, what do you think Gordon means when he says that one "doesn't *feel* a human being" without money? How does he think that he can somehow step outside of the commercial society he lives if he sees money as so connected to his very humanity? Does this make his efforts seem nobler or simply senseless?

2. **Poetry and literature:** What place in society does Orwell seem to be suggesting that literature occupies? Does he think this is the place it ought to occupy?

Think about the various types of literature discussed in *Keep the Aspidistra Flying* and how each type is represented. First, there is Gordon, who calls himself a poet. What kind of currency does this have in his society? What do others think of his work? Who actually reads it? Then, there is Gordon's first job in the bookstore, where he sells both highbrow and middlebrow works. What does he think of the patrons of this bookstore, and what do they think of him and one another? What types of books do the bookstore patrons most frequently take away with them? Which books sit and collect dust? Finally, there is the two-penny library Gordon works at when he is at his lowest point; the contents of that library are described as "yellow-jacketed trash," books "you could read at the rate of one an hour," and "real 'escape literature'" (204). Who reads this kind of literature? What does Gordon think of it?

With all this in mind, think about what the novel is really saying about literature and its readers. What is literature for? Who is it for? What makes one book highbrow and another lowbrow? According to the novel, is highbrow literature or lowbrow literature more valuable to society? Is literature valuable at all? In what way(s)? Finally, consider Gordon's prediction that film will one day replace literature. In what vein does he offer this prediction? While it may seem inevitable to him, what does he think it means about the direction in which society is headed?

3. **Love and sex:** Does the novel conceive of love as a timeless and universal force in human life or as a phenomenon defined dif-

ferently in different eras and by different social classes? What is the ultimate purpose of love in this novel? Is it concerned primarily with individual happiness, or does it have more to do with maintaining social structures?

Think about the romantic relationships the novel portrays— Ravelston and Hermione and, of course, Gordon and Rosemary. What is the relationship between the two wealthier people like? What do they do together? Where do they spend their time? What is their sense of values concerning love and sex? Compare and contrast their relationship to Gordon and Rosemary's. When and where do Gordon and Rosemary meet? What kinds of activities do they share? From what the novel reveals, do they treat romance and sex in the same way that Ravelston and Hermione do? Do they share the same morals? The same practical concerns? How does Gordon perceive love and sex? Contrast how dependent Gordon is on Rosemary's letters at the beginning of the novel to how completely indifferent he has become in the later chapters. What has changed? Then consider how Rosemary's pregnancy, the consequence of their single successful sexual encounter, changes his feelings about her once again. How do his opinions on these matters evolve through the course of the novel? All told, what would you say is the novel's main point about sex and love in 1930s England? What part do these things play in the proliferation of middle-class values and aspidistra culture?

Character

When writing about a character in a piece of literature, one of the first things you will want to ask yourself is whether or not that character changes in the course of the story and whether that change is presented as a positive or negative one. This can help you get at the fundamental concerns of the work. Take Gordon Comstock, for example. He definitely evolves through the course of the story, but is this transformation positive or negative? Answering this question will help determine what you take the main message of the novel to be. If a character, take Ravelston for example, seems the same at the end of the book as he did at the beginning, then your task is to figure out what function that character is playing in the novel. Is the author using him to illustrate a particular point of view? If so, you will want to determine whether that character is seen in a mainly positive or negative light; this may help you to ascertain what point the author might be trying to make by creating the character you have elected to study. Also think about how your character compares to others in the novel. Again taking Ravelston as an example, set him for a moment against Gordon. How does having Ravelston included as a character change how you feel about Gordon? Does he help to put Gordon's character into fuller perspective? How?

Sample Topics:

1. **Gordon Comstock:** A key to understanding this novel is getting a handle on main character Gordon Comstock. Is he, ultimately, a likeable hero? Do readers root for him? And is rooting for him wanting him to fly the aspidistra or to "sink" beneath the world of money as he intends to do before Rosemary announces her pregnancy?

   What are Gordon's philosophical views? Who, if anyone, in the novel shares them? How does Gordon attempt to live by these views? Is what he is attempting possible? Are his efforts commendable even if he what he aims for is not possible? At the end of the novel, Gordon feels relief in capitulating to normal, lower-middle-class life. How would you argue that Orwell intends readers to perceive Gordon's ultimate decision to give up his fight against money? One basic consideration when writing about Gordon is figuring out if he is more hero or antihero. As readers, what do we hope for Gordon? If we hope for him to rejoin the wider society, is the novel trapping us? Making us complicit in the shallowness of capitalism? Or is there something far more basic and humane happening if we are upset by Gordon's "sinking"?

2. **Rosemary:** Does Rosemary function primarily as a counterpart to and influence on Gordon, or is she a fully fledged character in her own right? If she serves primarily to be in concert with Gordon, what does she represent in his life?

How would you describe Rosemary? In what ways does she seem like every other Englishwoman of her time and station, and in what ways does Orwell present her as unusual? How does she feel about Gordon? Do you find Rosemary to be a realistic character? A sympathetic character? At one point, the narrator comments that "everyone who met her did take a liking to Rosemary" (158). Considering how misanthropic and gloomy Gordon often is, what is it that attracts a convivial woman like Rosemary to him? And what attracts him to her? When does Rosemary finally pluck out the three white hairs from her head? What does this action symbolize? Do you find that Rosemary changes from the beginning of the novel to the end? In what ways?

3. **Julia Comstock:** How does Julia function in the novel? Why does she provide such consistent support to Gordon? Considering her support of Gordon, how does she compare to Rosemary?

Record everything you know about Gordon's sister Julia. For the most part, Julia operates offstage in this novel; Gordon thinks about her a great deal and certainly relies on her, but she only rarely appears. Why is her invisible presence important? Clearly, she is not a character who changes and grows over the course of the novel, so what is it that she symbolizes? What are her most important character traits? How does she feel about Gordon? Spend some time thinking about how Julia is similar to and different from Rosemary. What do you think accounts for those similarities and differences? In the end, do you think Julia's support operates as a positive or negative force in Gordon's life?

4. **Philip Ravelston:** In many ways, Ravelston operates as a male parallel to Julia. He functions as a steady support for Gordon and seems to evolve very little. What is his fundamental role?

What do you know about Ravelston's background? His work? Relationships? He produces a socialist paper and claims to understand Gordon's desire to have anything but a good job and to live outside of the world of money, but Ravelston very much enjoys his own wealth and the luxury it buys him. How does the novel treat Ravelston's hypocrisy? Does he come off as a genuine character? As a likeable one? Why or why not? How does Ravelston serve as a foil to Gordon's character? Does his unwillingness to live out his ideals make Gordon more admirable? Or does Ravelston's comfort in facing the realities of economic and social life highlight how unrealistic and unworkable Gordon's philosophies are?

Biographer Michael Shelden writes that Ravelston's character is based on an actual person in Orwell's life named Sir Richard Rees. Shelden writes, "In his autobiography, published in 1963, Richard Rees took great care to present himself as an average man, while making it clear that he was fully aware of the position that his wealth had created for him among his less fortunate friends" (203). Does this sound like Ravelston? Is he not only aware, but does he also trade on the position his wealth creates for him among the less fortunate characters? If Ravelston is indeed modeled on Rees, what can you determine Orwell's feelings about Rees to have been?

History and Context

Doing some background reading is often helpful when you prepare to write an essay about a piece of literature; it can be particularly helpful if, as a twenty-first century student living in the United States, you are planning to study a writer from 1930s England. In the case of Orwell's *Keep the Aspidistra Flying*, some basic biographical research is definitely in order, particularly considering that Orwell and his protagonist Gordon seem to have a great deal in common. It would also be helpful to learn a bit about the culture Orwell was immersed in, the culture he portrayed in his work. What was London like in the 1920s and 1930s? What was the class structure like? What was a typical middle-class life like? What were women's social roles and how were they evolving? Knowing the answers to questions like these will help to make sure that you approach Orwell's novel with enough cultural and contextual knowledge to appreciate his distinctive perspective on the society in which he lived and worked. Finally, it would behoove you to understand a bit about the publication history of *Keep the Aspidistra Flying*, its journey from Orwell's pen to readers' hands, and how it was received by his contemporaries. Besides simply helping you to a deeper understanding of and appreciation of Orwell's novel, this type of historical context can also serve as the basis for an essay. You might devote your entire essay to studying the similarities between Orwell and Gordon or to speculating on the relatively poor reception of *Keep the Aspidistra Flying* by Orwell's contemporaries. Or you might take a social issue, such as the role of women, and, armed with enough cultural and historical contexts, explain how Orwell's take on the issue reflected or took issue with the mainstream point of view.

Sample Topics:

1. **Role of women:** How accurately does Orwell portray contemporary gender roles? What does his depiction tell us about what he thought about gender roles? Is he criticizing or commending how women are treated in his society?

How are women as a whole portrayed in Orwell's novel? What roles do they play in English society? Compare and contrast their lives with the lives of the male characters. How are they alike and different? Once you have established for yourself the respective roles of men and women in Orwell's fictional world, think about how Orwell's representation compares to real life. A good place to begin research into what life was really like for women in 1920s and 1930s London is Sally Alexander's "Becoming a Woman in London in the 1920s and 1930s," found in *Metropolis London: Histories and Representations Since 1800.* What roles did women play in 1920s England? What kind of status did they have in comparison to men? Would you say that Orwell's novel portrays gender roles accurately? Why or why not? From the narrative, does he seem to be critical of gender roles, approving of them, or simply neutral? How can you tell?

Analyze passages relevant to this question, such as the following exchange between Gordon and Rosemary:

> "Because one can't do that sort of thing. It isn't done."
>
> "It 'isn't done'! You'll be saying it's 'not cricket' in another moment. *What* 'isn't done'?"

"Letting you pay for my meals. A man pays for a woman, a woman doesn't pay for a man."

"Oh, Gordon! Are we living in the reign of Queen Victoria?"

"Yes, we are, as far as that kind of thing's concerned. Ideas don't change so quickly."

"But *my* ideas have changed."

"No, they haven't. You think they have, but they haven't. You've been brought up as a woman, and you can't help behaving like a woman, however much you don't want to."

"But what do you mean by *behaving like a woman*, anyway?"

"I tell you every woman's the same when it comes to a thing like this. A woman despises a man who's dependent on her and sponges on her. She may say she doesn't, she may *think* she doesn't, but she does. She can't help it. If I let you pay for my meals *you'd* despise me." (118)

What is revealed here about Gordon and Rosemary's perceptions of gender roles and relationships? Why do you think it is that Gordon is so concerned with rejecting the stifling and restrictive values of his society, particularly in regard to money, but is unable to slough off the idea that women must not financially support men?

2. **Reception of *Keep the Aspidistra Flying*:** What, if anything, can we surmise about the novel when we consider its very poor reception, not only by the book-buying public, but even by its own author? How does our reading of the novel change once we know that Orwell himself ultimately dismissed it? If it failed to gain contemporary success and earned the disdain of its own author, why are we still reading it more than 70 years later?

The first printing of *Keep the Aspidistra Flying* consisted of 3,000 copies, of which only 2,194 sold. Biographer Michael Shelden writes that Orwell was not surprised by the meager sales since "he quickly came to regard *[Keep the Aspidistra Flying]* as a book that belonged in the same category as *A Clergyman's Daughter*—'a silly potboiler'" (239). Critical reception of the novel was not terribly good either. The *Spectator's* Wil-

liam Plomer deemed the novel "crude" in his review, and Cyril
Connolly wrote in the *New Statesman* that the "writer of *Burmese Days* was . . . fond of Burma and included many beautiful descriptions of it, while the writer of *Keep the Aspidistra
Flying* hates London and everything there. Hence the realism
of one book was redeemed by an operating sense of beauty,
that of the other is not" (qtd in Shelden 238). Connolly wrote
a letter to Orwell, indicating that he felt badly about the negative review and explaining, "I felt that [the novel] needed more
colour to relieve the total gloom of the hero's circumstances &
self-hatred—there must be jam if people are to swallow the pill
because otherwise they choke" (qtd in Shelden 238).

What do you make of Orwell's characterization of this
novel as a "silly pot-boiler"? What would make him characterize it so? Do you agree with this assessment? Why or why not?
Far from dismissing the work as a potboiler, Cyril Connolly
appears to have viewed the book as a serious piece that missed
its mark; he argues that the problems with Orwell's novel were
that it evinced a hatred for London and that it was simply too
negative and dismal to get its point across to readers. Do you
agree with Connolly's assessment? Why or why not? What,
to your mind, probably accounts for the poor sales and the
poor critical reception of this particular novel? Likewise, what
accounts for its ultimate longevity?

3. **Gordon Comstock as representation of Orwell:** How closely
   does the character of Gordon resemble his creator? What
   implications do these similarities have for the novel? What differences are there between the two men, and what are the significances of those differences?

Biographer Michael Shelden notes the similarities between
a period of Orwell's life and that of main character Gordon
Comstock. Shelden writes:

> Gordon Comstock's plight is, in many ways, the same as Orwell's.
> He abandons a "good," steady job to pursue a literary career and
> while he waits to write his masterpiece, he works in a bookshop.

> His friends resemble Orwell's, as do some of his adventures, and he is preoccupied with ideas about art and society that are similar to those favored by his creator. He rages against the corruption in a society obsessed with money and power and takes refuge in a private world where high art is God. (220)

After pointing out these likenesses between Orwell and Gordon, Shelden offers his opinion on the reason Orwell created a character so like his younger self:

> Orwell turns on himself, so to speak, and satirizes the self-defeating aspects of his life in the early 1930s—his lack of self-confidence, his sometimes bitter cynicism, his romantic fatalism, and his unrealistic literary ideas. Gordon is defeated by these things. . . . He gives up on art because he cannot satisfy his own impossibly high standards and because he loses faith in its importance against the menacing background of world events. (220)

Spend some time reading Shelden's biography of Orwell and then compare and contrast Orwell with his fictional character, Gordon Comstock. Shelden spends some time pointing out their similarities. Are there any significant differences that strike you as well? And what about Shelden's assessment of Orwell's self-critique? Is this, to your mind, accurate? Why or why not? Write an essay in which you support and extend, modify, or argue against Shelden's claim that, in *Keep the Aspidistra Flying*, Orwell is satirizing his own unwillingness to find a way to deal with the practical realities of life while maintaining his principles.

4. **Advertising:** It is sometimes easy to think of the phenomenon of pervasive and aggressive advertising as a strictly late twentieth-century invention. Clearly, however, 1930s London was plastered with all sorts of advertising for every conceivable product. How much does advertising shape Gordon's life?

Gordon's "good job" is with the advertising firm of the New Albion, but it is work he despises. Interestingly, he often seems to be more upset by the poor quality of the ad copy than by the general phenomenon of advertising. Throughout the course of the novel, print and graphic ads are constantly capturing Gordon's attention. What kinds of products are being advertised? What are the ad pitches generally like? Do they typically tout the benefits of the product they are selling, or do they instead try to create insecurities in the viewer of the ad? Do some research into the history of advertising in England. Two good resources on the subject are T. R. Nevett's *Advertising in Britain: A History* and John Benson's *The Rise of Consumer Society in Britain, 1880–1980.* Just how important of a force had advertising become by the 1930s? Why, after looking at the books on infant development, does Gordon stop to peruse the advertisements in magazines in the library? What does his work on the "foot odor" campaign tell us about his principles by novel's end?

Philosophy and Ideas

One particularly illuminating way to approach a piece of literature is to examine the larger ideas with which it grapples. Much like working with themes, thinking about the larger philosophical concepts can help you answer that most fundamental question, What is this work about? Just as in real life, characters are driven by certain philosophies and ideas; their actions presumably are not merely random. Instead, there must be some sort of coherent worldview or ideology that guides them to act and react in somewhat predictable patterns. Often, in the course of a novel, something happens to challenge a character's personal philosophy, and much of the character's further development depends on how he or she responds. Likewise, you can also investigate the author's philosophical bent by examining the work for clues. It is often possible to see a work of literature as an extended testing of an idea, for instance—a way for an author to work out the implications of a particular philosophical musing as if the fictional world in the work were an ideological laboratory.

Sample Topics:

1. **Ideology:** Gordon Comstock clearly condemns the capitalist, money- and power-worshipping society in which he lives. He submits poems to *The Antichrist,* a socialist publication edited by his friend Ravelston but does not accept Ravelston's

socialist views. Ravelston, for his part, does not practice what he preaches, but if Gordon has such a disdain for capitalism and commitment to living out his principles, why does he not endorse and perhaps try to implement Ravelston's alternative, socialist views? What does he find objectionable about them? Finally, how do you think readers are supposed to feel about Gordon's rejection of both capitalism and socialism?

Begin by thinking about what criticisms of capitalism Gordon and Ravelston share. Then think about Ravelston's philosophical stance. Does he ultimately convince Gordon, or readers of the novel, of the virtues of socialism? How and why does Ravelston fail to put his beliefs into practice? Now think about Gordon's feelings regarding socialism. Locate passages such as the following in which Gordon comments on it: "Four hours a day in a model factory, tightening up bolt number 6003. Rations served out in greaseproof paper at the communal kitchen" (88). After locating and analyzing such passages, what would you say is Gordon's concept of socialism? What does he see as the potential problems with it?

   Now that you have spent some time analyzing Ravelston's and Gordon's positions, think about the message that the novel as a whole endorses. Does it seem to get behind Ravelston's socialism? To endorse Gordon's rejection of capitalism and socialism? Is Gordon's decision to abide by the capitalist rules of his society at the novel's end portrayed as positive or negative? What message is Orwell ultimately sending about political ideology and practical day-to-day living?

2. **Principles and practicality:** The characters of *Keep the Aspidistra Flying* put a lot of thought into their ideological principles; however, they do not always live true to them. In some cases, especially involving Ravelston, the character seems unwilling to make the sacrifices necessary to live up to his own principles. In other cases, the characters do try to abide by their principles despite the very impractical nature of those principles. What does the novel ultimately have to say about finding the balance between principle and practicality? Are we only to lionize those

who stick to their principles absolutely? Or does Orwell seem to acknowledge the need for practical considerations amid one's principles? If so, how much can one's principles be compromised in the name of practicality before the principles lose their meaning?

Read the following exchange between Rosemary and Ravelston regarding Gordon's refusal to take the good job available to him at the New Albion, where Rosemary still works:

> "It's so dreadful to see him like this! He goes absolutely to pieces. And all the time, you see, there's a good job he could quite easily get if he wanted it—a really *good* job. It's not that he can't, it's simply that he won't."
>
> She explained about the New Albion. Ravelston rubbed his nose.
>
> "Yes. As a matter of fact I've heard all about that. We talked it over when he left the New Albion."
>
> "But you don't think he was right to leave them?" she said, promptly divining that Ravelston *did* think Gordon right.
>
> "Well—I grant you it wasn't very wise. But there's a certain amount of truth in what he says. Capitalism's corrupt and we ought to keep outside it—that's his idea. It's not practicable, but in a way it's sound."
>
> "Oh, I dare say it's all right as a theory! But when he's out of work and when he could get this job if he chose to ask for it—*surely* you don't think he's right to refuse?"
>
> "Not from a common-sense point of view. But in principle—well, yes."
>
> "Oh, in principle!" We can't afford principles, people like us. *That's* what Gordon doesn't seem to understand." (197)

What does this exchange reveal about Rosemary and Ravelston's attitudes about acting on one's principles? Rosemary argues that she and Gordon "can't afford principles." Does the text bear out the idea that having money allows one to live in a way that respects his or her principles? What about Ravelston—does his life reflect the socialist principles he holds

dear? Thinking about this passage, others like it, and the overall tone of the novel, what do you think Orwell is trying to say
about the role of deeply held principles in the daily lives of
human beings? What happens when our principles are not in
line with the mainstream society in which we live? Are day-to-
day life and a deep devotion to principles mutually exclusive,
or does Orwell suggest a way that we can "get on" and abide by
our purer principles at the same time?

Language, Symbols, and Imagery

Language, symbols, and imagery are some of the most important tools
a writer possesses. Learning to analyze these elements in a work of
literature will help you dig deeper into the text and to probe its major
themes and messages. In the case of *Keep the Aspidistra Flying*, for
instance, you might try to get at the heart of the novel by analyzing
its major symbol, the aspidistra. Identify key passages that describe it
and analyze them carefully. What are the plant's major characteristics?
Figuring out what it means to Gordon and to the other characters in
the novel will help you to understand what's at stake to each of them.
In terms of language, you might set your sights on one of two specific
uses of language, each of which is accompanied by symbols and images:
Gordon's poetry and the advertising campaigns he disdains. You can
analyze either of these and use your findings to help shed light on Gordon's perspective and his relationship to the culture he lives in. Or,
you might even compare the two; setting Gordon's poetry against the
advertising jingles would make for an interesting essay. Just how are the
two similar and different? Further, what types of language, images, and
symbols does Gordon value? What, to his mind, makes these superior
to the advertising jingles he once helped to write? Would you agree
with his assessment? Why or why not?

Sample Topics:

1. **The aspidistra:** The aspidistra mentioned in the novel's title is
   definitely an important and recurring symbol in the book. For
   what exactly does it stand?

   Locate as many references to the aspidistra as you can. What
   are the plant's characteristics? What kind of meaning does it

hold for Gordon? Does that meaning change from the beginning of the novel to the end? If so, how exactly? What does the aspidistra seem to mean to other characters, such as Rosemary and Ravelston? For English society as a whole? What is the significance of Gordon's decision to purchase his own aspidistra at the novel's end?

2. **Advertising:** Gordon is a person who wants to use words to influence people, yet he despises creating copy for advertising. What makes advertising different than other forms of communication for him?

   Have a close look at the advertising that Orwell describes in *Keep the Aspidistra Flying*. What kinds of images and what sort of language are used to sell products? What does Gordon find objectionable about the advertising business? How would you say advertisements today compare with the ones referenced in Orwell's novels? Do they rely on similar images and language, or have they moved in a different direction? What differences are there in the language of advertising that disturb Gordon? Or does advertising use the same language as his poetry? What distinguishes them?

3. **Gordon's poems:** How are we supposed to evaluate works of literature—Gordon's poems—within a work of literature—*Keep the Aspidistra Flying*? Does the context of these poems change the way that we are reading them, and what do they tell us?

   What can Gordon's poems tell us about him? About his vision of the world? Why is *London Pleasures* so important to him? What sort of poem do you think he intends it to be? Are readers supposed to think Gordon's poems good or not? How can you tell, and why is this important?

4. **Christ imagery:** Though at times subtle, *Keep the Aspidistra Flying* is permeated with images referencing the story of the life, death, and resurrection of Jesus. What is the significance of this imagery?

In several places throughout the novel, references are made, sometimes ironically, to the story of Jesus. One of the most blatant references, of course, is the literary magazine Ravelston edits, *Antichrist*. More straightforwardly, there are signs of resurrection. Gordon sinks deeper and deeper into the abyss of his miserable life; however, during the spring of the year he turns 30—the age Jesus was when he began his ministry— Gordon is reawakened and reenters the world. Likewise, foreshadowing Gordon's resurgence is the rebirth of the aspidistra he thought had died in his room. Orwell even includes verbal play to this effect. It seems obvious that Gordon's "resurrection" is related to Rosemary's pregnancy. When she tells him that she is going to have a baby, Gordon responds, "A baby? Oh, Christ!" (225). What does all of this imagery mean? Who or what is the Christ figure in this novel? Or is there instead an Antichrist figure? How would it change your reading of the novel if you considered Gordon to be a Christ figure?

5. **Verbal substitution in the epigraph:** *Keep the Aspidistra Flying* opens with a lengthy epigraph drawn from a very famous biblical passage, 1 Corinthians, chapter 13. However, Orwell adapts the passage, by substituting the word *money* in each place that Paul, the author of Corinthians, had used the word *love*. Is this simply a joke, or does Orwell mean something serious by it?

Is the adaptation of this moving, often-quoted biblical passage intended to be a sacrilege, or is there a serious commentary going on here? Having read the novel, in whose voice do you hear this epigraph? Is this Gordon espousing his "money is at the bottom of everything" philosophy? If so, is it the Gordon of the beginning of the novel or the end? Is it the narrator? If so, how would Gordon respond? Does it matter that, in the original, Paul is speaking of the gifts given by the Holy Spirit, and the love he refers to is not romantic love but something wider and more enduring, such as the love that the Christian God showed through Jesus? Does this parallel the love if we can call it that, that Gordon shows toward his unborn child at the end? Why, then, does the altered epigraph still substitute *money* for *love*?

Compare and Contrast Essays

Comparing and contrasting can be a good way to get a broader perspective on the work you are studying. Take *Keep the Aspidistra Flying*, for example. You might compare Orwell's version to the movie made from the book in 1997. Seeing the choices the movie makes and what it emphasizes and downplays may well help you to see Orwell's novel in a new way. Likewise, comparing the novel, which was one of Orwell's earlier, less popular novels, to his later ones such as *Animal Farm* or *1984*, might enable you to notice aspects of the book that may initially have escaped your eye. The key to comparing and contrasting is to make sure that your essay does not turn into a simple list of ways that the elements or works you are comparing are similar and different. While this may be interesting, it should only be your starting point. Once you have compiled that list, it is up to you to synthesize your findings into a thesis that will help your reader to see one or more of the works you're comparing from a fresh perspective, to point out a significant pattern and discuss its meaning, or to trace the evolution of an image or idea from one work to another. After you have discovered what it is you want to say, you will use the points of comparison and contrast that you identified to help you make this point in the body of your essay.

Sample Topics:

1. *Keep the Aspidistra Flying*—**novel versus movie version:** Given that 60 years separate the publication of the novel and the release of Robert Bierman's movie, what is it that has allowed Orwell's novel to remain relevant for so long? What aspects of the novel has Bierman altered to make it even more relevant now? How does this help us read the novel with even greater insight?

   Watch the 1997 movie version of Orwell's novel, called *Keep the Aspidistra Flying* or, alternately, *The Merry War*. How closely does the film mirror the book? What elements of the film are different or new? What aspects of the novel would you say the film emphasizes? What aspects does it downplay? Does seeing the film help you to appreciate anything new about the novel? What surprised you about the film? Are there differences that are attributable to the differences in the times between the writing of the novel and the filming of the movie?

How, for instance, might the movie have differed had it been made much sooner after the book's publication? Ultimately, what do you make of director Robert Bierman's interpretation of Orwell's novel? Considering the poor reception that the novel received when it was published, what does it tell us about *Keep the Aspidistra Flying* and its ideas that a film version was made 60 years after its publication?

2. ***Keep the Aspidistra Flying* versus *Animal Farm* and/or *1984*:** Compare and contrast Orwell's early novel with one of his later, more famous works.

Compare *Keep the Aspidistra Flying*, published in 1936, to Orwell's more famous, later novels, *Animal Farm* (1945) and *1984* (1949). While Orwell's later novels have become cultural touchstones, *Keep the Aspidistra Flying* was not well received by Orwell's contemporaries and has not come to be generally considered a literary classic. Compare and contrast these works. What similarities can you find between Orwell's early novel and his later ones? What differences? What would you argue is the main reason for the different fates of these works? Did Orwell improve so drastically as a writer in 10 years? In what ways? Or is something else besides a honed craft at the heart of this issue? What might that be?

Bibliography and Online Resources for *Keep the Aspidistra Flying*

Alexander, Sally. "Becoming a Woman in London in the 1920s and 1930s." *Metropolis London: Histories and Representations Since 1800.* Ed. David Feldman and Gareth Stedman Jones. New York: Routledge, 1989, 245–71.

Benson, John. *The Rise of Consumer Society in Britain, 1880–1980.* New York: Longman, 1994.

Fitzpatrick, Shelia. *The Russian Revolution.* New York: Oxford UP, 2008.

Hollis, Christopher. *A Study of George Orwell.* Chicago: Regnery, 1956.

Lee, Robert A. *Orwell's Fiction.* Notre Dame, IN: U of Notre Dame P: 1969.

Miller, Martin A. *The Russian Revolution: The Essential Readings.* Hoboken, NJ: Wiley-Blackwell, 2001.

Nevett, T. R. *Advertising in Britain: A History.* London: Heinemann on behalf of the History of Advertising Trust, 1982.

Orwell, George. *Keep the Aspidistra Flying.* San Diego: Harcourt, 1956.

———. *Keep the Aspidistra Flying.* Accessed on 15 Nov. 2009. <http://www.netcharles.com/orwell/ext/336.htm>.

Patai, Daphne. "Political Fiction and Patriarchal Fantasy." *The Orwell Mystique: A Study in Male Ideology.* Amherst: U of Massachusetts P, 1984, 201–18.

Russell, Bertrand. "George Orwell." *World Review* 16 (1950): 5–6.

Shelden, Michael. *Orwell: The Authorized Biography.* New York: HarperCollins, 1991.

THE ROAD TO
WIGAN PIER

READING TO WRITE

FIRST PUBLISHED in 1937 in a Europe increasingly worried about the ever more powerful Germany under Hitler, *The Road to Wigan Pier* directly addressed current events in England and on the Continent, and yet it has continued to have meaning and resonance for readers in the twenty-first century. Among Orwell's catalog of pro-socialism works, *The Road to Wigan Pier* stands out as being the most explicitly ideological and propagandist of all his major works. This nonfiction work is divided into two quite distinct parts, a division so distinct, in fact, that it became the basis of the most scathing reviews of the book. In the first half of the work, Orwell presents a sort of anthropological study of the coal miners of north England. He lives among the miners and occasionally even goes down into the coal mines himself. Using this first-person experience, he reports on the harsh and destitute conditions the miners and their families face. In the second half of *Wigan Pier*, Orwell proposes a solution to the squalor and inequity he has described, namely socialism. The second half, however, goes far beyond addressing the miners' problems; it takes the form of a highly autobiographical and heavily ideological inventory of the need for England to adopt socialism in the face of rising fascist sentiments in Europe, while also criticizing much of the current membership of English socialism. The second part of the book was sufficiently controversial that Orwell's publisher took it upon himself to publish versions of *The Road to Wigan Pier* comprising only the first part to be sold to leftist organizations.

Despite its curious structure and attendant controversy, at its root, *The Road to Wigan Pier* is a call for the implementation of socialism in England. As you can imagine, comparing socialism favorably to fascism is one thing, but to try to convince people living under British democracy to adopt socialism is a much harder task. As a Briton himself, Orwell cannot deny that he was inculcated into the British social caste system and cannot easily escape it no matter how he tries. So, even for the author, there seems to be a bit of ambivalence and confusion about adopting socialism wholesale. Some of that ambivalence appears in passages such as the following:

> I sometimes think that the price of liberty is not so much eternal vigilance as eternal dirt. There are some Corporation estates in which new tenants are systematically deloused before being allowed into their houses. . . . This procedure has its points, for it is a pity that people should take bugs into brand new houses . . . but it is the kind of thing that makes you wish that the word 'hygiene' could be dropped out of the dictionary. Bugs are bad, but a state of affairs in which men will allow themselves to be dipped like sheep is worse. Perhaps, however, when it is a case of slum clearance, one must take for granted a certain amount of restrictions and inhumanity. When all is said and done, the most important thing is that people shall live in decent houses and not in pigsties. . . . On balance, the Corporation Estates are better than the slums; but only by a small margin. (64–65)

Can you untangle what Orwell's fundamental stance is on this relocation of miners and their families? Is he happy for the upgrade in housing, or is he outraged at how they are treated? Does he think the process of delousing is dehumanizing for the individuals, while the clearance of the slums is good for the group or not? Keeping in mind that one way to look at socialism is to think of it as putting the good of the group ahead of the rights of the individual, carefully read through the passage to see if you can determine where Orwell stands on the issue.

When Orwell proclaims that "the price of liberty is not so much eternal vigilance as eternal dirt," he certainly seems to be saying, if you want liberty, you have to deal with some dirt. On the basis of this statement alone, you should expect that he values liberty over cleanliness, and, therefore, he would prefer that the miners be treated with dignity even if they do bring bugs with them to their newly built houses. He does allow that "it is a pity that people should take bugs into brand new houses," but you still have the sense that he finds that a small price to pay for preserving people's rights and dignity. And, sure enough, he does go on to say that even though it is a pity to bring lice into a new house, the delousing process "is the kind of thing that makes you wish that the word 'hygiene' could be dropped out of the dictionary." So far, he appears to be consistently siding with the idea that dignity and liberty are more important than bug-free houses, although there is a sort of softness in the way that he is approaching it, almost as if he is strongly considering the merits of the delousing. With his next statement, however, he again sounds like the champion of the rights of the common man: "Bugs are bad, but a state of affairs in which men will allow themselves to be dipped like sheep is worse." Clearly, this is an unequivocal denunciation of the government program to delouse the miners who move into the new government housing. Not only does he state it without hesitation—bugs are bad, but this is worse—but he also invokes an analogy equating the victims of the delousing with sheep to let his reader know how inhuman he finds the process. His stance seems firm.

Notice, though, how the next sentence begins: "Perhaps, however." Even before you finish reading the rest of the sentence, Orwell has clued you in that a shift is coming. Using the word *perhaps* indicates that he is opening up the possibilities he is willing to consider. His opinion on the subject had seemed quite immutable—bugs are bad, the forced delousing of human beings is worse—but now, with that single word, some doubt creeps into his discussion. The next word, *however*, marks an even more radical shift in Orwell's thinking. As a contrastive, *however* signals that something in direct opposition to the previous sentence is about to be suggested. Given how forcefully Orwell has stated his case, the mere suggestion of an alternative, much less a recapitulation, is shocking, but, indeed, Orwell does suggest that "when it is a case of slum clearance, one must take for granted a certain amount of restrictions, and inhumanity." What in that sentence allows for such a radical departure from Orwell's earlier stance? He appears to be allowing for a special exception in the "case of slum clearance." Why is that? What does he mean by slum clearance? Thinking in terms of Orwell's socialist tendencies, who will benefit from slum clearance? How is it that slum clearance is a worthy excuse for a certain amount of inhumanity? What benefits does Orwell see in this process that can possibly be worth subjecting people to inhumanity?

Orwell offers his answer to this question when he says, "the most important thing is that people shall live in decent houses and not in pigsties." Why is living in a decent house "the most important thing"? What does Orwell mean when he uses the word *decent* here? Keep in mind that *decent* is frequently used to mean something along the lines of *socially appropriate*. Decent people, for instance, are those who have strong morals and who know their place in the social scheme and do not try to live outside their station. Can that possibly be what Orwell, the dyed-in-the-wool socialist, means here? Or does he simply mean housing that is structurally sound? Note the change in attitude that has crept into this passage. Whereas Orwell now says that "the most important thing is that people shall live in decent houses and not in pigsties," he began the passage proclaiming that "the price of liberty is not so much eternal vigilance as eternal dirt." If dirtiness is the price of liberty, but the most important thing for people is to get away from dirty houses, then, logically, Orwell must be suggesting that there is something more precious than liberty. What could that something be? Or is Orwell unintentionally contradicting himself? Does he not realize that he is espousing apparently opposite views just within the space of a few sentences? Both possibilities are worth considering. If he is unintentionally contradicting himself, what does that tell you about his deepest feelings regarding the implementation of socialism? Does such contradiction unmask some unresolved ambivalence? If the contradiction, however, is intentional, what is Orwell trying to tell us about socialism? If liberty is not the highest stated virtue—as it often is in democracy—then what is? What virtue is being upheld in the slum clearance and delousing procedures?

To answer these questions thoroughly, you will need to read the rest of the book, searching always for pertinent passages that you can then subject to more close reading. Each passage that you analyze in this fashion will bring you closer to answering your questions while simultaneously bringing up new questions and suggesting other passages that deserve similar scrutiny. Once you have settled on a specific topic you want to explore and write on, you can focus your close readings on those passages that are most pertinent to your topic. Your close readings will provide specific pieces of evidence to support your thesis, and, in the body of your essay, you will be able to present and expound upon these specific points in order to prove your thesis. The more effort and focus you apply in your close reading of passages, the stronger your evidence will be, which will result in a much better essay.

TOPICS AND STRATEGIES

The sections below present a variety of starting points from which to begin writing an essay on Orwell's *The Road to Wigan Pier*. Think of these more as prewriting prompts than as templates for a finished essay. The questions provided are not intended to give you a fully formed structure for an essay nor to lead you directly to a workable thesis. Instead, these topic suggestions, and the questions they pose, should spur your own thinking and introduce you to a general topic that you can then delve into in much greater depth. To that end, you should not feel compelled to answer each subquestion included, and you most certainly do not want to limit yourself to only those issues and idea that are explicitly provided here. See what questions, suggestions, or provided passages spark your own analytical thinking, then let your thoughts be guided by your own interaction with the novel, any research you may be doing, and your prewriting. As you work to answer some of the questions here, you ideally will be alternating between rereading the book, with your topic ideas firmly in mind, and working on prewriting activities, such as taking notes, idea clustering, even outlining if your ideas are structured enough. What you will find is that you will generate more questions on your own, subtler and more directed questions than the ones provided here. And as you continue to generate and answer those questions, you will end up constructing something interesting and meaningful to say about *The Road to Wigan Pier* and will, therefore, be well on your way to creating a good, solid thesis. While much of your prewriting will not be used directly in your final essay, do not consider it wasted effort; it is the invisible foundation on which any good essay is built.

Themes

Themes, quite simply, are the central ideas in a work of literature. They are what the work is about. And in any work of substance, there will always be multiple themes, even if one of them is clearly the most important. *The*

Road to Wigan Pier, for instance, is about any number of things. Orwell discusses poverty, housing, eating habits, class differences, social strata, imperialism, the merits and drawbacks of several ideologies including socialism, communism, and fascism, and quite a few other subjects. Any or all of these may be considered themes. When writing an essay about theme, you are likely going to be most interested in the major themes of the work. For instance, although Orwell mentions trains several times in *Wigan Pier,* the book clearly is not fundamentally concerned with rail travel, and so you probably would not produce a very compelling and enlightening essay if you chose that as your theme. Furthermore, another way to think of major themes in a work is to think of them as being the book's theses. Just as your essay has a thesis, so will a work of literature, particularly a work of nonfiction like this one. Thus, Orwell may mention rail travel, but he is not really commenting on it in any meaningful way. On the other hand, he has a strong message to deliver regarding fascism. Your job as the writer of an essay is not merely to point out the themes running through a work but also to interpret, for your reader, what the author is saying about that topic. What does Orwell mean when he says fascism, for instance? What is his stance? Does he have good reason to hold such a stance? Historically speaking, was he correct in what he said about fascism? These are the types of questions you want to consider when writing about theme.

Sample Topics:

1. **Revolution:** Unlike fictional writing, in which the narrator might observe characters' actions with a minimum of judgment, *The Road to Wigan Pier* is a work of nonfiction and is intended to be persuasive in its effect. What action does Orwell ultimately want his reader to take? Is a societal revolution his ultimate goal?

   Without doubt, Orwell is trying to convince his readers that socialism is the premier governing system available. In fact, in several places, he more or less suggests that the only way that England can possibly survive the fascist threat being posed by Hitler and Mussolini is to throw off its class distinctions and capitalist mentality and embrace socialism. Is this open advocacy for revolution? Is he suggesting that the imminent threats brewing on the continent call for a radical and immediate change in England's governance? Or does he suggest that such changes must happen more gradually? What does he see as the consequences of social revolution? Would such a radical change strengthen a society on the brink of war or weaken it?

At one point while discussing a wholesale breakdown of class distinctions in Great Britain, Orwell asserts that:

> [A]ll the while, at the bottom of his heart, everyone knows that this is humbug. We all rail against class-distinctions, but very few people seriously want them. Here you come upon the important fact that every revolutionary opinion draws part of its strength from a secret conviction that nothing can be changed. (138)

What does Orwell mean by this? Does he draw any distinction between those who talk about revolution and true revolution-aries, or is he speaking about everyone here? If the impossi-bility of change gives strength to revolutionary opinion, then where does actual revolution come from? Does this "safe" ver-sion of revolutionary thought accomplish anything ultimately, or is it completely static?

2. **Work and social value:** The first half of this book is intensely concerned with the lives of England's coal miners. Orwell lives among the colliers and their families for months and even goes down into the mines on a number of occasions. The sec-ond half of the book then goes on to call for the elimination of social inequities and class distinctions. What is the connection between the two parts of the book? If Orwell is ultimately con-cerned with making sure that people are not judged by the work that they do, what is it that he learns among the miners that reinforces this idea?

In the 1930s, coal occupied much the same position in the func-tioning of society as oil does today. Orwell goes to great lengths to make the point that the entire world depends on coal:

> Practically everything we do, from eating an ice to crossing the
> Atlantic, and from baking a loaf to writing a novel, involves the
> use of coal, directly or indirectly. For all the arts of peace coal
> is needed; if war breaks out it is needed all the more. In time of
> revolution the miner must go on working or the revolution must
> stop, for revolution as much as reaction needs coal. (30–31)

Given the fundamental necessity of coal, the obvious implication should be that coal miners are among the most important
members of society, and, logically, they should enjoy a very
exalted position in the social structure. Obviously, as *Wigan
Pier* demonstrates in great detail, that is not the case. The colliers live in squalid conditions, barely able to make a living for
their families and often having to rely on government assistance
just to survive. Their health is compromised by the work they
do, and the nature of mining means that they live most of their
lives filthy. As reward for this, they are looked down upon and
held in contempt by most of the rest of society. If the work that
they do is necessary to fuel the lives lived by the so-called upper
classes, why then are they not appreciated? How is it even possible for the rest of society to ignore their contributions? Who
gets to decide what work is appreciated and what work is not?
For that matter, how is it decided who will do the dirty, unap-
preciated work of a society? The second part of *Wigan Pier* is
a call for the implementation of socialism in England; if successful, how would that impact the miners? Would their lives
change in any appreciable way? Short of full-scale socialism,
where does Orwell see a chance for improvement in their lives?

3. **Liberty versus order:** It can be argued that the entire purpose
   of government is to try to find the balance between individual
   rights and the needs of the larger society. Orwell certainly looks
   at some of those struggles in *The Road to Wigan Pier.* On the
   whole, does he seem to come down on the side of individual
   liberty or social order?

On the surface, socialism appears to be all about privileging
the needs of the group over the freedoms of the individuals.

It calls for certain individuals to make great sacrifices for the benefit of others and for everyone to share equally. This may be an oversimplification, as Orwell certainly seems to be concerned with the rights of individuals in many of his works, most notably in *1984*. In *Wigan Pier*, more or less a work of socialist propaganda, what does Orwell seem to value more, individual rights or the good of the society at large? Take a close look at Orwell's descriptions of the clearing of the slums and the construction of Corporation housing in Chapter 4. Is it better for the individual miners to have the newer houses with a bit of garden in them rather than living in the crowded slums? What about the fact that the miner now lives so much farther from his work? The new housing is cleaner and sturdier, but the wider distribution of workers means that many shopkeepers and pub owners will lose their businesses. Who benefits from this arrangement? The larger society or the individuals involved? Are the miners given a choice about moving? How does Orwell seem to feel about the changes? Be sure to look through the book for other instances where individual rights and the good of the community come into conflict. What side does Orwell take in these clashes? Is he consistent? Does he provide justification for his stances?

4. **Appearance versus reality:** In several places, Orwell concerns himself with pointing out how appearance and reality do not necessarily match or, sometimes, how they do. What does he ultimately have to say about appearance and reality?

Orwell frequently points out the problems of appearances masking reality. Early in the book, he describes the lives of coal miners and tries hard to dispel many long-standing misconceptions about them. Because, for instance, the miners stay dirty much of the time due to the nature of their work, many people outside the mining community think that they are dirty by nature, that they enjoy being dirty. Orwell takes care to point out how fastidious the miners are in fact when it comes to their personal hygiene. Later in the book, Orwell bemoans that there is a particular type of socialist, what he calls at one point "that dreary tribe of high-minded women and sandal-wearers and bearded fruit-juice drinkers" (160) and that we might call hippies, who mislead other people about what socialism must be like. According to him, they put a face on socialism that belies what it really is. They are the appearance, but not at all the reality, and because of this, plenty of potential converts to socialism are scared away. In perhaps his most direct look at the problems of appearance and reality, Orwell writes, "perhaps it is not even desirable, industrialism being what it is, that it should learn to disguise itself as something else. As Mr. Aldous Huxley has truly remarked, a dark Satanic mill ought to look like a dark Satanic mill and not like the temple of mysterious and splendid gods" (97). However, he goes on to say that it does not really matter what appearance industrial buildings take; it only matters what goes on inside them and how they affect people's lives. Is there really an answer to the appearance vs. reality divide? How can appearances always match reality? What can we tell merely by looking at someone or a situation? If appearances can be deceiving, how are we supposed to go about discovering the reality? Are appearances ever useful in making judgments? What is Orwell suggesting? That we all wear our beliefs on our sleeves? How would that even be possible? Despite their appearance, are those "bearded fruit-juice drinkers" not truly socialists? What does he think a socialist should look like?

History and Context

The Road to Wigan Pier is one of those literary works that is impossible to separate from its historical context. That does not mean that it has no meaning today or even that you cannot get a great deal from it without doing some historical research, but your understanding of and appreciation for Orwell's message will be greatly enhanced once you have a grasp of the times and conditions in which it was written and first read. Understanding the historical and cultural impetus that drove Orwell to write *Wigan Pier* can lead to some very interesting brainstorming. One question to consider, for instance, is whether Orwell would have written the same book, or even something remotely similar, if he were writing today. Would a twenty-first century Orwell still be championing socialism, or would he have a different outlook given current conditions? Once you truly understand the working conditions, the threat of fascism Europe was faced with, and the social problems of a British culture that was losing its place as the premier world power, you should understand exactly how Orwell envisioned socialism as the ultimate solution to England's problems. Deepening your understanding of cultural and historical contexts will not only bring an enhanced sophistication to your treatment of the possible topics below, but it will also give you ideas about new, exciting topics to write about.

Sample Topics:

1. **Coal mining in the 1930s:** In *Wigan Pier*, Orwell chose to make coal miners emblematic of the exploited and ignored working classes in England. Once he decides to turn them into a symbol, the question arises: How much license did he take when presenting them? How accurate are his depictions of the lives and work of miners, and why did he emphasize, exaggerate, or minimize the details that he did?

Orwell presents some very persuasive portraits of the lives of the colliers of northern England in the first half of *Wigan Pier*. Part of the reason his depictions are so compelling and persuasive is that he took the extraordinary step of living among the miners for a period of time, and that kind of first-person research always seems quite genuine and convincing. How thoroughly accurate is his picture of mining life, however? Even Orwell himself admits that he is unable to get a full grasp of the lives of the miners he visits. From the fact that they tend to keep the downstairs rooms—where he often was greeted as a visitor—in better shape than their private upstairs quarters, to the admission that his few trips down into the mines did little to approximate the experiences of men who worked eight hours a day, six days a week in them, much about Orwell's accounts suggests that he only got a superficial look at mining life despite his best efforts. Still, he chose to make the miners a powerful symbol of the lower classes in England.

What was mining life really like at this time in England? Two good sources to begin researching are Barbara Freese's

Coal: A Human History and the Web site of the Coal Mining History Resource Center (www.cmhrc.co.uk/site/home/). Compare these very thoroughly researched sources to Orwell's accounts. What stands out as very different? What major details did Orwell leave out about the lives of colliers? Are there any aspects of their lives that he exaggerated? Why do you think he did that? Conversely, how do Orwell's experiences help round out these other, presumably more objective, sources?

2. **The rise of Hitler and fascism:** In *Wigan Pier*, Orwell advocates for socialism with a sense of extreme urgency. At times he appears to be suggesting that England must choose between socialism and utter destruction. What is the context for this heightened sense of urgency? Did history bear out any of Orwell's claims? What does the rise of fascism in Europe have to do with English coal mining?

Orwell does not mince words when he makes the case for the need for English socialism. According to Orwell, writing to his countrymen in 1937:

> It is meaningless to oppose Socialism on the ground that you object to the beehive State, for the beehive State *is here.* The choice is not, as yet, between a human and an inhuman world. It is simply between Socialism and Fascism, which at its very best is Socialism with the virtues left out. . . . For the moment the only possible course for any decent person, however much of a Tory or an anarchist by temperament, is to work for the establishment of Socialism. Nothing else can save us from the misery of the present or the nightmare of the future. To oppose Socialism *now,* when twenty million Englishmen are underfed and Fascism has conquered half Europe, is suicidal. (192–93)

In order to understand better the distinctions Orwell is making here, it is important that you have a sense of what he meant by fascism and why it differed from socialism. There are a number of good places to begin your research. One interesting starting point is the definition of fascism written by Benito Mussolini himself. A translation of his definition is available at the Internet Modern History Sourcebook at www.fordham.edu/halsall/mod/mussolini-fascism.html. Other sources for beginning your research include Piers Brendon's *The Dark Valley: A Panorama of the 1930s* and F. L. Carsten's *The Rise of Fascism*. What are the fundamental differences between socialism and fascism? In *Wigan Pier*, Orwell states the case very simply: Fascism is tyranny, and socialism desires the overthrow of tyranny. Does that description agree with your research? Given that England was in imminent danger of being taken over by a fascist dictator, was Orwell correct in putting forth socialism as a necessary antidote? What advantages would socialism give England that democracy would not? Did England, in fact, lean in a socialist direction during or after the war?

Philosophy and Ideas

Taking into consideration what a piece of literature has to say about certain ideologies or philosophies—or considering how a work of literature embodies certain philosophies—can be especially illuminating. In writing an essay like this, first think about what universal questions or ideological stances are presented in the piece of literature. Then attempt to determine what the author or work is saying about that particular idea or philosophy. Writing about philosophy and ideas is quite similar to writing about the themes in a work, though there are some important subtle distinctions. Writing about philosophy in a work, for instance, is often more abstract and open-ended. Sometimes the distinction can be as subtle as an author taking a definitive stance on an idea, a theme, versus an author honestly questioning an inscrutable idea, a philosophy. In other cases, philosophy and ideas are caught up with whole-scale ideologies. This is often the case with Orwell whose favorite topic of all is the sprawling, and sometimes disparate, set of political, ethical, and economic ideas known as socialism. In order to write about philosophy and ideas, it is sometimes necessary to do outside research, much as you might have to do when writing about historical and cultural contexts. In other cases, however, you may want to examine the author's ideas strictly within the context of the work itself. In either case, an examination of the "big ideas" an author is grappling with is usually a very rewarding experience that offers plenty of material for a good essay.

Sample Topics:

1. **Socialism:** As a writer, Orwell agitated for socialism for most of his career, and *The Road to Wigan Pier* is his most blatantly pro-socialist propagandist major work. What exactly does Orwell mean when he refers to socialism? And would socialism have benefited England in the ways that Orwell suggests?

It can be difficult at times for a contemporary reader to inject him- or herself fully into Orwell's works because of Orwell's insistent championing of socialism as a political structure. In the United States in the twenty-first century, the word *social-ism* tends to carry a lot of negative connotations. Often it arises in the context of proposed taxation or in health care reform. Politicians use charges of socialism to imply that their opponents favor a wholesale move away from free-market capitalism and representative democracy in favor of a large-scale redistribution of wealth and a huge government bureaucracy that oversees every aspect of citizens' lives. In fact, somewhat ironically, the vision of socialism often evoked resembles nothing more than the government of Big Brother in Orwell's *1984*. These particular connotations are probably impediments to understanding Orwell's vision of socialism. The first thing you will need to do in order to write an essay on socialism in Orwell's works is to research what Orwell's concept of socialism looks like. The best places to start are Orwell's own works. A careful rereading of *Wigan Pier*, along with some of this other works, in particular "The Lion and the Unicorn," *Homage to Catalonia*, and *Keep the Aspidistra Flying*, will tell you a great deal about Orwell's own understanding of socialism.

You will also want to do some outside research. Keep in mind that "isms" like socialism and Marxism tend to change meaning over time, and a current description of socialism may not accurately describe socialism as it was embodied in the 1930s. A good place to start your research is a book in the Political Systems of the World series, simply titled *Socialism*, by Thomas Fleming. Be sure to consult his bibliography for further, more in-depth resources as well. As a political and philosophical system, socialism has its roots in the French

Revolution and had come to stand for many different things by the 1920s. As Fleming writes, "By the 1920s and 1930s socialism had assumed many forms, some of them quite antagonistic to each other" (48). Which of these multiplicity of meanings had Orwell latched onto? Given your newfound understanding of socialism, was Orwell right to push so doggedly for it? How would the adoption of socialist policies have affected England's participation in the Second World War? How would socialist policies have helped or hindered England's long and slow recovery from the war?

2. **Aesthetics:** Throughout *The Road to Wigan Pier*, Orwell paints scenes of the environment in Lancashire and Yorkshire in vivid detail. He then often passes judgment on those scenes. What are Orwell's aesthetic judgments based on? What qualifies as beautiful, and what as ugly, for him? Does he appeal to a universal standard of beauty or something more personal?

Orwell writes that, as you travel northward in England, "you begin to encounter the real ugliness of industrialism—an ugliness so frightful and so arresting that you are obliged, as it were, to come to terms with it" (94). While the idea of a frightful ugliness seems simple enough, what does Orwell mean by an arresting ugliness? And how does it force one to have to "come to terms with it"? Orwell provides more precise detail: "A slag-heap is at best a hideous thing, because it is so planless and functionless. It is something just dumped on the earth, like the emptying of a giant's dust-bin" (94). According to this statement, it sounds as if beauty, in Orwell's estimation, requires planned form and some kind of utility. Does this make sense as a foundation to a theory of aesthetics? Can randomness be beautiful? And as for function, who gets to decide whether something serves a useful function or not? And should function be a determining factor of beauty?

Interestingly, a little later Orwell claims that he does "not believe that there is anything inherently and unavoidably ugly about industrialism" (96). Does this make sense in the context of what you already know about his aesthetic sense? Is he somehow leading the reader on when he says this? Perhaps the single most revealing comment he makes about his sense of aesthetics is that he believes that a "belching chimney or a stinking slum is repulsive chiefly because it implies warped lives and ailing children" (97). What does this statement imply about Orwell's sense of beauty and ugliness? Is there, in Orwell's view, an overlap between ethics and aesthetics?

3. **Classism and racism:** What does *Wigan Pier* reveal about Orwell's views on classism and racism?

The Road to Wigan Pier is a work very explicitly concerned with the prevalence of class distinctions and prejudices in England. In it, Orwell makes plea after plea for the end of classism, including the rather famous final sentence:

> And then perhaps this misery of class-prejudice will fade away, and we of the sinking middle class . . . may sink without further struggles into the working class where we belong, and probably when we get there it will not be so dreadful as we feared, for, after all, we have nothing to lose but our aitches. (204)

The implication of this last line is that only artificial and meaningless markers—such as the pronunciation of the letter *h* or not—separate the people of the various classes and that all will be fine when such differences are tossed aside. Rereading *Wigan Pier* carefully, can you find instances where Orwell engages in prejudicial assumptions based on a person's class? Does he practice what he preaches?

While Orwell does not address questions of racism, twenty-first century readers of his work will recognize the close resemblance between classism and racism. Does this work have anything to say about racism? What can you tell about Orwell's thoughts on racism? Locate and analyze all passages in which Orwell mentions race at all. You might begin by examining Orwell's discussion of the miners—and other poor people of the area—who have begun living in caravans. As he is describing the incredibly low standard of living these people are enduring, he notes, "One must remember that these people are not gypsies; they are decent English people who have all, except the children born there, had homes of their own in their day" (56). What is Orwell implying in this contrast between "gypsies" and "decent English people"? The Roma, as so-called gypsies are more correctly and respectfully known, are an ethnic group that has suffered immense discrimination. In fact, the very fascist dictators against whom Orwell is railing in *Wigan Pier* would, in the next few years, slaughter as many as half a million Roma in an attempt at "ethnic cleansing." What then do we make of Orwell's implication that the Roma are somehow lesser people than the English? How does this fit in with his anticlassism? Is it possible to be a genuine seeker of class equality and a racist at the same time?

Form and Genre

All writers work within the confines of particular forms of writing that have been established, defined, and redefined by countless writers who preceded them, and the conventions of each form and genre strongly influence how the finished work will look and sound. Just because a particular genre of writing comes with a set of established conventions does not mean, however, that writers slavishly adhere to those conventions. In fact, writers are often very explicitly working to subvert or transform the genre in which they are writing. Often, there is an important message in the form, not just the words, of a piece of literature. Think about it in terms of your own writing. If you send an e-mail to a close friend of yours, you likely do not employ the conventions of formal business letters. It is unlikely that you open the letter with a salutation like *Dear* or close it with *Sincerely.* You may not use standard English capitalization and spelling or pay that much attention to paragraphing. However, what if you did send your close friend an e-mail that did all of this? There is no doubt that your friend, so used to your much less formal e-mails, would take notice of the change in form and would see some meaning in it. Perhaps you were doing it for comedic effect, parodying someone, for instance. Or, perhaps your friend had done something to hurt you, and you adopted the more formal stance to show the distance you feel. In any case, your tinkering with the normal genre of e-mail writing would carry a meaning all its own, and this is exactly what goes on in works of literature where good writers are always very cognizant of how they are shaping their message. The more you pay attention to the form and genre being employed, the more you will understand about the work you are studying.

Sample Topics:

1. **Genre:** While it does seem clear that *The Road to Wigan Pier* is a piece of nonfiction, what is less clear is what type of nonfiction it is. What genre would you place *Wigan Pier* in? What effect does that choice have on your reading of the book?

   Is *Wigan Pier* a memoir? Orwell not only writes about his personal experiences living in the mining communities of northern England, but he also relates much of his life story in the second half of the book. What is the purpose of a memoir? What is a reader supposed to take away from a memoir? Does *Wigan Pier* provide this? If it is not a memoir, then what is it? A sociological study? A sermon? Journalism? Philosophical musings? Political propaganda? How do you determine its genre? How well does it succeed at fulfilling the expectations of its genre?

2. **Structure:** One of the most notable features of *The Road to Wigan Pier* is its unusual, bifurcated structure. While there is a nominal connection between the first and second parts of the book, in many ways they seem to be utterly discrete works. Why did Orwell structure his work like this? What effect does this have on your reading of the book?

   On at least one level, of course, there is a connection between the first and second parts of *Wigan Pier;* in the first part, Orwell has presented a vivid and thorough picture of the inequities and miseries of capitalism under the prevailing English social system, and in the second part, he offers the remedy to those ills. However, the styles of the two sections are so radically different that it can be hard to reconcile them into a single, unified reading experience. The first half of the book is, more or less, a journalistic account of Orwell's anthropological data gathering among the miners. The second half of the book switches gears entirely, laying out the arguments for the implementation of socialism in England. The second half is further complicated by the fact that Orwell relies heavily on autobiographical detail—charting his own personal development as a socialist—rather than strictly appealing to intellectual or logical arguments. The differences between the two sections are so jarring that they even negatively impacted the original reception of the book. As Orwell's biographer tells it:

> When Orwell's book came out, various writers on the Left criticized it for failing to let the facts speak for themselves. They charged that he was at fault for putting too much of himself in the narrative and that the heavily autobiographical Part 2 was a travesty that tried to shift the reader's attention from the really important social problems. . . . [O]ver the years the book has frequently been portrayed as a misshapen creature with one "good" section (Part 1—a cool, realistic presentation of the facts) and one "bad" section (Part 2—a vague, idiosyncratic discussion of political ideas). (Shelden 230)

The split perceived between the two parts of *Wigan Pier* was so great, in fact, that Orwell's publisher took the extraordinary step of publishing some copies of the book that were composed solely of the first half for distribution to more left-leaning readers.

Given that Orwell was a very talented and thoughtful writer, what do you make of this criticism of *Wigan Pier?* Is it possible that Orwell made a huge mistake in structuring his book like this? Could there have been an explicit strategy for doing so? If so, what do you think it was? Is there a way to read the book that reconciles the disparities between the two pieces? How might Orwell have structured the book differently to avoid these criticisms? What would have been gained by this different structure? What might have been lost?

Symbols, Imagery, and Language

Paying attention to the symbols, imagery, and language in a work of literature is an exercise in noticing the very nuts and bolts of the author's craft, the small details that all come together to make the overall work what it is. Good writers always use language, symbols, and imagery with great care and meticulous attention to detail. Sometimes, it is possible to get so caught up in the larger brushstrokes of a piece of literature that you miss a lot of what is going on below the surface. Forcing yourself to take note of these smaller details will deepen your understanding of the work. As a writer, Orwell is quite fond of describing scenes in his works; these passages give you a great opportunity to examine the way he uses imagery and symbols. Furthermore, not only does Orwell, like all writers, pay a great deal of attention to his own use of language; he also often addresses the use of language in a culture directly. This provides you wonderful opportunities to explore his views on language in great detail.

Sample Topics:

1. **Orwell's use of scenes:** Even in the midst of the heavily sociological first part of *The Road to Wigan Pier*, Orwell has a habit of stopping to describe a particular scene in great detail. Is this an effective strategy or a distraction? Why does he do this?

For the most part, the first half of *Wigan Pier* is an anthropological and sociological study of poverty and the coal miners of England. Much of the time, Orwell goes to great lengths to appear objective in his descriptions, and he often presents raw data to his readers. There is a general journalistic, if not exactly scientific, tone to this part of his narrative. However, he occasionally breaks this tone up with careful descriptions of particular scenes that he feels are charged with meaning. On the day that Orwell leaves the Brookers' boarding house, for instance, he describes the following scene he observed from the train:

> At the back of one of the houses a young woman was kneeling on the stones, poking a stick up the leaden waste-pipe which ran from the sink inside and which I suppose was blocked. I had time to see everything about her—her sacking apron, her clumsy clogs, her arms reddened by the cold. She looked up as the train passed, and I was almost near enough to catch her eye. She had a round pale face, the usual exhausted face of the slum girl who is twenty-five and looks forty, thanks to miscarriages and drudgery; and it wore, for the second in which I saw it, the most desolate, hopeless expression I have ever seen. (16)

From this brief glimpse of a woman to whom he has never spoken, Orwell goes on to make some fairly wide-reaching conclusions about the inner lives of the impoverished. He claims to have divined exactly what the woman was feeling, not only about that particular moment but about her life in general. This stands in stark contrast to the carefully presented data Orwell compiles elsewhere. There is no doubt that descriptions like this can be quite persuasive, but do they undercut the veracity of Orwell's project? Is the use of individual scenes like this counterproductive to the otherwise objective tone Orwell is trying to convey? Are they too subjective? Or are they a nice counterpoint to the more objective observations and data? Find other instances like this and consider how well they work at persuading you as a reader.

2. **The image of the "quack" socialist:** On more than one occasion, Orwell paints the picture of what he claims is a common adherent to socialism, a sort of eccentric who drives level-headed people away from socialism. Examine the details with which Orwell conjures up these people. Why is the image he creates so derogatory and insulting?

In more than one passage in the second half of the novel, Orwell complains that too many current socialists are weirdoes, eccentric kooks who give socialism a bad name, or at least a bad image. In one instance, Orwell laments that

> there is the horrible—the really disquieting—prevalence of cranks wherever Socialists are gathered together. One sometimes gets the impression that the mere words 'Socialism' and 'Communism' draw towards them with magnetic force every fruit-juice drinker, nudist, sandal-wearer, sex-maniac, Quaker, 'Nature Cure' quack, pacifist, and feminist in England. (152)

He goes on to relate an instance in which "two dreadful-looking old men" got on a bus with him. They were "hatless" and "dressed in pistachio-coloured shirts and khaki shorts into which their huge bottoms were crammed so tightly that you could study every dimple" (152). The immediate assumption of everyone on the bus is that the men are socialists. Reread the second half of *Wigan Pier*, noting carefully all the instances where Orwell describes this sort of socialist. What types of details does he always use when describing them? What exaggeration is obvious? Why does Orwell create this image? What do these caricatures symbolize for Orwell? How is he using this symbolism?

Bibliography and Online Resources for *The Road to Wigan Pier*

Branson, Noreen. *Britain in the Nineteen Twenties.* Minneapolis: University of Minnesota Press, 1976.

Brendon, Piers. *The Dark Valley: A Panorama of the 1930s.* New York: Vintage, 2002.

Carsten, F. L. *The Rise of Fascism.* Los Angeles: U of California P, 1982.

The Coal Mining History Resource Centre. Accessed on 15 Nov. 2009. <http://www.cmhrc.co.uk/site/home/>

Fleming, Thomas. *Socialism.* Political Systems of the World. New York: Benchmark, 2008.

Freese, Barbara. *Coal: A Human History.* New York: Penguin, 2004.

Hollis, Christopher. *A Study of George Orwell.* Chicago: Regnery, 1956.

Lee, Robert A. *Orwell's Fiction.* Notre Dame, Ind.: U of Notre Dame P, 1969.

London Museums Hub. Exploring 20th Century London. Accessed on 15 Nov. 2009. <http://www.20thcenturylondon.org.uk/server.php?show=nav.40>.

Mussolini, Benito. "What Is Fascism." Internet Modern History Sourcebook. Accessed on 15 Nov. 2009. <http://www.fordham.edu/halsall/mod/mussolini-fascism.html>.

Orwell, George. *The Road to Wigan Pier.* New York: Penguin, 1985.

———. *The Road to Wigan Pier.* Accessed on 15 Nov. 2009. <http://www.netcharles.com/orwell/books/wiganpier.htm>.

Ross, Cathy. *Twenties London: A City in the Jazz Age.* New York: Philip Wilson, 2003.

Shelden, Michael. *Orwell: The Authorized Biography.* New York: HarperCollins, 1991.

INDEX